Dietrich Bonhoeffer

Dietrich Bonhoeffer

AN INTRODUCTION TO HIS THOUGHT

Sabine Dramm

Translated by Thomas Rice

HENDRICKSON
PUBLISHERS

Dietrich Bonhoeffer: An Introduction to His Thought
English translation © 2007 by Hendrickson Publishers, Inc.
P. O. Box 3473
Peabody, Massachusetts 01961-3473

ISBN 978-1-56563-762-7

Translated from *Dietrich Bonhoeffer: Eine Einfürung in sein Denken.*
© Chr. Kaiser/Gütersloher Verlagshaus, Gütersloh, Germany, 2001.

Printed in the United States of America

Second Printing — May 2008

Cover Photo: Portrait of Dietrich Bonhoeffer, 1935. Photo Credit: Hulton Archive/Getty Images.

Library of Congress Cataloging-in-Publication Data

Dramm, Sabine, 1943–
  [Dietrich Bonhoeffer. English]
  Dietrich Bonhoeffer : an introduction to his thought /
Sabine Dramm ; translated by Thomas Rice.
    p. cm.
  Includes bibliographical references.
  ISBN-13: 978-1-56563-762-7 (alk. paper)
  1. Bonhoeffer, Dietrich, 1906–1945. I. Title.
  BX4827.B57D7213 2007
  230'.044092—dc22
                2006020474

Table of Contents

Foreword

"Every book has its history," I wrote in 1998, when beginning the foreword to my book about Dietrich Bonhoeffer and Albert Camus, which I dedicated to my mother. The present book's history began, at least in part, in a conversation I had with Eberhard Bethge in the spring of 1999, when I shared with him my idea for *Dietrich Bonhoeffer: An Introduction to His Thought*. He encouraged me wholeheartedly and emphatically to begin the work.

This book deals with a body of thought for persons who are perhaps interested in theology but not necessarily well-versed in it; for persons curious about Bonhoeffer; for persons whom he has already touched; naturally for students of theology and related fields, but also and above all for non-students; for persons of all confessions—or none—who are politically and philosophically open-minded; for persons who, for whatever reason, desire a better understanding of what we would normally call Bonhoeffer's "life and works," his thought, his faith, and his actions. The intention here is not to reconstruct his life's journey in detail, with an excursus here and there into his thought. Rather, his life and the death he encountered and accepted in resistance and open-eyed surrender will serve here as the backdrop against which his faith and thought become comprehensible as a whole. This does not include, however, aspects and statements that belong to the realm of the personal; most of these have been excluded out of respect for the person of Dietrich Bonhoeffer.

The individual chapters and blocks of material in this book naturally build upon one another; however, they can also be read and understood singly. The unavoidable repetitions that often result are cross-referenced in each case in the endnotes. Unless otherwise mentioned, the official collection of *Dietrich Bonhoeffer's Works* (abbreviated in this book as DBW) served as a textual basis and guideline for orthography, punctuation, and accentuation of passages in the quotations. Several of Bonhoeffer's individual writings are also available in paperback, for instance, *Life Together,* the *Ethics, Resistance and Surrender* (German: *Widerstand und*

Ergebung), and the *Sermons—exegetical texts—Meditations.* The DBW "predecessor," Dietrich Bonhoeffer's *Collected Writings* (Vol. I–VI, Munich 1958–1974, edited by Eberhard Bethge), however, is now found only in libraries. In view of the different textual editions, and especially to make clear the *Sitz im Leben* of Bonhoeffer's sayings, I have in most cases briefly mentioned the place, time, and situational context of the quotations. In listing secondary literature I have deliberately confined myself for the most part to those works that are still available in bookstores or can easily be found in public libraries. This information should be understood as a possible guideline for further study and often suggests the names of works that elaborate on this or that topic more deeply.

Eberhard Bethge passed away in March of 2000. He was able to read only a very small part of the manuscript for this book. My mother, Elisabeth Zapp-Gerr, was able to read the complete manuscript before she too passed away only a short time ago. I dedicate this book to the memory of both. With the hope that in every ending there is a new beginning.

Sabine Dramm
April 2001, First Sunday after Easter

Abbreviations

ed(s).	editor(s), edited by
e.g.	*exempli gratia,* for example
et al.	*et alii,* and others
i.e.	*id est,* that is
trans.	translator, translated by
vol(s).	volume(s)
DBW	*Dietrich Bonhoeffer Werke* (See bibliography for individual volumes)

1

Approximation and Accents

> Every view that we take of the world and every
> selection we make of what is important to notice
> is simply one way of looking at things, and
> there are infinite ways of looking.
>
> *Alan Watts*

Understanding him is both easy and difficult at the same time. Dietrich Bonhoeffer never "practiced" theology merely for its own sake. Rather, for him theology was a window that opened onto the world. It was the dimension through which he understood the world and wanted to make the world understandable. His theology was faith in thought, thought in faith, with a great partiality for ethics, which for him was more than merely a specialized branch of theology and life. But while these two—his theology and his ethics—are inseparably linked together, they are not a closed system. He expressed them—and himself—in unmistakably clear, unambiguous, and succinct terms.

Nevertheless, his statements sometimes seem paradoxical and difficult to follow. Both are part of the same whole of course: on the one hand, his direct and immediately understandable, literally "striking" way of expressing himself, unconditionally and to the point; on the other hand, his highly abstract, sometimes complicated and terse diction, with manifold elements from the history of thought—above all from theology—sometimes commingled with wordplays as well, all of which are constantly varied, rejected, and taken up anew. Indeed it is sometimes astonishing to see how the simple and the complex go hand in hand for Bonhoeffer, the way the one becomes understandable in light of the other.

Other contradictory elements, no less astonishing, become understandable only when viewed as "contra-dictums," opposites conjoined, and not necessarily mutually exclusive or reconcilable with one another: man abandoned by God, God seeking man; the religion-less Christian, the follower of Christ; the communion of saints, the overriding guilt of the church; God who melds us together, God who is powerless; man come of age, man the failure, the lost one; the childlike ease of an ethics of love, the complexity of an ethics of responsibility; death the adversary of life, death the gateway to freedom.

Bonhoeffer's theology, in the truest sense "thought-full," often nearly "high-flying," was matched—although perhaps not at the beginning—by a down-to-earth, rectilinear, practical way of living life that finally culminated in political action. It was truly an "embodied theology,"[1] in several senses, for it was paired, perhaps likewise not from the very beginning, with intense personal piety.[2] His particular alloy of a very individual spirituality and a fully thought-out theology, of mandates of faith and enduring personal commitment, was nonpareil. Bonhoeffer's theology and piety had the potential to support criticism of the church and state when more general concerns such as social criticism or religious conscience threatened to pale.

Seemingly contrary lines of thought and living were inextricably woven together in his person, his thought, his faith, and his actions: his rational, easy-to-follow, conceptually polished, and convincingly formulated theology, and an emotionally grounded faith of immense affective and activating power; theoretical existence as a Christian and practical existence as a Christian; a theological existence which became simultaneously and undeniably political; and, last but not least, the idea of "religion-less Christianity" and the self-evident presence in him of a piety which was "religious" in the deepest and best sense of the word.

There is no way to unravel, either vertically or horizontally, this fabric of Bonhoeffer's thought, faith, and action. To try to do so, or even to "play off" the individual elements against one another,[3] would cause us to miss his meaning. It is of course tempting to break his thought down into its component parts and label them, for example, according to early and late Bonhoeffer, to the extent that the terms "early" and "late" can be applied to a life that was broken off after thirty-nine years. Or perhaps we might counterpoise the components according to the "man of piety" and the "man of the world"; the "theological thinker" and the "politically active Christian"; the "conservative theologian" and the "progressive theologian"; the "classical thinker" and the "modern thinker." All this would, however, do injustice to his identity as a theologian and a thinker, if not destroy it entirely.

Bonhoeffer was a Protestant theologian par excellence; but at the same time that he practiced a faith whose foundations were theological to the core, he developed a theology of his own within Protestantism. He was also a man far ahead of his time, for the dimensions of both his theology and his faith were ecumenical, transnational, and pioneering in every sense of the word, having implications in some cases yet to be fully explored. He is certainly one of the most famous Protestants of the twentieth century, for both Protestants and non-Protestants alike. Still, the question arises whether or not he is in fact a forgotten Protestant, especially within the very concrete, existing world of the church and Christianity. Does Christian existence in our own day reflect—at the individual, congregational, and ecclesiastical levels—the Bonhoeffer to whom we so often and so gladly refer? Bonhoeffer: Is he sand or oil in the gearwheels of theology and the church? Does he inspire and spur us on? Or does he serve us as an alibi and window dressing? Bonhoeffer: Is he on the one hand a rebel but on the other a concrete role model? Or is he only a rich source of quotations for Sunday sermons and other discussions, that is, quoted far more often than taken seriously in practice?

For now, we return to the man himself. No system of thought, no pattern of action that arises from a system or points back to it—above all, no system of theology and ethics (including actions that result from them)—stands alone in a vacuum. "In other words," as Bonhoeffer himself emphasizes in a somewhat different context in *Discipleship*, "no insight can be studied in isolation from the existence in which it was gained" (DBW 4, 38). The thought of any person must always be described and understood against the backdrop of his or her concrete existence. This does not mean, however, (1) that it can be understood only and exclusively by turning to that person, or (2) that there is no ongoing interplay between the thought and actions of a human being. So also with Bonhoeffer.

Although there are many methods that might bring to light both the interdependence and the mutual dependence that existed between Bonhoeffer and his thought, this book is not the proper setting for a sociological treatise or psychological analysis of Dietrich Bonhoeffer. Instead, the central theme here will be—and how could it be otherwise when speaking of Bonhoeffer?—the relationship between his life and his thought, his biography and his theology.

The quintessential aspect(s) of his theology and thought as a whole cannot be brought to light without tracing the commingling of his thought with the life he lived. The weaving together of the abstract with the concrete was for Bonhoeffer an essential part of theological perception, intrinsic to the perception of another person's existence, an existence we know consists of being *and* consciousness. The interplay between being and consciousness, between the world of consciousness and that of being, invariably creates a constant "to and fro" in the life of every human being, as well as in society as a whole; they are searching movements and determinants rolled into one. These interactions are more pronounced in Bonhoeffer's thought than that of almost any other theologian. To put it differently: his theo-logically centered life is inseparable from his life-centered theology.

Viewed from another standpoint, we can say that Bonhoeffer "realized," that is, made real in the truest and ultimately the bitterest sense of the word, the theological insight that had become one of the basic features and unshakable certainties of his life. His ethics were made transparent by his existence; his thought was legitimized by his actions; his theology, authenticated by his biography. To be sure, questions have often been raised—with vehemence, and rightly so—with regard to using this congruity between "dictum and doing," this intimate interweaving of his theology with his personal biography, as the starting point for understanding Bonhoeffer. In response, it need hardly be said that there are gaps and contradictions in his thought and life: How could it be otherwise? Perhaps we would do better not to refer, as is so often done, to the "unity of his life and work," but to say more modestly that in many respects his views harmonized with the way he lived his life (and that, after all, says a great deal!). Be that as it may, we can in any case recognize in Bonhoeffer a bit of what it means to live an authentic life.

This very specific relationship between theology and personal biography that we find in Bonhoeffer necessitates an overview, a synopsis, of his life and thought; thus his personal biography plays an important part in our further explorations, especially at the beginning.

However, we cannot and should not speak here of yet another "half-biographical" work, so to speak, in which one half of Bonhoeffer is studied as a springboard to the other half, namely, the study of his theology. Rather, our purpose here from the very beginning is to present *An Introduction to His Thought*. After all, we already have the great (in every sense of the word) biography written by Eberhard Bethge and the corresponding illustrations published by him elsewhere,[4] which are both inexhaustible troves of information; and we also have numerous "smaller" biographies that are valuable reading.[5]

Nor is our purpose here to present a comprehensive view of his theology, but only to present an *Introduction* to his thought, for Ernst Feil wrote a still-unsurpassed work on Bonhoeffer's theology[6] from and for the "High School of Theology." The almost-endless flood of literature on Bonhoeffer also includes programmatic and detailed Forewords and Afterwords inscribed in the individual volumes of *Dietrich Bonhoeffer: Works*, which was completed in 1999. There are also numerous studies on the individual aspects of his theology; indeed the recently published *International Bibliography*[7] contains nearly 4,000 titles! Of necessity, therefore, an additional work conceived as an introduction and approach to the thought of this man can only delineate contours rather than claim to be comprehensive.

Moreover, this introduction to his *Thought* must of course sketch not only the theological but also the philosophical side of Bonhoeffer, along with what we refer to today as his political ethics, or more generally, the way he viewed the world. Our purpose here is to pave a way into his theology, into his manner of thinking and believing, above all for those who, sad to say, are so often still regarded as "the laity" (a truly meaningless term for Protestant understanding!) or describe themselves as such. Perhaps our project will serve as a bridge both back to him *and* into the future, as well as provide incentive for the reader to take up his works, either for the first time or once again; an opportunity to let Bonhoeffer—perhaps again—"infect" us, or to view him from a greater distance in time and thought than before, and in this way to relativize him. In any case, the reader may personally come to grips with Bonhoeffer here, and thus arrive at a personal opinion about him.

By the very nature of the matter there is no need to emphasize that this *Introduction to His Thought* is not objective. It cannot be so nor does it wish to be so; and such a claim would in any case be fictitious, since every such introduction is also *nolens volens* an interpretation. However, the hope is to maintain a balance between proximity and distance: the goal is to make Bonhoeffer's thought understandable from the viewpoint of an inner, but hopefully critical, proximity and at a remove in time, albeit an undeniably involved one for those who are now going on about their lives generations after he lived. Its aim is to present his unique manner of thinking and believing, along with the consequences that resulted from actually putting them into practice, consequences which for *him* were deadly.

As for us, we find ourselves today in a historical and political situation incomparably more comfortable than what Bonhoeffer experienced. But at the same time we live in an even more "cult"-ivated Northern Hemisphere, whose mankind- and life-threatening dimensions often appear to stifle us. Can Bonhoeffer's "Theology of Life," as I have called it elsewhere,[8] still touch us in today's world?

Regarding *Dietrich Bonhoeffer: An Introduction to His Thought*, I agree with what Helmut Gollwitzer, one of my theology teachers, wrote in 1970, in the foreword to what is probably his most important book: ". . . We already have more than enough 'professorial theology' for instructors of theology, unavoidable as that may be, and I hope to continue making my own contributions to it. But the function of science is to serve, no more and no less; and after science has come to the end of any journey through scientific reflections, it must remain possible to discuss in everyday language the topics with which science has wrestled."[9] A preceding *personal* passage through the scientific reflections Gollwitzer spoke about is, of course, indispensable. But the task of imparting an understanding of Bonhoeffer's thought on this basis, without using technical theological terms, resembles a high-wire act: as little technical terminology as possible, as much technical terminology as necessary! This also applies to the historical perspective: an understanding of Dietrich Bonhoeffer's thought makes an orderly awareness of the circumstances of his life and time almost imperative. But here too, selection becomes nearly a high-wire act: as little data and facts as possible, as much as required—such that their selection is already a form of exegesis.

For this reason, I take my stand in *Dietrich Bonhoeffer: An Introduction to His Thought* with Dietrich Bonhoeffer himself: I am aware that this book cannot help but interpret him as well. "Personal interpretation," he wrote during his travels in Italy in 1924, "is one of the most difficult of all problems; but still it accompanies all of our thinking; we must have our own interpretations, we must give meaning if we are to live and think at all" (DBW 9, 106).

2

Rings of Years

Blessed are those who have lived before they died.

Marie-Luise Kaschnitz

Dietrich Bonhoeffer. Born: 1906 in Breslau (today's Wroclaw), Poland. Early years in Berlin. Studied theology with rapid success in
a theological career. Active in the Confessing Church and actively ecumenical. Sanctions from the State. Contact with the Resistance. A conspirator. Arrested 1943. Killed at Flossenbürg concentration camp in
April 1945. His works: some publications during his lifetime, others
posthumously and in fragments. These are the brief headings of an existence. How are they to be fleshed out with life?

Dietrich Bonhoeffer was born in an era before the break in time
ushered in by the First World War—the first mechanized and superbly
organized slaughter of the masses, the (un)worthy opening of a century
that continued to outdo itself in inventing and applying means of mass
destruction. He did not even live to see the end of the first half of that
century, because he tried to stem the inhumanity of a system of terror
that originated in "his" land, in "his" city. Although Breslau, now in Poland, was his place of birth, Berlin became and remained the center of
his existence. His family moved there when he was six years old.
Dietrich's father, a prominent psychiatrist and neurologist, as well as a
professor in a university department of international renown, automatically became the Director of the Charité Hospital in Berlin. These were
the years when the psychoanalytic methods developed by Sigmund
Freud in Vienna, another European metropolis, began to cause earlier
paradigms of psychology and psychiatry to crumble. Karl Bonhoeffer's
orientation, however, was too neurological to allow him to sympathize
with Freud's radically new approach to understanding and helping the
fragile human psyche get back on its feet, even had he wanted to. The
aversion Dietrich expressed in later years toward psychoanalysis and
psychotherapy, and his—as he put it—"distaste for soul analysis" are
rooted here (DBW 8, 235).[1]

Dietrich was the youngest son in his family. He had a younger sister, Susanne, and also a twin sister named Sabine. (She later married Gerhard Leibholz and emigrated with him to England for fear of arrest—he did not match the definition of the "Arian" race.) It requires little imagination to guess that the twins were emotionally close to one another as children. He also had two older sisters, Ursula and Christine. (The Nazis later murdered both of their husbands, Rüdiger Schleicher and Hans von Dohnanyi, in April 1945.) Finally, at the head of the line of siblings were Dietrich's three brothers: the oldest was Karl-Friedrich, an enthusiastic and later highly respected natural scientist; followed by Walter, who lost his life at the age of eighteen in the First World War; and Klaus, five years older than Dietrich, who was executed exactly two weeks after his brother's death. We can only imagine the emotional trauma endured by Dietrich's parents, and the other survivors in the family, at their decimation by war and Fascism. Can such things be "coped with" at all, or—to use more contemporary language—can they be "processed"? These are questions that cannot be answered by outsiders.

Bonhoeffer's family was the never-to-be-forgotten backdrop of his existence and remained so through the very last phase of his life. For him, family was something like a home and hearth that existed in no particular part of the world, something he carried within himself, no matter where he happened to be. The family atmosphere was one of liberalism, Prussian (self-)discipline, a natural but unostentatious form of Protestantism with no exaggerated bonds to the church. This Protestantism fostered narrow-mindedness neither of confession nor of any other ideology. It was without doubt one of the culturally and educationally most productive "dynasties" of the German upper middle class, from which the intellectual, political, and financial elite of the time were recruited. Its roots were in the prosperous but thrifty, well-educated middle class whose conservative values did not *merely* correspond to the idealized, after-the-fact image so easily constructed by a gaze into the past.[2] This family—and this is all that interests us here—clearly had a highly beneficial influence on Dietrich Bonhoeffer's identification of himself inwardly and outwardly. Tolerance and respect for others, no matter of what provenience, and a basically open-minded attitude toward the world and in forming a world view constituted the foundation stones of this humanistically stamped family's world. It was a world that had its own successfully functioning mélange of expectations, and one that provided help in fulfilling those expectations: both components were invariably present simultaneously and generously. To this extent, Bonhoeffer lived a *jeunesse dorée,* a golden youth, albeit one that was checked by self-discipline and crystal clear limits set by the family's un-questioned—as was usual for the times—family hierarchy. The positive aspect of this world was that children were empowered toward personal self-development. Dietrich Bonhoeffer's parents gave free reign to the full development of his musical, intellectual, and athletic abilities; his father, for example, accepted (albeit unenthusiastically) his son's early decision, apparently at the age of fourteen or fifteen years, to study theology, even though he himself was an agnostic.

His mother, whose own family esteemed theology as a career choice (both her father and grandfather were professors of theology), was un-usual for her time and its conventions in that she had completed train-ing as a teacher and instructed her children personally in particular subjects up to a certain age, with the result that they quickly jumped ahead in several classes when they entered the German Gymnasium, or university preparatory school. Dietrich, for example, was only seven-teen when he entered the university in Tübingen and began his study of theology. A year later he returned to Berlin. In 1927, at the age of twenty-one, he had already completed his dissertation there: *Sanctorum Communio,* "The Communion of Saints."

He spent the following year as curate to the German community in Barcelona. But by 1929 he was already back in Berlin and again at the university. While serving as an assistant to the faculty of theology, he worked on his professorial dissertation *Act and Being,* an exploration of the border area between theology and philosophy, which he submitted in 1930. At the same time, he passed his second theological examina-tions. He was, however, still far too young for ordination, and so had no prospects for pastoring a church. But in truth, the academic world was more important to him at that time, and he received approbation as an assistant professor of theology at the age of twenty-four years. He en-titled his inaugural lecture "The Question of Man in Modern Phi-losophy and Theology."

Thereafter, the continuation of his years of teaching and traveling the world took him first to a year's sabbatical study in New York, where he made initial contacts with churchmen from other countries and other modes of faith. In the United States, he experienced theology in earnest: experienced faith hardened in the fire and experienced ecumenism first-hand. He encountered a pacifism that was rooted in the Sermon on the Mount—personified in the French theologian and friend Jean Las-serre—and the Social Gospel Movement, which sought on the basis of the Gospels to combat the explosive issues of social injustice and racism that were taken for granted. In England, he participated for the first time in an international church conference, namely, the annual meeting

of the World Alliance for Friendship of the Churches and Reconciliation, and from this time forward served as its Secretary for Ecumenical
Youth Work. His area of responsibility was Central and Northern Europe, work that now began to take him across many borders; ten years
later he would continue this work subversively for the politically conspirative circles of the time—conspirative circles was still a contradiction in terms within the church at that time!—as well as on his own,
very personal initiative.

Bonhoeffer's path now begins unmistakably to take on its later contours. Concrete Christian living has its place both in this world *and* before the countenance of God. In practice it is oriented toward theory,
and in theory it is oriented toward practice. More stations follow in his
life: Berlin again, and again the university. The beginning of the 1930s,
as Germany was "forming" itself, was, for Bonhoeffer, a time full of contacts and activity. In addition to teaching at the university, he was given
responsibility for pastoral care of the students. "Extracurricularly," so to
speak—and indeed in quite an extraordinary manner—he took on the
task of instructing those awaiting confirmation in the social cauldron of
Berlin's Wedding suburb, where he also initiated a project for the unemployed. He worked during this time with tireless energy, both in Berlin
and at ecumenical encounters within and outside of Germany. His out-
standing talent, which emerges again and again, was the written and
spoken word: in university classes; in lectures, sermons, and letters; in
documentation, drafts, talks, theses, memoranda, and essays. One of his
university courses, Creation and Fall, appeared as his third book in 1933.

This phase of Bonhoeffer's life, which was productive on so many
different levels, continued into the middle of the 1930s, when he became a founder of the Confessing Church, a social frontline combatant,
and—in the end—an outsider. At the same time and with the same
single-mindedness, he attempted to win over the ecumenical movement
of his time with his descriptions and visions of the church and the
world, of faith and life (after the Second World War, the Ecumenical
Council of the Churches emerged from the World Alliance for Friendship of the Churches and Reconciliation and other ecumenical federa-
tions). For a time, he had a pastorate in London, but then returned to
Berlin. The next stations: Zingst, Germany, then Finkenwalde, high in
northeastern Germany, where the Confessing Church established its
own seminary for preachers and a training center for curates. Bonhoeffer, not much older than his own students, became its director.
There he put into writing what he himself was practicing: *Discipleship*
(published in 1937) and *Life Together* (published in 1939). Finkenwalde
became a "House of Brethren," an experimental non-Evangelical com-

munity that was nevertheless Evangelical in the deepest sense of the word, and one that bore Bonhoeffer's stamp at every turn.

This life together did not last long. The Confessing Church was forced to close its institutional Preaching Seminary and instead had to train its curates in a type of "wandering seminary" called the Group Vicariate. Bonhoeffer wrote circular letters, organized group meetings, and visited the curates in their respective churches, which were far away from Berlin, in Pomerania, Germany's remote region near the Baltic Sea. In the summer of 1939, he once again received the opportunity to travel to the United States. But this time the situation was not as it had been nine years earlier, with an academic stipend; this opportunity included the prospect of a teaching position and, even more, of an unendangered, long-term, assured basis for his private, professional, theological, and political existence. Bonhoeffer made his choice—and broke off his plans for a stay in America.

Finally, after the outbreak of the war he had long prophesied, he decided once again to live his life in the shadow of constant risk that would eventually bring that life to an abrupt end. His manifold contacts with the Resistance among his family and friends—even if the latters' goals and motives were in some cases very different from his own—played a part in his journey into an incognito existence of conspiracy.[3] He entered into a kind of double life inasmuch as he continued on the one hand to work for the—now "tamed"—Confessing Church and, above all, officially for military intelligence, but in reality for those and with those who elected resistance within military intelligence and were making preparations for a *putsch*. During travels to Switzerland, Scandinavia, and Italy, Bonhoeffer attempted to use his ecumenical connections to inform the rest of the world about this organized military resistance and his own intentions. He began to write again, knowing full well that he was not allowed to write, beginning work on his *Ethics*.

The Bonhoeffer File: the State dictatorship had long since begun to focus on him: move for move, step by step. 1937: forbidden to teach at the University of Berlin, closure of the Preaching Seminary in Finkenwalde. 1938: forbidden to remain in Berlin (except for visits to his parents). 1940: forbidden to speak publicly, required to report regularly to the police. 1941: forbidden to print or publish his writings. Mail and telephone surveillance apparently since 1942 at the latest.

In January of 1943, Dietrich became engaged to eighteen-year-old Maria von Wedemeyer, against the will of her mother, who demanded a year's separation as a sign and test, so to speak, of their love. Theirs was a love, however, that would soon encounter a much more absurd test: Bonhoeffer was arrested in April the same year and held for interrogation in the military prison in Berlin's Tegel suburb. As his fiancée, Maria was given visiting rights, and during the eighteen months he was imprisoned there, the two were allowed to see one another, albeit only rarely and only under the supervision of prison personnel. Nevertheless, an inner closeness grew and developed between them through their letters, where they wrote themselves into a future that would never come. After a long silence on the part of Maria von Wedemeyer, she consented to the publication of this correspondence after her death, and years later it appeared as *Love Letters from Cell 92*.

And there was another exchange of letters during those months in Tegel Prison that kept Bonhoeffer alive in the truest sense of the word: his correspondence with his friend Eberhard Bethge. These letters document a singular experience of existence and a singular existential reflection on faith. The letters and notes sent by him were first published by Bethge in 1951, bearing a title that was borrowed from a phrase that appears in them: *Resistance and Surrender* (German: *Widerstand und Ergebung*). It is through these letters that Bonhoeffer's imprint on the world remains. And even more, they made him known throughout the world, which was unusual enough for an Evangelical theologian in the twentieth century. They also call attention to his earlier books, which had previously remained in the shadows. They cast light on his specific path of resistance and make it remembered—along with its drastic end.

After the attempt to assassinate Hitler failed on July 20, 1944, the possibility of a putsch became so remote as to be almost out of the question. Thereafter, the chances that members of the Resistance who were already imprisoned would receive a trial that was even partially fair utterly deteriorated—and along with them their chances of surviving. In October of 1944, Bonhoeffer was transferred to the basement of a Gestapo prison in Berlin. Shortly thereafter, all contact between him and the outside world was terminated. At the beginning of 1945, the National Socialist machinery of death took on a life of its own. From February to April, Bonhoeffer lived a wild journey from which he would never return alive:[4] incarceration in a bunker in Buchenwald concentration camp, "shipped" to the Flossenbürg concentration camp, inadvertently sent off with a group of prisoners, and then the finality of death. After being sentenced in a courtroom farce, on April 9, 1945, in the final weeks of the war, he was brutally hanged on the gallows at Flossenbürg concentration camp, together with Canaris, Oster, and other members of the military resistance group.

3

Facets of a Life

"Entirety" is a deception.
Theodor W. Adorno

The totality of his life—and the sum of his written fragments—lies hidden behind biographical sketches. The life and work of Dietrich Bonhoeffer were fragmentary due to the involuntary discontinuation of his work and his inexorable progress toward a violent and early death. Studies of him have pointed out from time to time that his theology is only a torso, a work incomplete.

This viewpoint is both correct and incorrect. Above all, his letters from Tegel Prison and the notes that echoed around the world as *Resistance and Surrender* are naturally not a *Summa theologica* like that of Thomas Aquinas, nor do they make up a *Church Dogmatics* like that of Karl Barth. In addition, Bonhoeffer's *Ethics,* which he was working on before his arrest, is unfinished; of necessity, it too first appeared in print posthumously and as a fragment. But this in no way waters down the message of either, not even after half a century. Then too, by the very nature of the situation, they drew and continue to draw legitimation and fascination from the permanent situation of a man who lived on the edge during conspiracy and imprisonment, deliberately incurring the risk of isolation, the fear of torture and death, and finally death itself.

It may be true that there was and still is a danger that this forever incomplete body of work is used and will continue to be used in an arbitrary and dilettantish fashion. But can we not say this about the "finished" works of other authors as well? And is it not also true, to put the question more generally, that the body of thought conceived by most human beings is only a "torso"? Is it not true that the lives of many persons remain forever fragmentary, even when they extend over more years than Bonhoeffer's and finally shatter in a manner less brutal?

Bonhoeffer himself was soberly and painfully aware of the fragmentary character of his thought. However, his response to this circumstance was acceptance rather than lament. All the less do we therefore have a right to "superior" interpretations from the vantage point of an "informed" retrospective. In a letter to his parents from Berlin's Tegel Prison dated February 20, 1944—which is, by the way, one of the few letters in which he makes no bones about the fact that he would often like nothing better than simply to remain silent—Bonhoeffer writes: "The unfinished, fragmentary side of life is felt . . . with special poignance here. But it is exactly this fragment that can in turn point to a consummation no human power can achieve" (DBW 8, 330–31). And shortly thereafter, on February 23, 1944, he wrote to his friend Eberhard Bethge that their intellectual existence was still only a torso—he uses this exact term in this context—the only real point to it all probably being to ensure that this fragment of life will reflect ". . . how the whole structure was designed and conceived, and of what material it is made" (ibid., 336). Moreover, some fragments are intended to be and remain fragments because their completion can come only from God. He thinks, for example, of the art of the fugue and comes to the truly joyous conclusion: "If our life represents even the remotest reflection of such a fragment's beauty, . . . then we have no desire to lament our fragmentary life, but instead rejoice in it" (ibid.). He himself attempted, he writes, not only to accept the fragmentary character of his life but also to see it as the seal of his existence and a sign of hope.

Perhaps this is the proper context to raise a frequently asked question, one that often generates heated discussion among Bonhoeffer scholars: do Bonhoeffer's theological ideas represent a continuum of thought, or an unevenly dictated landslide?[1] It would be a waste of time to attempt a response to this question here, for it is answered best precisely *through*, and not *before*, an encounter and confrontation with his thought. But what can be offered here is Bonhoeffer's own view of his thought, development, and life. When discussing ethical questions and decisions, and an ethical understanding of existence, in the *Ethics* (DBW 6, 388), he speaks at one point about the "*flow* of life from conception to grave," of "life's gnarled growth." Do these images perhaps express or reflect his own personal understanding of existence? We have a note written by him in May 1943, that is, from the weeks just after he was brought to the military interrogation prison in Berlin. In it he speaks of "[c]ontinuity with past and future interrupted" (DBW 8, 64). Is this perhaps the kind of sensation one can have (only) in the chaos of a dissociative life experience?

An explicit response to the question of a continuum or discontinuum in his understanding of himself, his mental and real existence, is found in two letters Bonhoeffer later wrote to Bethge. On April 4, 1944, he wrote retrospectively about his decision to return from America to

Germany in the face of gathering clouds of war: ". . . I have never regretted the decision I made in the summer of 1939; rather, I have the strongest impression that my life—curious though it may sound—has proceeded in a completely straight, unbroken line, at least with respect to outward guidance. I view it as an unbroken series of enriching experiences for which truly I can only be thankful" (DBW 8, 391).

On April 22, 1944, he wrote that, although he had certainly learned a great deal since his incarceration, he himself had changed very little: "Neither of us has in fact experienced a break in his life. . . . Continuity with one's own past is indeed a great gift" (ibid., 397–98). Without exception, he arrives at the same conclusion again and again, "that all was determined by the unyielding and unswerving guidance of a higher source" (ibid., 398). To judge by his own statements, Bonhoeffer accepted his own existence as fragmentary and understood it—"curious though it may sound"—as a continuum that reflected both an inner logic *and* the logic of God. And for this reason he also attempted to interpret the future possibilities for his life—in *both* of the plausible alternatives—as the further progression of a continuum that was full of meaning.

He had not had much time to live. Nevertheless it appears to have been a rich life, marked perhaps by changes in intensity but with a sense of identity that remained for the most part unbroken. What constituted the core of this wide-ranging life that was so full of contrast, a life lived out between the poles of faith and reality with the reality of faith at its center? Where are the other components which gave it its stamp and constituted it? We will take up some of these like pieces of a mosaic, without trying to put them together to form a complete, a precise, or a full picture. The goal is not to typify his character as a person, for the only one who has the right to answer the question "Who am I?" is each person himself. For his part, Bonhoeffer used this question *expressis verbis* for the title of a poem he wrote in prison in the summer of 1944, answering it in his own way.

But from an outsider's perspective, who, what, and what kind of person was he? A thinker in the forefront and train of faith. A master of theology. A philosopher by choice. A pacifist by persuasion. A preacher by calling. An unconventional professor. A fascinating teacher. A radical in the service of the church. A troublemaker in the Confessing Church. An ecumenical activist. A mystic. An ascetic. A bit of a hedonist. A spiritual counselor and pastor, i.e., a shepherd. Disobedient toward authority. Subversive. Dubious as a military intelligence courier. Officially a traitor to his country. A martyr. A hero of faith, and extremist in faith. An aristocrat. A middle-class nationalist. A socialistically-tinged idealist. A progressive. A conservative. Pietistic. A rationalist. An elitist.

Democratic. An experimenter in Christian brotherhood. A loner in person. A man of faith.

And who, what, and what kind of person emerges from his own statements about himself and the photographs we have of him? In studying the *Pictures from His Life* one is struck by the fact that Bonhoeffer is often seen in discussion, in joint activities, in thinking something through with others: with members of the congregation in Barcelona; with students at Union Theological Seminary in New York; with "his" Berlin students; with confirmation candidates in Berlin's Wedding suburb; with participants in ecumenical conferences in the Carpathians, in Switzerland, in Denmark; with seminarians in Zingst and Finkenwalde, and on the way with and to them. Even the final photographs, taken early in the summer of 1944, show him in a group, together with Italian prisoners in the prison courtyard. As he wrote to his friend on August 14, 1944, "There is . . . almost no happiness greater than the feeling that one is valued by others. What is important is not their number, but the intensity of this experience. After all, human relationships are simply the most important thing in life, and even the modern 'career' person cannot change this" (DBW 8, 567).

The spoken and written word must have been unusually important to Bonhoeffer. He read extensively and widely, and as frequently as possible during his months in prison. Indeed it was during this time, when he was driven to psychological and physical limits, that the activity of writing became an inner, and apparently a successful, attempt at self-rescue.

But as important as the *Letters and Notes from Prison* (the well-known subtitle of *Resistance and Surrender*) became for others, they were—above all—a life-saving port in the storm for him! It must have been especially painful for him when, long before his imprisonment, he was forbidden to lecture, publish, or preach. Possibly out of an unconscious desire for self-reassurance in Tegel Prison and, as the French say, for *enracinement*—a term that almost cannot be translated but means more or less "to find one's roots"—he embarked on several adventures in writing that were new for him: narrative, novel, drama. But then he abandoned them. (In 1976, before they appeared for the first time in print, the literary scholar Walter Killy asked whether this really makes sense as a means of "rounding out our understanding of the author"; and in a 1978 analysis of the literary and psychological aspects, Ruth Zerner characterized these experiments by Bonhoeffer as "his way of reestablishing contact with his own past.")[2]

We put aside the question as to whether or not these fragmentary texts—a novel, drama, and narrative texts—which were published in full as *Fragments from Tegel Prison* (German: *Fragmente aus Tegel*) in the critical edition of his works, can help one gain a better understanding of Bonhoeffer. Unlike all of his other writings in Tegel Prison, he himself put these aside, deliberately leaving them unfinished. Even under living conditions that are difficult for us to imagine, he apparently remained capable of taking a step back and critiquing his own work. "I am, after all, no poet," he remarked to Eberhard Bethge in the summer of 1944 (DBW 8, 572) regarding other attempts at writing that may be regarded as poetically far more powerful, in particular the poem "Stations on the Way to Freedom." (Bonhoeffer's poems, above all, the poem *By Goodly Powers Wondrously Sustained* [*Von guten Mächten wunderbar geborgen*], which was later set to music many times, are certainly among the texts that have become his best-known.)

The sense of belonging to a group—the members of his family, those who shared his goals, his fellow believers, his friends—was just as important as the written word for one who was forced to live through inner *and* outer loneliness. He practiced *Life Together* (*Gemeinsames Leben*) first at the House of Brethren in Finkenwalde and had an unquenchable longing for innovative New Testament-like forms of Christian community, that is, for community lived in conformity with Christ. Bonhoeffer seems to have understood how to move between discourse and contemplation, discussion and meditation, public life and isolation, as if this were matter-of-course; the different "musical keys" of communication and personal commitment on the one hand and contemplation of himself and God on the other; in short, the medieval monastic rule of *ora et labora* (prayer *and* work!) were clearly not new to him.

Bonhoeffer's own words indicate that he was also interested in another aspect of monastic life, an experience writers in the Middle Ages, Martin Luther, and Bonhoeffer himself called *acedia* or *acediatristitia*. This Latin word refers in particular to a feeling that would overcome monks who lived cut off from the outer world, and it was characterized by a profound sense of one's impending loss of God and the self. The same word was also used to describe psychic suffering in general: a paralysis of the soul, bitterness, and capitulation of the will to live—in today's terminology what we would call depression. Bonhoeffer experienced traces of this spiritual breakdown,[3] along with the self-destructive impulses that sometimes accompanied it, and he recognized it clearly for what it was. Long before his time in prison he had spoken about depressing moments to his friend Eberhard Bethge. These developed a life of their own under the extreme trauma of imprisonment, and cast a fully different shadow over him.

Such experiences were, however, offset by Bonhoeffer's joyous experience of intense, long-lasting friendships. These are documented in *Scenes from His Life*, as well as in the entire body of his correspondence from the time of his university studies to the last phase of his life. Bonhoeffer's family later helped his friend from student days, Franz Hildebrandt, who was stigmatized as a non-Arian, leave Germany before it was too late. During his stipendium stay in the United States, Bonhoeffer met Erwin Sutz, Jean Lasserre, and Paul Lehmann, who became his friends and fellows in later ecumenical work. In England, he developed strong bonds with Julius Rieger and George Bell, the bishop of Chichester. His ecumenical work and, above all, his work in the Preaching Seminary of the Confessing Church, led to friendships with men such as Otto Dudzus, Winfried Maechler, and Albrecht Schönherr, and of course Eberhard Bethge. (There is no pathos in the observation that this was for both men the most meaningful friendship of their lives.)[4]

Even more than the photographs, Bonhoeffer's diaries and letters call attention to another line of contact he maintained with the world: travel. Relative to the customs and circumstances of that time, Bonhoeffer traveled a great deal. For the most part these were working trips (including those he undertook from 1940 on, in the guise of a military informer). But there were also private trips, especially in his younger years, and these opened up new horizons of experience that left a lasting stamp upon him: Italy, Spain, Mexico, Cuba. . . . Writing to Bethge from prison on March 24, 1944, he described Italy, in particular Rome, as "that piece of land on earth that I love so much" (DBW 8, 365). Twenty years earlier, he had undertaken a trip to Italy with his brother Klaus, and his diary reflects his impressions of it. "My imagination is turning into reality. . . . But the reality is actually more attractive than any pictures in my imagination," is how he describes his first encounter with the Italian landscape (DBW 9, 81–82); in Rome, previously unknown dimensions of Catholicism and art opened up to him; he experienced Sicily as a premonition of the Orient: "A new world opens up inside oneself, it grows upon one from every side, from every street corner" (ibid., 97).

For Bonhoeffer, discussion and music, games and sports, were—if such a thing is possible—as natural as breathing. He was at home in seven foreign languages: Hebrew, ancient Greek and Latin, English, French, Spanish, and Italian. (In the chaos of his last weeks and days of life, he took beginner's lessons in still another language, from a Russian fellow prisoner, a nephew of Vyacheslav Michailovich Molotov, by the way, by striking an original bargain: he gave lessons in Christianity in return for lessons in Russian.) Bonhoeffer's musical talent appears to have been unusual even within his own family, where playing and discussing classical music were part of daily life. Indeed for a time he and his family considered training him as a pianist. Music remained an inseparable dimension throughout his life: it was simply a part of him and remained present even—indeed all the more—in the isolation of his imprisonment. On March 27, 1944, he wrote to Bethge: "It has been a year since I have heard a chorale. But the curious thing is that when one gives himself up totally to it, music heard only with the inner ear is almost more beautiful that that heard physically (DBW 8, 367–68).

In a letter Bonhoeffer wrote to his parents from Barcelona in 1928, he commented on his talent for games and sports: "I play a lot of tennis . . . , am invited to join others in music, and play chess. But one thing I still greatly lack is skill at the card game 'Skat.' Here, one is expected to be good at it; maybe I will learn it yet!" (DBW 10, 38). In the winter of 1932, he described to Erwin Sutz his own way of working with his young confirmation candidates in Wedding, Germany: "I've been living here in the north since the beginning of the year and have placed the boys in different groups every evening. We eat our evening meal together and then play some game. I've taught them chess, and now they play it *molto con brio*" (DBW 11, 64). Sometimes he arranged for a similarly unconventional daily schedule in the Preaching Seminary in Finkenwalde: "When the weather was good, he sometimes cancelled lessons abruptly and went off with the seminarians into the countryside, or to the coast."[5]

There are two documents in *Scenes from His Life* that at first glance appear to contain nothing out of the ordinary, but on closer look prompt reflection. The first brings a smile; it is Bonhoeffer's school grades from the autumn of 1921.[6] The fifteen-year-old pupil in university preparatory school was rated "Very Good" in Religion and Gymnastics, but lacking in orderliness and Writing. ("Writing" is explained in more detail as "legible handwriting"). The other document evokes sadness, for it refers to plans he made several times to visit Mahatma Gandhi in India. "My dear friend," Gandhi wrote on November 1, 1934, "I have received your letter. Provided you and your friend have enough money to pay for the trip back home . . . , you may come whenever you like."[7] Bonhoeffer never went; but the reason the trip never became a reality had nothing to do with money and everything to do with the dark clouds that were ominously gathering on Germany's horizon.

Later, these dark clouds overshadowed an event that was far more important in Bonhoeffer's life, finally obliterating it entirely: his marriage. It would remain utopian, a "Not yet!" that eventually became a

"Never!"; a promise never fulfilled by and in the reality of his life. The correspondence between Maria von Wedemeyer and Bonhoeffer matured into a fully unpretentious, thus all the more authentic, manifestation of love for one another. At the end of April 1944, after his first year in prison, Maria wrote to him: "Often when I wake in the night and you are so much in my mind, I feel as if perhaps a thought of you has awakened me. And if so, that would be welcome. In the morning, when I get up at 5:30, I make every effort to think very gently and tenderly of you, so that you can sleep a little longer. I have drawn a circle in chalk around my bed, about the size of your cell. A table and chair stand there, the way I picture it" (*Love Letters from Cell 92*, 174).

In his feelings for Maria von Wedemeyer, Bonhoeffer discovered music in human existence previously unknown to him, a promise and more: an answer to an indefinable longing for a reality and a fulfillment. He dreamt of the day when they would see one another again outside the prison walls, as in his letter of January 14, 1944: "Then I see the two of us . . . as we walk together through the forest, side by side, seeing as one, taking it all in as one, in touch with the earth and with real things" (*Love Letters from Cell* 92, 119). When she reached her twentieth year, he pictured to her and himself the twenty-year-old that he himself once was: "In those days I still thought that life consisted of thoughts and books. I wrote my own first book and was, I fear, quite proud of it. . . . Luckily, you write no books, but instead you act, you live, and you fulfill in real life what I only dreamed of. To realize, to desire, to act, to perceive, and to endure patiently are not broken shards in you, but a great unity," he wrote to her on April 16, 1944 (ibid., 167, 169). In another letter, he expressed his fear that her perception of him would place him and the love he had for her upon a pedestal, far removed from reality. "The desires I have . . . are very earthly and tangible," he wrote to her on August 20, 1943 (ibid., 42). And in the same letter, a few lines earlier, he said to her with affectionate (self-)irony: "You need to know what I'm really feeling and not view me as one born to be a hermit on a pillar. By the way, I cannot imagine that you would want to marry someone like that, and in light of my church history studies, I wouldn't recommend it either."

No, Bonhoeffer was no saint, certainly not one on a pillar, nor did he have any desire to be one. He was—a theologian.

4

Calling: Theologian

I did not learn my theology all at once; I had to
brood my way deeper and deeper into it.

Martin Luther

Bonhoeffer's decision to become a theologian was probably made in childhood; it was a decision that became final when he was in school at the age of fourteen or fifteen, one that was reached completely on his own; his parents put no pressure on him in this respect. But they accepted his decision. In 1934, when his son was already in the midst of a very active theological life, Karl Bonhoeffer admitted to him: "Back then, when you made your decision to study theology, I often thought to myself that a quiet, sedentary existence as a pastor . . . was really almost not good enough for you," but then he added immediately that he had certainly been ". . . gravely mistaken regarding the 'sedentary' part" (DBW 13, 90).

And indeed he had been mistaken, for Bonhoeffer's life was never that of a quiet, sedentary pastor in Berlin, Barcelona, or London; and even less so thereafter. On the contrary, it isn't going too far to say that Dietrich Bonhoeffer's curriculum vitae resembled that of a theologian "without a permanent address," both in the figurative sense of that expression and—at the end—in the literal and most tragic sense. Speaking figuratively, he wrote to his theological friend Erwin Sutz in the autumn of 1932 (DBW 11, 117) that his visit in Switzerland had been a long-yearned-for asylum in his "theological rootlessness"; from his point of view, both of them were leading "existences somewhere on the outskirts of our church" (ibid., 118). Speaking more literally, from the end of the 1930s on, after he was forbidden to stay in Berlin, except to visit his parents, and after the closing of the Preaching Seminary of the Confessing Church, Bonhoeffer's life resembled that of a "theological outlaw." And finally, from 1940 on, when he was actively connected to the military resistance, his life became that of a "political outlaw" as well.

Nevertheless this existence was one he was able to identify with fully. In 1941, when he learned that one of his relatives had been diagnosed with a terminal illness, he asked himself, "What would I do if I knew that it was going to be over for me in four to six weeks? The question keeps going through my mind. I believe I would try to teach theology as before and to preach often" (DBW 16, 153). His assessment of his own life could not be stated more clearly. What Bonhoeffer formulated both with deep conviction and very dispassionately about his chosen profession in the hypothetical case of an imminent death matched his less dispassionate, deeply felt declaration to study theology as a profession; he once wrote in retrospect that even as a very young man he had found his road laid out before him, a way "which he already knew with certainty as a fourteen-year-old boy that he would travel" (DBW 11, 371). But beyond this, we have no statements from Bonhoeffer himself, no details that explain how and why he decided to study theology. We do, however, know something about his later theological development.

Bonhoeffer was simultaneously a passionate theologian on the one hand and a thorough professional on the other, and his theology no less. Theology was the cornerstone of his life. At the same time, it was a highly individual mixture, specifically Bonhoefferian: his theology was academically grounded through and through, but rooted in and directed toward nothing other than the practice of theology in faith, in the congregation, in sermons, and in the care of souls.[1] This was the constant compass direction, the aim and focus of his theology. As he expressed to Erwin Sutz at the beginning of August 1932: "What occupies me so much at present is the problem of making the Good News concrete" (DBW 11, 100). His theology was eminently intended for practice, not at all meaning "practical theology" in the sense of an academic discipline found within theology and among theologians.

How, then, do we categorize him? Nearly any appellation is conceivable. The course listings taught by any Protestant faculty of theology suggest that "Bonhoeffer" as a topic, as well as the composite mixture of theory and practice—of the deeply abstract reflection and concrete, practical usefulness—his theology represents, could be included among almost all of the disciplines. And this is exactly the case time and again at institutions of theological learning: in systematic theology; in ethics, more precisely in social ethics; in practical theology; in homiletics; in religious instruction; in congregational pedagogy; in ecclesiology; and in ecumenical theology.

Bonhoeffer's theology was theology in practice from yet another perspective: its consequences went beyond the classical terrain of theological thought and action within the church. It subverted the "Two Kingdoms" theory Luther developed, which was based on the letters of St. Paul, and transgressed the unwritten law that commands, "Thou shalt not show resistance!" It swelled like a wave from biblical to systematic theology, and from there to ethics and social ethics. In short, for Bonhoeffer, theology in theory merged seamlessly into a theology of practice. By its very nature, Bonhoeffer's theology automatically drew lines that led from God to the world—and back again.

Yet another force moved in his being. Bethge mentioned three steps in his biography of Bonhoeffer and used these steps as an outline for the biography he wrote: *Theologian—Christian—Man of Our Time;* three unusual steps which are of course to be understood not merely and not strictly chronologically. But they do justice to the basic direction of a process of development. Bonhoeffer's (de-)tour to faith led through theology, not the other way around. His (de-)tour to political thought and action led from theology *and* faith to personal ethical commitment, to political protest.

This dynamic is succinctly reflected in the title Bonhoeffer gave to a long section of his *Ethics*, "On the Last and Next-to-Last Things." His first—theologically distilled—statement is "The source and essence of all Christian life lies contained and determined in a single event the Reformation calls 'justification of the sinner by faith alone' " (DBW 6, 137). In the lines that follow, he delineates the significance of this event, not only for his own life but for that of any person drawn into the Christ-event: "Here the length and breadth of human life are brought together in a single moment, at a single point; the whole of human life is encompassed in this event. . . . The past and future of the whole of life flow together in the present of God" (ibid.). The swings of the pendulum that move between personal faith and authentic piety—between God and one's own life, and back again to God—can never take place without theological reflection. Rather, they are a consequence of it. They go hand in hand with the swings of a political existence which, firmly grounded in theology *and* faith, makes freedom possible in the movement from God to the world and back again to God. Bonhoeffer writes: "The labyrinth of one's previous life folds inward upon itself. The person is free for God and his brother" (ibid.).

Shining through these lines is the image of the double helix of faith and freedom invoked by Martin Luther in his work *On the Freedom of a Christian,* and it is as if Bonhoeffer were taking words out of the mouth of that great reformer when he formulates in this context: "Faith means grounding my life upon a ground outside myself. . . . Faith means consenting to an event and acting only in light of this consent" (ibid., 138). And this action, which in our world becomes part of the sacred precinct of the Last Things, more precisely, what Bonhoeffer calls the "Next-to-Last Things," is guided by the coming of Christ. It is not the precondition for that coming, nor can it cause it to happen, but it is shaped by it. It prepares the way.

In this respect, to be sure, Bonhoeffer goes his own way, following less in the footsteps of Martin Luther. Otherwise he shared much in common with the author of the Reformation. For instance, both theologians wrote with clarity and precision, using language creatively. Both placed enormous emphasis on the centrality of the cross and a *theologia crucis*, whose power derives from the signature of the risen Christ. Both manifest intense despair *and* faith in God. And both men were stubborn about maintaining their specific, respective hope in God. But with regard to the question of preparing the way, of the relationship between ethics and eschatology, Bonhoeffer's thought parts company with Luther the Reformer and follows instead that of another theologian, *the* reformed theologian of his own century, Karl Barth. But more about this later.

In the section of his *Ethics* entitled "The Last and Next-to-Last Things," Bonhoeffer writes that "When for example a human life is bereft of the conditions that are intrinsic to humanity, justification by grace and faith may not be impossible, but it is nevertheless gravely hampered" (DBW 6, 152). And the conclusions he then draws anticipate the liberation theology that grew up decades after Bonhoeffer, following in many respects in his footsteps. The imitation of Christ means action in this world; it always *also* aims at true liberation, always *also* at ensuring that human life can unfold under those "conditions that are intrinsic to humanity" (see above). Action concretizes the consent of faith which conforms to grace and correspondingly prepares the way (ibid., 155). This is what Bonhoeffer means with his postulate and verdict that it is blasphemy against God and one's neighbor to let others go hungry, because God draws nearest precisely in our moment of deepest need: "We break bread with one who hungers, we share our dwelling out of love for Christ, who belongs to the other just as much as to me. If one who hungers does not come to faith, then the guilt for this falls upon the one who has withheld bread from him. Procuring bread for one who hungers is the same as preparing the way for the coming of grace" (ibid.). No more, but also no less.

Here we will not go more deeply into the details of the place Bonhoeffer's theology holds with respect to Christian traditions, in particular its relationship to Evangelical theology, nor how it also distances itself from those traditions. The more important issue here is the way his theology moves in new, original directions and how it opened up, and will continue to open up, new paths into the future. Suffice it to say here that Bonhoeffer's theological provenience was Lutheran, and Luther's influence on Bonhoeffer's theology[2] was unquestionably enduring and identifiable to the end. But this is true of the differences between them as well, especially toward the end.

In the history of theology and the church, it is of course no coincidence that within the broad spectrum of what has been—and still is—called "Protestantism," it is Lutheranism that has demonstrated particular difficulty with respect to protesting. Because of their respect for the authority of those in office, it never entered the minds of Lutherans to protest against those within their own ranks who proudly called themselves "German Christians," much less outside their own ranks, that is, against National Socialism. On the contrary, loyalty to the throne and altar, and a comfortable chumminess between worldly and church officialdom, had become second nature to those in the great Lutheran branch of German Protestantism to the extent that they helped the leaders of "Greater Germany" into the saddle without hesitation, and even with enthusiasm, sometimes celebrating frenetically in their own homes the union of swastika and cross as the new emblem representing the "Faith of German Christians."

Bonhoeffer was unable to (further) identify himself with this kind of Lutheranism and its heritage. However, this did not prevent other, more worthy aspects of Lutheranism from being incorporated into his theology and faith. We find above all Luther's bedrock Evangelical Good News of the unreserved Incarnation of God in the "ungodly" Jesus of Nazareth, a Christ who did not at all correspond—and even today still does not correspond—to the conventional human picture of incarnation but placed himself at odds with it in every respect! Bonhoeffer's ideas about God's logic of crib and cross and the unconditional, unconditioned forgiveness that define justification, which is more accurately called the "certainty of justification," were certainly imbibed from Luther's theology (and the theological emotionality of his poems written in prison is especially close to Luther's piety). But for Bonhoeffer, *Lutheran* elements were less formative than *Luther* himself. This is especially true with respect to Luther's fanatic insistence against all reason on a God of unique and irresistible love who clothes Himself in such laughable, such fearfully inadequate, insignia as the crib and cross and the indefatigable references to the unspectacular life and almost absurd death of Jesus of Nazareth. And it is also true of the "already" and the "not yet" of the kingdom of God, where our own existence falls into the "here and now," but whose biblical promise is what really counts, and this in spite of everything to the contrary.

In general, however, Bonhoeffer's relationship to Lutheran theology was not as ambivalent as his relationship to liberal theology. The reference here is to an Evangelical theological tradition that appeared at the end of the nineteenth and early twentieth century, which was represented by the school where Bonhoeffer studied theology. In spite of later distancing himself from this tradition, Bonhoeffer always considered himself, as he wrote to Bethge on August 3, 1943, "a 'modern' theologian who still carries the heritage of liberal theology within himself" (DBW 8, 555). Berlin's theological faculty was the bastion of this theology, whose most respected representative was Adolf von Harnack, but also included Karl Holl and Reinhold Seeberg. The latter became Bonhoeffer's dissertation supervisor and decades later, with a simultaneous sideswipe *and* kudo, Karl Barth said that if there were any justification for Seeberg it was "in the fact that this man [Bonhoeffer] and this dissertation were able to come from his school"![3]

There can be no question that liberal theology was very beneficial, that it probably had a salutary, immanent influence on the history of theology in contrast to the movements that preceded it, and that it was, in the final analysis, a necessity of the time. It bore within itself above all humanistic and rationalistic, but also idealistic and in any case cultural, Protestant elements. Its greatest advantage was that it did not attempt to avoid the historical critical method, but supported it with might and main. It was also liberal in the best sense in that it attempted to lay aside the blinders of theological orthodoxy and maintain an open viewpoint toward the other sciences. It did, however, have some serious drawbacks. For instance, it ran the danger of an all too zealous *aggiornamento,* an accommodation with the spirit and direction of the times, in overeager obeisance. It ran the danger of rendering the scandal of the cross harmless and—still more—of losing sight of the kerygma, the core of the Christian faith: namely, that, strange as it may seem, it is man who, in spite of everything, is the object of God's great love and that the cross, strange as it may seem, is His declaration of that love. Herein lies not only the dilemma of liberal theology in that day, but also the dangers of the (roller-coaster) ride between the Scylla of accommodation and the Charybdis of resistance, dangers to which a theology and a preaching of the Good News, if they are open (to the world), are apparently always exposed if they do not wish to dwindle to a self-contained system, a "closed mind."

The most important movement that opposed liberal theology was dialectic theology, whose foremost theologian has already been named above, Karl Barth. Shortly after the end of the First World War, Barth's *Letter to the Romans* sounded the death knell to peaceful times for liberal theology. To put it more bluntly, his *Letter to the Romans* was like a hammer blow for many in the world of theology. It ignited a battle, first among theologians and then, with the usual delay, in the Evangelical churches over the "what" and "how" of Christian proclamation. Next to the ensuing tumult, the battle over Rudolf Bultmann's demythologization (German *Entmythologisierung*) during and after the Second World War was nearly a model of politeness and good manners.

It was in the winter of 1924–1925 that Bonhoeffer made "the theological discovery of his life":[4] he read Barth for the first time. But years passed before his first direct meeting with him. In 1931, just before he began lecturing at the University of Berlin, Bonhoeffer went to Bonn for three weeks to hear and see Barth. A long report he wrote to his colleague and friend Erwin Sutz on July 24, 1931 (DBW 11, 18ff.), reveals the deep impression this visit made on him. Likewise, the impression Bonhoeffer made on Barth's seminar is revealed in an entertaining report from Winfried Maechler, later one of Bonhoeffer's students in the Preaching Seminary: "I met him [Bonhoeffer] for the first time during an informal evening at Karl Barth's residence. We were discussing the contents of Barth's 'Dogmatics' lectures. Suddenly a blond, Germanic-type stood up and said, 'There is a passage from Luther which says, "the godless man's curse can be more pleasing to God than the hallelujah of the pious!"' Barth shot out of his chair: 'That is wonderful! Where is that passage, and just who are you?' "[5] For his part, the "blond, Germanic-type" who cited the passage Barth called "wonderful" viewed himself, as he once told Erwin Sutz, as "somewhat bashful" (DBW 11, 21) among "Barthian thinkers" (ibid., 18) because of his "bastard theological origins" (ibid.). He experienced himself quite literally as being between Bonn and Berlin, between the chairs of dialectic and liberal theology. Writing from Bonn, he describes the latter as sadly lacking: "Here is a person from whom there is truly something to be gotten, and people just sit there in pitiful Berlin, feeling blue and bemoaning the fact that there's no one there to learn theology from, along with a lot of other 'profound' insights" (ibid., 20–21). For Bonhoeffer, this meeting with Karl Barth—with his theology and his person, with the theologian "without his books" (ibid., 19)—had the effect of unexpected liberation: "It becomes easier to breathe; I no longer fear suffocating because the air is so thin. I think I have almost never regretted anything so much in my theological past as the fact that I did not go there sooner," he wrote to Sutz (ibid.). He then describes in detail what impressed him the most about Barth, what today we would call his "authenticity": "I am impressed by his discussions even more than his writings and lectures. He is really 100 percent present. I have never before experienced such a thing, nor would I have thought it possible."

That meeting was followed by others, some during the brief period when the Confessing Church was beginning to make itself heard; others even after Bonhoeffer's suspension from his duties in 1935 and Barth's emigration to Switzerland; and a final meeting held at the end of May 1942. This last meeting between Bonhoeffer and Barth had been preceded—fortunately only briefly—by a measure of apprehension. It was Bonhoeffer's third trip to Switzerland as a conspirator, and during it he was informed that his [Bonhoeffer's] stay in Switzerland made Barth "uneasy because of Bonhoeffer's secret assignments," as he recounted the rumor he had heard in a letter to Barth on May 17, 1942 (DBW 16, 267). The nuances of this letter and their immediate responses from the Barth residence, formulated by Charlotte von Kirschbaum (ibid., 269ff.), are impressive; each of the two letters expresses mutual trust, each writer's confidence that he could rely on the other and the will to do so, in spite of richly nourished dissent that was not without its own dangers. And this effort succeeded.

Years after the end of the Second World War, Barth mentioned Bonhoeffer in his typical unorthodox, sharply-worded, provocative, and nearly contradictory Barthian manner: in 1952, immediately after the first publication of *Widerstand und Ergebung* (*Resistance and Surrender*), he wrote in a letter to Regional Superintendent Herrenbrück that Bonhoeffer had been in his eyes an "aristocratic Christian," an "impulsive, visionary thinker": "Now he has left us with the enigmatic statements in his letters—clearly confiding at more than one point that he had a presentiment, but by no means clearly knew, how his story was to continue. . . ."[6]—an assessment, however, which he thereafter severely retrenched in the course of this exhaustive letter. Barth's *Church Dogmatics* also renders judgment much more favorably, for instance, in the context of his thoughts on the Communion of Saints, in a passage concerning Bonhoeffer's dissertation *Sanctorum Communio:* "I confess openly that I worry whether I can maintain here the level reached there by Bonhoeffer: from my own standpoint and in my own language not to say less nor speak with a weaker voice than that young man did then."[7]

With regard to their theologies, there were points of major agreement and substantial disagreement between Bonhoeffer and Barth. These cannot be discussed in detail here. But, with all due care and some reservations, one thing should be understood about these two very individualistic theologians: above and beyond the labels of "Lutheran" and "Reformed," both men were Protestant reformers through and through; yet at the same time there was within both men a distinct affinity for elements of Roman Catholicism, so rare in Evangelical theology, and different in outlines.

The heart of this was the experience of the church as a communion of the faithful, a dimension both men apparently felt was inadequately prominent or experienced in the *concept* and *being* of the Evangelical Church. It was in Rome (!) that Bonhoeffer began, as he himself wrote, to comprehend the idea of "church" (DBW 9, 89). On the next-to-last day of his nearly three-month stay in Italy, a stay, as his diary of that trip richly documents, that awakened thoroughly ambivalent feelings in him concerning the different confessions, after experiencing the great *Te Deum* in St. Peter's Cathedral, he noted: "It left an almost indescribable impression. Once again, I saw at the end what Catholicism is, and once again my heart warmed mightily to it" (ibid., 111).

One assertion, however, can be made with certainty: basic to the theological stance of each of the two theologians was something Anselm of Canterbury, that most philosophical of the Scholastic theologians of the Middle Ages, had characterized as *fides quaerens intellectum:* faith seeking understanding, a faith that prods the intellect (and also makes use of it, one might add). It is no accident that Barth's book on Anselm, which appeared by coincidence in the same year as Bonhoeffer's professorial dissertation, bears precisely this title: *Fides quaerens intellectum.* But this is also where the line of separation between Bonhoeffer and Barth must be drawn. Bonhoeffer's theology is unwilling to violate the precincts of revelation in the name of theology or to bestow too much importance on "positivism of revelation," as he calls it in his letters from Tegel Prison. As one writer explained, "The task of theology is to lead us to the mystery of the Divine as the ever-receding center of reality, without babbling on about its eternally given truth, as if the latter could be grasped logically. In light of this basic difference between Bonhoeffer and Barth, however one may wish to evaluate it, the later verdict concerning Barth's 'Positivism of Revelation' is anything but surprising."[8]

Bonhoeffer had found his own theological path. His fellow travelers along this way were (and remained) Martin Luther *and* Karl Barth—a nearly impossible combination in the eyes and ears of the Faculty of "Evangelical" (that is, in its own view "Liberal") Theology in Berlin. As Bonhoeffer wrote to Erwin Sutz on December 25, 1931, in the midst of his first semester as a lecturer, "My theological origins are gradually becoming suspect here, and they seem to have more or less the feeling of having nourished a snake in their bosom" (DBW 11, 50).

A third person accompanied Bonhoeffer on his way, from beginning to end. Although Bonhoeffer mentions him less often, his influence is not to be underestimated. This was Søren Kierkegaard, an "extraordinary" theologian, a Protestant solitary. In the oversaturated Lutheran State Church in Copenhagen, the city of the Danish king and bishop, the middle-class view was that he had lived "a failed existence," or at best a theologically, literarily, and philosophically strange one. Many of the titles of his works sound like his constant companions: *The Concept of Irony, The Concept of Fear, Sickness Unto Death, Either-Or, Exercises in Christianity*. . . . From the time he began to think and feel, Kierkegaard suffered abysmal depths, a loss of self and loss of God, which he countered and overcame by constantly reinventing himself—with a conscious, desperate, but salutary leap of faith. He lived only to the age of forty-two (and lived, by the way, almost exactly one hundred years before Bonhoeffer) and is regarded as the trailblazer, the forerunner, and the fore-thinker for both dialectic theology and existential philosophy of the twentieth century.

We can only indicate here that the theologies of Bonhoeffer and Kierkegaard are similar in structure, intention, and immediacy; both men were masters of theological language. In his dissertation *Sanctorum Communio,* Bonhoeffer said of Kierkegaard that ". . . our critique of the idealistic concept of time and reality is very close to his. However, it parts company with him at the point where *Kierkegaard* speaks of the origins of the ethical person" (DBW 1, 34 note 12). In another footnote (ibid., 104 note 20), Bonhoeffer characterizes him as one "who was able to speak of the burden of loneliness as few others could"; and he singles him out elsewhere as the man "who spoke of the individuality of each human being as no one else did" (ibid., 171).

Bonhoeffer's affinity with Kierkegaard is documented undeniably and *expressis verbis* in many passages of *Discipleship*. Bonhoeffer himself once put his finger exactly on what it is that characterizes this inner affinity between Kierkegaard and himself, as well as the inner affinity between their common albeit very different theologies of existence, not at all with respect to Kierkegaard but only in speaking of himself. In a letter he wrote to his brother Karl-Friedrich on January 14, 1935, Bonhoeffer remarked: "It may be the case that I appear to you in many things to be somewhat fanatical and even a little unbalanced. I too often fear this side of myself a bit. But I know that if I were to start being more 'level-headed' and honest with myself, the next day I would have to hang up all of my theology like an unused coat" (DBW 13, 272).

But Bonhoeffer did not grow more "level-headed"; instead, he continued to work out a theology whose development did not run smoothly or uniformly either before or after. Several statements by Bonhoeffer himself reflect his theological development and his own understanding of himself as a theologian. In the above-mentioned letter to his brother, for example, he added that he had originally envisioned theology as an academic affair, but it then turned into something quite different: "Now

I think I can finally say that I have found the right track—at least this once—for the first time in my life. And this often makes me very happy" (DBW 13, 272). Bonhoeffer explained this more clearly in a letter he wrote to a woman colleague a year later, when he spoke about a decisive turn in his life, something "that changed my life and turned it around down to the present day. I hit upon the Bible for the first time. . . . I had given many sermons, had a good deal of experience with the church, had spoken and written about Christianity—and was still not a Christian; rather I was totally wild, untamed, and my own master. . . . It was a great liberation" (DBW 14, 113). It is clear that he was reluctant to speak to others about what today is commonly called an experience of "conversion" or "calling." But these statements are further evidence of *his own* stairway in life: from theology to faith. And then from and for the sake of faith, back to the study and teaching of theology!

A self-portrait of Bonhoeffer the theologian also appears between the lines of an essay he wrote during the summer semester of 1933, when he was a university lecturer, which bears the title "What Does It Behoove Today's Student of Theology to Do?" Many of the statements in this essay apply exactly, and from beginning to end, to the theological existence and "existential theology"[9] of Bonhoeffer himself. "It is not an experience of calling but rather a firm decision for sober, earnest, responsible theological work that stands at the beginning of a course of studies in theology," he wrote (DBW 12, 416); the student of theology "is not to think that he must wait for a certain special experience of 'calling.' Rather, he is to accept as his calling the occasion when the questions of theology rivet his attention and refuse to let him go again." Here he is unmistakably speaking of himself, of his own passionate, clear-eyed manner of thinking and practicing theology.

But what were the questions and issues, the content and goal of his theology? What was distinctive about them, at their innermost core? Perhaps the best and possibly "quite simple" answers are to be found in the three classical steps outlined in the Christian credo. Following the Trinitarian triptichs of the credo of the early church, each word contains and tells its own story: *I* believe. I *believe.* In *God.* In *Jesus Christ.* In the *Holy Spirit.*

5

The Language of Faith

> What they utter is Spirit, and the Spirit is what they
> utter—an identity beyond all powers of thought.
>
> *Wilhelm von Humboldt*

Dietrich Bonhoeffer's faith has an unmistakable profile: full of surprises, astonishingly stringent, often impressively clear and consistent, but also enigmatic and at times confusing. It speaks through insinuations whose consequences are not always immediately discernible, if at all. This is only natural in a life that came to an end so quickly that the "instructions for use" for much of his basic thought remained unwritten. All the more respect is commanded by the intensity and unerringness with which his faith was lived out in his brief life.

A note written by Bonhoeffer in July 1944, while he was in Berlin's Tegel Prison, outlines his own understanding of all confessions of faith: "A confession of faith does not express what others *must* believe but what the believer himself *believes*" (DBW 8, 506). Faith, for him, is not a dictate, nor is it donned *pro forma* only to remain, in the final analysis, foreign. On the contrary, it is the deepest of convictions. A confession of faith is the proclamation of what holds an individual existence, if not the world, together in its innermost depths. It can only be spoken in the first person singular because nothing and no one can be held responsible for it other than the speaker; only he can speak for himself. To the extent that a confession is a Christian confession—that is, a confession of Christ—it is the response to the one and only proclamation of God's love, the proclamation of a history that unfolded between Bethlehem and Golgotha and from whose echo the believer draws his life.

In his last-known letter to Eberhard Bethge, written on August 23, 1944, Bonhoeffer expressed his own personal faith, *his own* credo, in words that require no further commentary: "For me, God's hand and guidance are so certain that I hope to be preserved for ever in this certitude. . . . My life up to now has overflowed with God's goodness, and the forgiving love of the crucified One is above all trespasses" (DBW 8,

576). The road that led to this credo had been neither easy nor smooth, nor did it wind its way behind walls or in isolation. Bonhoeffer traveled a road of faith *and* thought that was unprotected and open in all directions. His journey involved modes of understanding, of speaking and acting. These two—being and action—were, in his view, the constitutive elements of faith. There were other elements as well: doubt, fear and despair, surrender *and* resistance.

In Bonhoeffer's thought there were no compartments, no filing cabinet drawers clearly dividing knowledge from confession, *ratio* from *pietas,* understanding from piety. For him, belief and knowledge are the avenues that grant us access to reality; they are neither in competition with one another nor are they accessory methods, but rather "teamworkers" of the Spirit. Understanding illuminated by faith, faith illuminated by understanding: the young theologian who wrote the highly abstract and theoretical academic treatises *Sanctorum Communio* and *Act and Being* held the firm conviction that these two go hand in hand; and this remained his conviction years later when he was a prisoner occupying a cell in Berlin. As he expressed to his friend in August 1944, "At present I am working on the three chapters of which I wrote. It is as you say: the 'moment of understanding' is the most exciting thing in the world, and for that very reason I am completely fascinated by the work" (DBW 8, 563).

Just as for him faith could not exist without understanding, so also faith could not be mute. Faith for Bonhoeffer always involved two things: putting faith into words and making faith understandable, both to oneself and to others. The spoken and written word played an eminently important role in his life and theology, and this all the more so with regard to faith. It was the primary vehicle by which faith expressed itself and poured itself out. This is the only possible explanation for his viewpoint that silence plays a role of major importance, namely, as a contrast to the spoken and written word. Thus he more or less imposed periods of silence on the young men in the Confessing Church's Finkenwalde Seminary. This silence was intended to help stabilize a faith that was coming into its own.

In his dissertation *Sanctorum Communio,* Bonhoeffer makes a statement about himself, and this not only with regard to himself but all persons in general: "Each person finds himself embedded in an inexhaustible wealth of possibilities for expressing and understanding" (DBW 1, 41). Bonhoeffer explored this inexhaustible wealth throughout his life. Indeed, he reveled in it: first through music and the fine arts, then through history and natural science, sociology and philosophy, foreign languages, and literature. He felt a special affinity, for instance, with the French author Georges Bernanos and—above all—with certain trends in nineteenth-century German literature set by authors such as Adalbert Stifter and Theodor Fontane. Their use of language served as his model, although he knew he could not always conform his own use of language to theirs. In a letter to his parents, written in July 1943, he characterized their particular exercise of language, which he found "most congenial": "In the most delicate matters not to be sentimental, in the most serious matters not to become frivolous; not to be pathetic in voicing one's own convictions, never to use oversimplification or exaggerated complexities" (DBW 8, 117).

This description applies in many respects to Bonhoeffer's own use of words. But above and beyond this, he gradually found his own language of faith: it was to the point and original, albeit at times long-winded; it was circumspect and factual, but also at times more than a little equivocal; it was self-reflective *and* impulsive; full of pathos *and* conciseness. Bonhoeffer was not fond of pre-fabricated and polished turns of phrase, but he knew and appreciated the effort that underlies authentic speech: "It is not easy to speak of God's love for the world if one does not wish to bog down in formulaic language," he declared in a sermon he presented in 1940 (DBW 15, 572). He wanted to tell the story of God's great love in the language of the world without losing it in that language. His books differed one from another, as he constantly renewed his attempt to do nothing other than—in the final analysis—speak of this love and its consequences, as far as possible without formulas and platitudes.

One might assume that Bonhoeffer's thought would be transmitted to succeeding generations most compactly and directly through these books. But in his case, a rapid reading of his books cannot convey an accurate perception of his thought, nor even a full understanding of the man himself. Bonhoeffer opens himself up to us at least as much, if not more so, through writings that were originally spoken by him or intended for use in actual situations: his letters and sermons, his university lectures, and his speeches. Above all, he comes alive—and remains alive for subsequent generations—through the letters and texts that were published after his death, under the title *Resistance and Surrender*, and through his unfinished *Ethics*.

The two books he was able to finish, and those he intended to be read by a so-called normal theological public within the church, were *Discipleship* and *Life Together*. His two first books, *Sanctorum Communio* and *Act and Being*, were distinctly academic works, or more precisely, his doctoral dissertation (in slightly modified and shortened form) and his professorial dissertation. This context should not be overlooked, since from the beginning they were written for a special purpose and a corresponding special audience. (*Creation and Fall* also belongs among his academic works, since it was not specifically conceived as a book but is a set of his university lectures that were subsequently published.) Bonhoeffer was unable to finish his *Ethics*, as already mentioned; this book has come down to us in the form of individual segments he had worked on, as far as possible, up to the day of his arrest.

Without a doubt, the book that has had the most widespread impact is *Resistance and Surrender*. Strictly speaking, this is not one of Bonhoeffer's "books," but a compilation of his *Letters and Notes from Prison*. Whether or not some of his other books, such as *Life Together*, which has also been widely read, and *Discipleship*, have exerted a similarly widespread influence on individuals and spirituality must remain a moot question; it is, after all, only natural that the echo from these books was not articulated so loudly. Other, more belletristic manuscripts begun by him in prison, as already mentioned, were deliberately broken off and published posthumously as *Fragments from Tegel Prison*. Bonhoeffer did not write these—at least not in their original versions—with the intention of publishing them. For him, their purpose was to provide an existential anchor from the past in light of his isolation and life-threatening situation in the present.

Bonhoeffer's style of writing is not uniform in either his shorter texts or his books, perhaps because his subjects were so dissimilar. Thus *the* language of Bonhoeffer is not to be found in them. Rather, the development of his written language reflects the different phases of his life and has as many facets as the places where his texts came into being and their purposes; one is a scientific treatise, the other a sermon; one is a personal letter, the other a theological reflection; one is a lecture presented before a live audience, the other a plan for a book. But whatever the nature and purpose of the writing, there are two characteristic elements that remain invariably present in Bonhoeffer's language of faith: "theological expressionism" and paradox.[1]

Theological expressionism refers to Bonhoeffer's manner of putting God's reality into words, because at its core this is in a process of fermentation; there is an expressivity, a power of expression and impact, that probably has no equal in theology even today. This expressionism appears to be based on an unrelenting, self-imposed rule: Bonhoeffer, it seems, wanted to determine the authenticity of his faith and bear witness to it by constantly attempting to verify whether or not his inner world was identical to the outer language of his faith; whether his *impression* of faith equaled his ability to *express* it. In other words, he tested whether or not the language he used to proclaim and announce the

Good News—regardless of how inadequately that language may have fully expressed the essence of that Good News—was consistent with it, at least to some extent.

Examples of theological expressionism crop up often enough in any study of Bonhoeffer or his work; only a few need be mentioned here. Several instances appear in the notes of his university lectures delivered during the winter of 1932–1933 which, as we have already mentioned, appeared in print in 1933 under the title *Creation and Fall*. These particular lectures, focused on the first three chapters of the Bible, were delivered during a time when Bonhoeffer—to put it cautiously—seems to have experienced something like a conversion or calling. He himself was very reticent about this. But Eberhard Bethge later remarked that something took place in Bonhoeffer's life during this time that was very difficult to identify; clearly a change took place, one that carried within itself the seeds of "everything that was to come in this time period."[2]

This *Theological Commentary on Genesis 1–3* (as it was called in the subtitle of the lecture series) begins with the opening lines of the Bible, followed by a strongly worded passage: "At the place where the most passionate waves of our thought curl and break, are cast back upon themselves and lose themselves in foam, this is where the Bible begins" (DBW 3, 25). When asked what it means that in the beginning God was, Bonhoeffer replied: "What is the meaning of these first words of the Scripture? Are they the deluded fantasies of a coward, a human being who at the core is incapable of living proudly and resignedly, and thus the person we ourselves all are, we who cry out from the cowardice of our lives, without beginning or end, to a God who is our own ego?" (ibid., 28–29). The infinite difference between Creator and creature has infinite consequences, and only a single bridge can resolve them: ". . . if the Word is not present, then the world plunges into the abyss" (ibid., 38).

The other characteristic element of Bonhoeffer's language of faith, namely, his partiality for paradox, is also readily present in his thought and writings. Ordinarily, we associate the word "paradox," according to its Greek roots, with all that is highly curious and strange, with the grotesque and the absurd, with all that goes against reason, and in particular with anything that is contradictory. But the word "paradox" originally meant "aside from (official) teaching," or "contrary to appearances." Thus a paradoxical statement contains truth in spite of being contradictory; indeed, it contains truth precisely when and *because* it appears to be contradictory. Bonhoeffer's attempts to translate faith into words are shot through with paradoxical turns of phrase. In fact, his ideas are most successful, that is, most provocative, when they are expressed in paradoxes. Often enough, this was Bonhoeffer's instrument of choice when attempting to speak with a modicum of truth about something that is ultimately unfathomable, namely, the reality of God. To this extent, his theology can be characterized as a paradoxical theology, and this on more than one level.

Bonhoeffer himself liked to use the term "paradox" often—accompanied, by the way, with references to Kierkegaard[3]—and he spoke explicitly of how fundamentally paradoxical the Christian Good News is. In his dissertation he singled out "the paradoxical reality of Christian community in the cross" as a community that harbors within itself the opposites of "extreme loneliness and closest community simultaneously" (DBW 1, 95); "thus the cross becomes the center and paradoxical sign of the Christian Good News. A king who goes to a cross must reign over an odd kingdom. Only those who understand the profound paradox in the idea of the cross can fully understand Jesus' meaning when He says: 'My kingdom is not of this world,'" said Bonhoeffer in 1928 (DBW 10, 320) in one of the sermons he preached to his congregation while a vicar in Barcelona (entitled "Jesus Christus und vom Wesen des Christentums" ["On Jesus Christ and on the Essence of Christianity"]). In a Christmas meditation he wrote in 1939, he said that he admired the "Old Church," that is, Early Christianity, because its credo bore witness "to the mystery of the living person of Jesus Christ" and "did not shy away from uttering the final conceptual paradoxes" (DBW 15, 539). Particularly during the last phase of his life and faith, he was convinced that there is a paradoxical commingling of the theology of the cross and the world's coming of age, between the "uncomplicated paradox of the *theologia crucis* and man's assumption of responsibility for himself."[4] In short, Bonhoeffer himself continually chose statements that are truly paradoxical (and not merely paradoxical in appearance), precisely in order to translate his central insights in faith into words.

A few examples from different phases in the progression of Bonhoeffer's thought and faith, with no attempt to delve into their content and intention, demonstrate Bonhoeffer's partiality for paradoxical formulations. To sum up the relationship between Jesus Christ and the Christian church in terms of time, he wrote in his dissertation *Sanctorum Communio* (DBW 1, 97) that the church comes to fruition in Christ; that time no longer exists; *and* that the church is to build upon Christ in time as its immovable foundation. In light of the impossibility of thinking about God as we do an object or a thing, independently of the existence of the subject or the self, he sums up his view of God in his professorial dissertation, *Act and Being*, accordingly: "A God who is 'out there' does not exist; God 'is' person in relationship; His being is His being as person" (DBW 2, 112).

As if anticipating one of the most important paradoxes he later developed in prison, his lecture on the opening lines of Genesis stated with respect to this God: ". . . He is never in the world except as one who is utterly beyond the world" (DBW 3, 39). Later, in a letter he wrote on April 30, 1944, he modified this position, thus firing the opening shot of his prison theology: "God is in the midst of our life beyond it" (DBW 8, 408). Bonhoeffer's partiality for paradox has also left its traces in *Discipleship*, where we read for example: "The cup of suffering will pass by Jesus, *but only by being drunk*" (DBW 4, 83). Without a doubt, the most telling paradoxes, however, are found in *Resistance and Surrender*, for example his "religion-less Christianity"—that famous and difficult phrase to which a full chapter will be devoted later in this book.[5] Or the no less famous and no less difficult description of the God who is with us *and* is the God who abandons us. In a letter he wrote on July 16, 1944, he draws the following conclusion: "The God who lets us live in a world devoid of God as a working hypothesis is the God before whom we stand without pause. Before and with God we live without God" (DBW 8, 533–534).

Theological expressionism and a proclivity for paradox were apparently the immutable personal characteristics of the specifically Bonhoefferian way of believing. But there was also a further, ultimately decisive, characteristic of his faith: it was never a passive, introverted faith nor did it ever deteriorate into mere activism. On the contrary, his faith was a dialectic union of the *vita contemplativa*, the life of contemplation, and the *vita activa*, neither one being more important than the other. Introverted faith constantly interacted and alternated with extroverted faith according to various phases of his life. Being a Christian includes the basic understanding that faith is lived—or it is not faith. The man or woman of faith is impelled to implement that faith in the world. But only a faith that constantly reaffirms itself and looks inwardly can manifest itself outwardly; thus it is always "my" faith, not simply one among others: credo means "*I* believe. . . ." Bonhoeffer transformed Decartes' "*Cogito ergo sum*" ("I think, therefore I am") into "I believe, therefore I am." And for him, an inescapable conclusion followed: "I am, therefore I act!" Faith, thought, being, action—for him, these were like the four fixed points of a parallelogram: side by side, opposites, one above the other, each related to the other. To further this image, the entire parallelogram represents a life that comes from God and is ever on the way to God.

6

God—Truly Near, Truly Far

"There is a God" and
"Whale calves are born alive":
Few of us think twice about such things.
They remain for us just the way
we learned them in school.

Kurt Tucholsky

Both latently and manifestly, the central theme of Dietrich Bonhoeffer's life was the reality of God. Not an abstract divinity, a
higher being, an absolute beyond time, but the reality of the living God
in the world: herein and hereby the whole of reality revealed itself. In his
view, God bears witness to this reality, even as it bears witness to God.
God's reality is irrevocably a part of the horizon of personally experienced reality. As Bonhoeffer himself expressed the focus and goal of his
thought and life, "the reality of God manifests itself everywhere as the
final reality" (DBW 6, 32). At the very core of his personal existence,
Bonhoeffer was convinced of the personal existence of God, a God who
is "not merely our fate beyond time" (DBW 8, 31), but a being who becomes real in the midst of this world's coordinates, in the midst of time,
space, and human existence. The reality of his own human existence was
inextricably derived from the reality of God, which he in turn identified
with the reality of the world. The whole of his life and thought revolved
around the proclamation of God as this reality in this world, for the men
and women of this world.

Christian existence is simply participation in the reality of God.
Expressing this reality of God in words, making it transparent, living
in accordance with it, was a constituent part of Bonhoeffer's hopes and
actions, and for him it constituted the root of Christian existence. In
all his books, but most explicitly in his *Ethics,* he speaks either directly
or indirectly of God's indispensable, ineluctable reality: "*Participation
in the indivisible whole of God's reality*" (DBW 6, 38). To this end he di-
rects all of his coiled energy, meaning "the reality of God as the final

reality without and within all that exists; it is thus the reality of the existing world as well, a world that has reality only through the reality of God" (ibid., 39).[1]

If the lines of thought sketched here were extended, they would reach back to the (Christ) event, in which God's reality culminates *as* the reality of the world, and from there they would continue on to the consequences of this for our understanding of *post-Christum* reality. Since the time of Jesus, and through Him, the world has ceased to be a "dual system": transcendence and immanence converge in Him beyond and within it, and God is once and for all not a God who dwells merely in the preserve of metaphysics, in a realm only nebulously perceived behind the reality of the world. It is God Himself who is unwilling to wall himself off from the world or be separated either from it or within Himself. Reality is an undivided whole, and a God who is responsible only for parts of it would not be—God. God is the author of the proximate, real "here and now" *as well as* the remote, seemingly unreal, "there and then." Therefore there is no division within this reality according to a principle of "bi-compartmentalization," however it may be named, and this because thinking and living in such a bi-compartmental system, in Luther's "two kingdoms," has become obsolete for Christian men and women. A duality of the spiritual and the worldly, of a Christian existence and a political existence, is in the final analysis an outmoded construct that must be revised.

According to Bonhoeffer, the notion of two realms, which is found throughout the history of the church, cannot be found in the New Testament. There, "the single, most important issue is the emergence of Christ's reality as a reality in the world which it has already embraced, taken possession of, taken unto itself, the world of the present" (DBW 6, 44). Too often, this world of the present is perceived as the factual world before which we are to bow down or whose rejection has become for us almost a cardinal principle. On the basis of his theory of identity, Bonhoeffer argues against this: "To recognize the factual and to contradict it are inextricably connected characteristics of a life lived in conformity with reality; the reason being that *reality* is first and last not something neutral but *that which is real*, namely God become man" (ibid., 261).

To pursue this further at this point would be to anticipate a later discussion and divert our attention away from the real topic of this chapter, which originally was meant to be "Bonhoeffer and the Question of God 'As Such.'" In truth, for Bonhoeffer there is no such thing as a God "as such," for God as very God is never in His essence simply God by Himself; instead God is before time, at all times, and beyond all times, in life for me, for us. This is the meaning of the theological terms *pro me* and *pro nobis*. On the other hand, God is not absorbed into the subjectivity of the believer. God is real, and God is real not only in faith but also, in Himself, God *is* God *pro me*, that is, "for me." The reality of God comes to meet me—comes to meet us—in the very God who became real man and seeks real men and women. Community is experienced when the "every-man-for-himself" law of human existence is broken. For Bonhoeffer, the loneliness of the believer, as intensely as he himself sometimes experienced it, is superfluous in God's eyes, precisely because the Christian community embodies the company and communion of believers, and this communal solidarity of Christians is founded on God's solidarity with us: togetherness is the reverse side of loneliness.

These pairings are reminiscent not only of the works Bonhoeffer was able to complete, from *Sanctorum Communio* through *Act and Being*, *Discipleship*, and *Life Together* but also—as already emphasized—of his *Ethics* manuscripts and *Resistance and Surrender*. Each of these works will be discussed in its own right, but some of the basic principles and core ideas presented in them undeniably belong here as well, since Bonhoeffer's thoughts move, as it were, in concentric orbits around the reality of God, the reality of Christ who manifests it, and the reality of the world encompassed by it. In the reality of Christ we become participants in the reality of God. This, and nothing other, is what is meant by faith.

In his dissertation *Sanctorum Communio,* Bonhoeffer transformed Hegel's dictum of "God existing as the community of believers" into "Christ existing as the community of believers."[2] Here the reality of God becomes identical to the reality of Christ and becomes nearly palpable in the communion of the faithful. In his professorial dissertation *Act and Being*, Bonhoeffer writes that "God's word does not exist independently from His revelation of Himself to man, nor from its being heard and believed by man" (DBW 2, 77). This line of thought includes the central thesis of this work, also cited above, that God is not *a given*.[3] Bonhoeffer affirms that "the path of theological thought runs from God to reality, not from reality to God" (ibid., 83–84). And the indirect and direct link with *Sanctorum Communio* again becomes evident when he writes, "God is free—not from man, but for man. Christ is the word of God's freedom. God *is* present, not in the form of an eternal spirit but He is 'haveable' and 'graspable'—provisory though these expressions are—in His word in the church" (ibid., 85).

Similarly, in *Discipleship* the reality of God, of Christ, and the community of believers are all mentioned in the same breath: "The temple is the site of God's merciful presence, it is God's abode among us. At the same time, it is where the community of believers is accepted by God. Both have become reality only in Jesus Christ become man. This is where God's presence is real and corporeal" (DBW 4, 238). By the same token, in *Life Together* Bonhoeffer characterizes the brotherhood of the community of believers as God's abode in our world: "Christian brotherhood is not an ideal that remains yet to be realized; rather God in Christ has already made it reality—and we are allowed to participate in it" (DBW 5, 26). As if to continue this thought, he writes in the section entitled "Christ, the Reality and the Good" of the *Ethics*, "In Christ we are offered the opportunity to participate simultaneously in both God's reality and that of the world, the one not without the other. God's reality opens itself up to me only by placing me wholly within the reality of the world; for my part, I will always believe that the world's reality is founded upon, accepted by, and reconciled in God's reality" (DBW 6, 40).

Bonhoeffer's faith in God's reality had its own history. It was not an erratically tumbling boulder; it was rather a certitude attacked, but one which constantly reconstituted itself. His faith is not to be viewed as one that was at his disposal, unchanging, and fully self-evident from his early years throughout the vicissitudes of his life. To be sure, there were times and situations when Bonhoeffer appeared to lose his grip on this certitude, times and places he referred to as "the dark side of the moon"; but by no means did he escape the experience of this dark side of faith. No one, however certain he may be of God's nearness, can be certain of never falling away from this certainty. There are events and periods in life when both conventional and eccentric interpretations and attempts to clarify or explain things run aground, and "God" exists only as a cry or an empty word. This remoteness from God was not unknown to Bonhoeffer. In rhythms we cannot fully explore here, and at points of crisis and major decisions in his life, however different their intensity may have been, he experienced something he once described as "his personal '*acedia tristitia*,' with its menacing consequences."[4]

By *acedia*, a term we have already mentioned, he meant the monastic susceptibility to passivity, the leaden heaviness sometimes experienced in the early church, which Luther later painted in dark colors; a temptation of a special kind. Fully in accordance with the meaning of the word, Bonhoeffer understood *acedia* as an acidic bitterness of the soul, the gray odium of an evaporating faith. In March 1936, while at the Preaching Seminary of the Confessing Church, he spoke about this malady in more general terms. As one hearer wrote in his notes on the lecture, "*The believer is at odds with himself.* He grapples with the Other in himself; it drives him into *loneliness.* Everything between him and

God loses meaning, becomes useless, is completely dark; he loses sight of God entirely. Not doubt of salvation, but doubt that God is there at all" (DBW 14, 583).

Although it is clear that Bonhoeffer never experienced a "total eclipse" of God's presence, he did experience the blackness of God's remoteness. There are indications of longing for a faith that was more constant than that which—at times at least—was his own. In his dissertation (DBW 1, 32), he speaks of God as an impenetrable "You" (but, it must be added, as a "*You*" nevertheless). And at the beginning of a sermon he delivered in the autumn of 1931, he spoke of a desperate struggle to find meaning, to find God: "The pillars of life have begun to crumble; where one thought he would find a firm handhold one grasps nothing but thin air. God, where are you? God, who are you? God, who am I? My life disintegrates, falls into a bottomless pit. God, I grow afraid" (DBW 11, 377).

Similarly, in a letter he wrote to a colleague at about the same time, he describes the state of his inner and outer life as follows: "I am presently the student chaplain at the Theological Academy. How is one to preach such things to these people? Who still believes them? The unseen does us in. When we cannot see in our own personal lives that Christ came, we would at least like to see it somewhere else, like India; but this crazy, ongoing experience of coming up short against the unseen God himself—nobody can endure it" (DBW 11, 33). Once again, by the way, we see here Bonhoeffer's gaze toward India and Gandhi, another life project that would remain only a dream.

In a sermon he wrote for the first Sunday of Advent that same year, 1931, he used the leitmotif "Waiting for God" to delineate again and again the fundamental situation of one who awaits the God whose presence, when it comes, surprises and overwhelms him: "We cannot wait for God with the same resignation, the same patience, the same reasonability we would show in waiting for a raise in pay," he says, as a way of differentiating the lack of reasonability and patience in waiting for God (DBW 11, 391). Place is made for God only by one who abandons himself fully. And he continues, "Rather, such a one sees himself wrenched out of the waiting in which he wished only to aggrandize himself; he is forcefully pulled into a foreign, irresistible, wonderful event that simply happens without his doing" (ibid., 392). But even then, the fact is that "No one ever possesses God in such a way that there is no longer any need to await Him. And no one can wait for God unless he knows that God has long been waiting for him" (ibid., 393).

Bonhoeffer's faith moved between these two poles: waiting for God and being caught up in God's reality. The nearly boundless dynamic between the nearness and remoteness of God's reality is what makes Bonhoeffer's faith so plausible—not to say moving; or, to use two of his favorite expressions, so "down to earth" and "honest." Later, when he was in prison, he jotted the following on a piece of paper: "I am waiting for God" (DBW 8, 507). But in that same place he also spoke of being caught up in the following of Jesus and the messianic event (see ibid., 535–36).

This ambivalence of the hidden, the loving, the remote and near God and the ambivalence of his own faith is reflected, for example, in another sermon given by Bonhoeffer in May 1935; its basic theme is that God is mysterious and the world is lacking mystery. The world desires a God it can take the measure of and make use of, "or no God at all" (DBW 13, 361). It molds gods for itself according to its own wishes, "yet it fails to recognize the God who is near, secret, hidden" (ibid., 362). God's mystery, however, is both sealed and revealed in that "God does not remain remote from man but comes *close* to him and loves him" (ibid.).

In spite of much experience with the brittleness of faith, Bonhoeffer always felt himself held fast by this extra-ordinary love of God. It was clear to him that this love has no expiration date, sets no conditions, cancels all criteria, and breaks through the barriers of reality. In the section of his *Ethics* manuscript entitled "Ethics as Creation," he—almost jubilantly—put his finger on this out-of-the-ordinary story of God's love for man in a single sentence: "The love of God became death's death and man's life" (DBW 6, 78). This love became the center of Bonhoeffer's own life. The result was a one-of-a-kind constancy in faith and—above all—a clear distance from fear.

Especially during the last few months of his life, Bonhoeffer seems to have experienced a freedom from fear that, from the perspective of an outsider, was almost uncanny. It was not that he did not know the meaning of fear and self-doubt, nor that he never had any doubts about God; it was not that he did not question himself, nor that his self-confidence was not at times shaken to its very core. But it seems that *with* his fear and *in* his isolation (perhaps precisely because of them?) Bonhoeffer was also conscious of the reality of God; and he was able both to draw life from this reality and to direct his life toward it, even in the shadow of fear and the assaults on his faith. Bonhoeffer's prison poems, "Who Am I?" and *By Goodly Powers Wondrously Sustained,* bear witness to his deeply personal relationship with God, a witness that needs no further commentary here.[5]

About a month after the assassination attempt against Hitler failed on July 20, 1944, thus sharply increasing the risk that hidden channels of conspiracy would now be uncovered, Bonhoeffer wrote to his friend Eberhard Bethge, "It is certain that we are allowed to live always in God's nearness and presence . . . ; that for us, there is no longer anything that is impossible, because nothing is impossible for God; that no earthly power can touch us except by the will of God, and that danger and need simply impel us to draw closer to God; it is certain that our joy lies hidden in suffering, our life in death; it is certain that in all these things we stand in a togetherness that supports us. In Jesus, God said 'Yes' and 'Amen' to all of these things. And this 'Yes' and 'Amen' is the firm ground upon which we stand" (DBW 8, 573).

Bonhoeffer wanted to make God's "Yes," spoken only once and once-for-all, audible in every moment of the present. The Alpha and Omega of the Christian proclamation is God's "Now," the actualization of His reality in the present. Lot's wife looked back and turned into a lifeless pillar of salt; but God seeks living men and women to carry his message, men and women—each with his or her own past, with his or her own personal history—who have been touched by God's love, and in response devote themselves to the "Now," to liberating God's Good News from the imprisonment of traditional nomenclature. This is the only way the fullness of life promised in the Good News can be opened to us. Only in this way can the concrete will of God be recognized and answered, not in a "heaven" of abstraction and ideas, but on earth and through our deeds. The concretization of God's genuineness in Jesus Christ is mirrored and echoed in our concrete proclamation. This is what Bonhoeffer was referring to when he spoke at an ecumenical youth conference for peace in 1932, in a speech he entitled "On the Theological Foundations of Work in the World Federation": "Therefore the church may not proclaim immutably true principles, but only mandates that are valid today. For that which is true 'forever' is precisely untrue 'today': God is 'forever' *God* for us precisely '*today*.'" (DBW 11, 332).[6]

More than anywhere else, it was in *Discipleship* that Bonhoeffer urgently returned, again and again, to the *hic et nunc*, the "here and now," of God's call in the person of Jesus of Nazareth. In so doing, he pointed out the fact that the reality of God is always concrete. One corresponds to the other: flight into a revelation from the past is nothing other than flight into revelation as an abstraction; it puts the whole matter superbly and forever on ice. Jesus, on the other hand, calls us "into concrete situations where He becomes credible; that is why He calls so concretely and wants to be understood in just this way, because he knows that only in concrete obedience do we become free for faith" (DBW 4, 73). The important thing is that Jesus Christ is alive today: "He is present to us today, in the flesh and in His word" (ibid., 215).

Once again, it becomes clear that for Bonhoeffer, the reality of God cannot be had without Jesus Christ. Nor can it be had without or beyond the reality of this world. God exists only in Jesus Christ, and it is in Him that the world opens itself up for Bonhoeffer. The central theme of his theology, as summed up by scholars of Bonhoeffer's life and work, is "the union of God with the reality of the world as realized in Jesus Christ."[7] Throughout Bonhoeffer's life, the quest for God and the questions of the world were closely linked—how could it have been otherwise?—to one question: Who was and who is this Jesus Christ?

7

Jesus Christ—God Incarnate and Incognito

Abandoned at the end of crucifixion, what
bottomless love on both sides!

Simone Weil

In a kaleidoscope, the same individual elements always come together in new ways to form a unique whole that consists—when all is said and done—of the same original parts. Similarly, the individual elements of Bonhoeffer's theology produce countless variations but always according to the same basic pattern: Jesus is the Christ and God has come to us in Him. To oversimplify: Bonhoeffer's whole theology is Christology. The Archimedean point in his entire body of thought is the point where the vertical line of God's reality crosses the horizontal line of the world's reality: on the cross of the Nazarene. The reality of God becomes concrete in the man Jesus of Nazareth. It is in Him that we can see that and how it is God's will to be for us.

According to Bonhoeffer, without Jesus of Nazareth, the word of God would remain only a word; but through Him it is filled with life; it becomes corporeal and real. The Incarnation of God forms an arc that extends from the crib to the cross, but this Incarnation is God incognito; God stripped bare of the attributes of divinity so familiar to us; a Savior who does not choose the King's Highway but the byways of salvation; a Savior who rewrites laws that were previously considered holy and who—so utterly ungodly and unsightly—traffics with the pariahs of religion and society. In the end, he is killed in the most gruesome manner possible. But it is precisely in Him that God's love is made manifest and this love is, as the Song of Songs from the Hebrew Bible declares, "stronger than death." It aims to be the center of man's life.

To be sure, Bonhoeffer was not the first theologian to view Jesus Christ as the focal point of reality, as the mediator between God and man, and the mediator between man and man; nor is this viewpoint peculiar to Bonhoeffer's thought alone. But it is so central to his thought that the other elements crystallize into a whole only as they radiate from it. It is no coincidence to read in *Life Together* (20) that Jesus is "forever the one and only mediator," and as Bonhoeffer emphasizes in *Discipleship,* that "*He is the Mediator* not only between God and man but also between man and man, between man and reality" (DBW 4, 88). The central theme of a monograph by Ernst Feil, devoted to a detailed historical overview of Bonhoeffer's Christology, is entitled "Jesus Christ as Middle and Mediator."[1] Another monograph on Bonhoeffer's theology even bears the overall title *Christ As Reality.*[2]

The Man from Galilee appears in Bonhoeffer's writings, books, lectures, and sermons so frequently that it would be impossible even to attempt to present a full catalogue here; however, a few examples may serve to highlight Bonhoeffer's understanding of Christ. One of the lectures Bonhoeffer presented when he was a curate in Barcelona clearly indicates the extent to which Jesus of Nazareth was the key figure in his thought. Not immodestly, he entitled this lecture, given in December 1928, "On Jesus Christ and the Essence of Christianity"—certainly with a glance toward Ludwig Feuerbach's criticism of religion in his portentous work *The Essence of Christianity,* and Adolf von Harnack's famous work on liberal theology, which bears the same title. We will return to this lecture later,[3] inasmuch as Bonhoeffer's resentment of "religion," which was heightened by dialectical theology, already plays an important part in it. But for now, it is the way the contours of Bonhoeffer's interpretation of Jesus begin to take shape that is of interest to us.

Following in the footsteps of Barth, Bonhoeffer classifies knowledge, morality, the church, religion, and other high-flying human projects as hopeless attempts to build a stairway to God, just like the Tower of Babel; thus he rejects them out of hand: "If man and God are to come together, there is only one way: the way of God to man" (DBW 10, 315). Such high-handed attempts on the part of man point in the wrong direction. Christ alone speaks of the *other* direction; he *alone* speaks of the other direction. "No," says Bonhoeffer, therefore, "the Christian idea is that of the way traveled by God to man, with its visible concretization: the cross" (ibid., 319). Jesus catches up to us even and—precisely— at the point where He is annihilated. It becomes clear in Him that God seeks the company of man; He follows after him in unconditional love. The meaning of Jesus' life, according to Bonhoeffer, lies in the documentation of this divine will: "Where Jesus is, there is God's love" (ibid.).

This love does not shrink back from the last and lowest point of human existence but takes upon itself the final disaster "that looms over every life, namely, death" (DBW 10, 319). Only through truly dying and through the true death of Jesus does it become certain that God's love is not an illusion but reality—namely, a lifelong love unto death. This is the only way, Bonhoeffer emphasizes, that we can be certain "that God's love goes with us and guides us through death" (ibid., 320). And he reminds us here of the words spoken by Jesus as he hung on the cross, the often-quoted New Testament saying that Jesus prayed from his depths when he desperately cried out the opening words of Psalm 22: "My God, my God, why have you forsaken me?" Since that time, and because of it, we can be certain, Bonhoeffer says, "that the eternal will of God in love does not abandon us even at the point where we are about to despair, thinking God has abandoned us" (ibid.). It is precisely here that the infinite love of God manifests itself, by falling into despair with us— in the person of the man Jesus—and refusing to let go of us even in death. But this implies love's defeat: death is rescinded precisely in Jesus' death. In Bonhoeffer's words, "And it is only because Jesus on the cross withstands the test of His own and God's love for the world that the resurrection follows upon death; death cannot hold love fast" (ibid.). He quotes here from the Song of Songs—"Love is stronger than death"— and continues: "That is the meaning of Good Friday and Easter Sunday: God's road to man leads back to God" (ibid.).

During the summer semester of 1933, when Bonhoeffer was an assistant professor at the University of Berlin, he taught a course in Christology that again explicitly took up the topic of Christ in theology and the history of theology; in other words, this time he took up the topic in a classical manner.[4] The comments he made in that course are preserved only in notes taken by his auditors, but even so one clearly hears the "original Bonhoeffer" in them. His minutely arranged exposition begins by isolating the central question about the meaning of Christ, "Who are you? Are you God Himself? The only purpose of Christology is to answer this question" (DBW 12, 282). What is decisive, Bonhoeffer explains, is to remain with this question of "Who?" without "losing one's way between the Scylla of the 'How?' and the Charybdis of the 'That' questions" (ibid., 285). The old church ran aground on the first, modern theology on the second, while Luther, Paul, and the New Testament went straight through its center. Bonhoeffer's attempt to answer the "Who?" question is dialectic in structure. The category of the Present is of decisive importance to him here; it implies simultaneity of both time and place, that is, being present. The presence of Christ, His simultaneity in time and His actual presence, result from His being man *and* God.

Bonhoeffer assumes that God can be present to us only because he is man. "But," he elaborates, "the fact that He is forever present to us, forever simultaneous to us: that is His presence as God. Only because Jesus is God can He be present to us. The presence of Jesus Christ forces us to say that Jesus is wholly man but also that Jesus is wholly God; otherwise He would not be present" (DBW 12, 294). Bonhoeffer turns this thought over and over, modifies it, and rephrases it anew in words that are nothing other than a repetition and a match for the credo the early church formulated as "true God and true man." He even spins this in negative form: "God in His timeless eternity is *not* God. Jesus Christ in His humanity within the confines of time is *not* Jesus Christ. Rather, God is God in the man Jesus Christ. Only in Jesus Christ is God present" (ibid.).

But—aside from the danger of becoming fixated anew on the "How?" question—all this has not yet fully plumbed the depths of the decisive element; this takes place only when something is added, which Bonhoeffer calls the "*pro me* ('for me') structure": "The being of Christ's person is in its very essence directed toward me. His being as Christ is His being '*pro me*'" (DBW 12, 295). There is for Bonhoeffer no question that Christ cannot be conceived of in His being as such, but only in His being "for me," only in a mutual personal relationship; or, to express it another way, only in an existential dimension. And only within the community of believers! The "Church," as a dimension in Bonhoeffer's eyes, is by its very nature intrinsically situated in the dimension of Christ's presence.

We may pass over the question as to what extent Bonhoeffer's approach in "thinking" about Christ (ibid.) is trapped in a hermeneutic circle: God's presence in the man Jesus is affirmed, described, called upon as evidence and confessed—whereby that which is to be understood is, in the final analysis, taken as a given. Therefore it is more correct to ask, how it is possible to believe in Christ instead of "thinking" about Christ? This question is also much more consistent with the whole of Bonhoeffer's theology.

In a masterful march through the history of dogma and theology, Bonhoeffer discusses in his lectures on Christology the attempts made over the centuries to make, as he says, "the incomprehensibility of the Person of Jesus Christ comprehensible" (DBW 12, 315). Put more simply, they have absolutized either His being as God or His being as man; that is, they view it in isolation from His specific manner of being. Since these attempts have always run into insurmountable obstacles and could indeed in their one-sidedness and inadequacy not do otherwise, and have ended as heresy, he calls them "critical" or "negative" Christology. Nevertheless, in Bonhoeffer's eyes these critical or negative Christologies—the plural seems to be more appropriate—serve a useful purpose in several ways. First, simplistic, positive statements about Jesus Christ have become impossible as a result of them; alone the apparent contradiction between "true man and true God" has detonated simplistic solutions once and for all. Second, they have resulted in a liberation from thinking in terms of "things"; and third—above all—they have led to a liberation of the "How?" question. He means by this that it was, is, and will remain henceforth impossible to conceive of Jesus Christ simultaneously as "true man and true God," that is, true(ly) God and true(ly) man at the same time. He cannot be encompassed or described in normal coordinates. To put it informally: we cannot conceive of him in the categories of chemical alloys. The result of critical and/or negative Christology, according to Bonhoeffer, is "the realization that it is not possible to frame this 'How?' of the interconnection in thought" (ibid., 340).

Against the backdrop of those—forever futile—attempts in regard to Jesus Christ to deal with the "How?" question, Bonhoeffer unveils his own panorama of a "positive Christology," as he calls it, by declaring the fatal "How?" question superfluous. Into the center of the arena of his reflections about the triad of God, Jesus Christ, and man, he throws the "Who?" question: Who are you, God? Who are you, Christ? What do the answers have to do with me, a human being? We can hear Bonhoeffer the theologian in this last part of his Christology lectures; his thought is a synthesis of the professor's chair and the pulpit. This "positive Christology" contains the quintessence of his own, very original Christology. The final part of the lectures makes the reader completely forget that the text that has come down to us consists "only" of notes by a hearer; in content and in style, it is Bonhoeffer "to the life!"

The paradox lies in the fact that God is present in Jesus, who was human through and through, and to whom, as Bonhoeffer says, "nothing human was foreign" (DBW 12, 340)—and this precisely *because* He was human with no reservations. The essence of faith that is specifically Christian is the belief that the human being Jesus is God, "precisely as *the* human being, not in spite of His humanity or above and beyond His humanity," as Bonhoeffer affirms (ibid., 341). The fundamental conviction of a powerless and suffering God, to which Bonhoeffer later gives expression in prison, is already making itself heard in the lecture hall of the university when he states, "To describe Jesus Christ as God, we may not speak of His omnipotence and omniscience, but rather of His crib and His cross. 'Divine being' does not exist as infinite power, as infinite knowledge" (ibid.).

The *curriculum vitae* of this ungodly God leads from one scandalous event to another, from the crib to the cross. He is a child in a crib (meaning not a sentimentally designed animal stall but the bitter existence of one seeking asylum on the fringes of an outwardly functional world); and He is the one condemned to death before the gates of the city. He *is* Jesus Christ, this abased man raised up on high. And Christianity says of this Jesus Christ that He is God. Bonhoeffer speaks of him as a God in disguise: "He goes incognito among beggars as a beggar, among pariahs as a pariah," as sinner and sinless in one (DBW 12, 343). For Bonhoeffer, there is no doubt: "Jesus does not cast off His incognito, not even as the Risen One" (ibid., 347–48). It will be cast off only beyond time and the future. It is only natural that the figure of Jesus Christ is always directly or latently present in the books Bonhoeffer wrote in the years thereafter, namely, *Discipleship* and *Life Together,* where he deals explicitly with the *praxis pietatis,* with the union of personal faith and the Christian life to which faith leads. This fact will later play a major role in the description of these two books.[5] For now, however, attention is called only to a few characteristics that are particularly salient in the picture of Jesus Christ presented there.

Some of the passages in *Discipleship* and *Life Together* are difficult for a rationally and discursively trained thinker to follow. They contain Bonhoeffer's picture of Christ in unusually intense colors and reveal an inner bond with Jesus Christ that can perhaps best be characterized as "intimate." These passages are situated so very much in the realm of personal piety and spirituality in practice that they are incapable of normal theological analysis—and rightfully so. Nevertheless, there is reason for going into them in this context, for they too belong to Bonhoeffer's thought, to his reflections as a believer, and not merely marginally.

In the first part of *Discipleship,* Bonhoeffer speaks of "Discipleship and the Cross," deriving from the words and texts of the Synoptic Gospels[6] Christ's unconditioned and unconditional call for his followers to suffer with Him. He writes, "Just as Christ suffers and is rejected, and is Christ only in this, so also the disciple can only be a suffering and rejected disciple, one crucified in unison" (DBW 4, 78). Only when the disciples of Jesus are ready to deny themselves can they fully forget themselves and, finally, no longer know themselves; only then and then alone will they be ready "to bear the cross for His sake" (ibid., 79). The cross is, for Bonhoeffer, the seal of being a Christian, and suffering for the sake of Christ is not an extreme case but a matter of course—to the extent that one enters upon the discipleship of Christ. What is very much at issue for Bonhoeffer is in fact the "*If* anyone will come after me" (ibid., 78). But under this condition, the disgrace of rejection, along with suffering and the cross, are among the insignia of Christian life. Thus Bonhoeffer affirms categorically, "To be cast out in suffering, despised and abandoned by men, . . . this essential characteristic of the suffering of the cross cannot be comprehended by a Christian mentality that is unable to distinguish between civil and Christian existence. The cross means suffering the suffering of Christ with Christ" (ibid., 80).

Bonhoeffer describes in ever new turns of phrase and images not only the wounds and scars, the shame and guilt, that become part of the fabric of life for disciples in and through their suffering in the discipleship of Christ, but also the "purest joy and happiness" (DBW 4, 83). He points out that it is precisely the acts of the first martyrs of the church that bear witness to the fact that "Christ clarifies for those who are His own the moment of deepest suffering through the indescribable certainty of his nearness and fellowship." Suffering, Bonhoeffer emphasizes, is still an experience of God's remoteness, "but suffering is overcome by suffering in the fellowship of suffering with Jesus Christ, and fellowship with God is given as a gift precisely in suffering" (ibid., 84). In this context, Bonhoeffer comes finally and explicitly to his own form of a theology of vicarious suffering when he says, "Thus Christ in suffering takes the place of the world . . . and the family of believers in Jesus Christ stands in place of the world before God by following after Him under the cross" (ibid.).

Aside from the fact that the idea of vicariousness, even in various nuances, is familiar as one of the basic elements in the Christian interpretation of the event on the cross, the postulatory sentences that precede it nevertheless raise questions. Must we not ask—in spite of all due respect and appreciation for Bonhoeffer's postulate of suffering and, above all, for his own readiness to suffer—whether the biblical God does not perhaps become reduced in this way to a God of suffering? Must we not ask whether the glorification of suffering does not also have elements that are inimical to life and humanity? Does not the call for self-sacrifice also have critical, or at least problematic, consequences for human beings? Has not the readiness to deny oneself also been misused in the most un-Christian manner? Does not Bonhoeffer move here undeniably toward a theology of suffering that runs the danger of glorifying suffering for its own sake?

Life Together contains similar statements of "self-forgetfulness" that bear witness to an unconditioned personal piety. Bonhoeffer describes its foundations with the affirmation, "There is no need for God's help and presence to manifest themselves first in our lives; rather God's presence and help for us have manifested themselves in the life of Jesus Christ" (DBW 5, 46). For Bonhoeffer, the consequence of this is the ineradicable coupling of one's own person to that of Jesus Christ and vice versa. "That Jesus Christ died," Bonhoeffer writes with deliberate provocation, "is more important than whether I die; and that Jesus Christ was raised from the dead is the only basis for my hope that I too will be raised on the Last Day" (ibid.). This is the *pro me,* the subjective side of the event of salvation. Nevertheless and with the same emphasis, he emphasizes the significance of *extra nos,* that is, that the event of salvation exists outside our own selves: "Our salvation is 'outside ourselves' (*extra nos*); it is not in my life history, but only in the history of Jesus Christ that I find it" (ibid., 47). Following this we have the sentence that bestows on the center of life—for Bonhoeffer, Jesus Christ—its unique place and sums up the nearness of man to God and the nearness of God to man: "Only one who lets himself be found in Jesus Christ, in His Incarnation, His cross, and His resurrection, is with God and God with him" (ibid.).

Bonhoeffer's *Ethics* is written in a somewhat different key:[7] much less frequently in the "I" or "We" form; and more distanced, more "objectively," so to speak, but nonetheless unambiguously, confessionally, with challenge and proclamation at the same time. They are grounded—so typical of Bonhoeffer—in Christology. This becomes apparent in the self-contained section entitled "Ethics as Creation," in a way that may appear surprising in a work of ethics—as the gradual revelation of a nearly hymnical confession of faith in Christ. Why? Prior to any search on the part of man for an ethics, God's initiative to become man in Jesus Christ has for Bonhoeffer absolute priority. The world in which we live is reflected in Him, and God is reflected in Him. In Him, we learn how to live, for He is the very quintessence of man—and the quintessence of God's love for man as well.

Bonhoeffer selects as his basic theme words from the Gospel of John: "*Ecce homo*—Behold, what a man!" We all know these words as the statement ascribed to Pontius Pilate when the derided Jesus of Nazareth was "adorned" with the crown of thorns and sentenced to death. (This is also, by the way, the title of one of Friedrich Nietzsche's works, a fact of which Bonhoeffer will hardly have been unaware.)[8] "*Ecce homo*" appears four times in this text, which has four sections, and it always appears at the beginning or end of a train of thought. This Bonhoefferian hymn to Christ contains at its innermost core a statement in which the "Center" is again mentioned: "The figure of the Mediator, the God-Man Jesus Christ, steps into the center between God and the world, steps into the midpoint of all that happens. In it the mystery of the world becomes unmasked, just as in it the mystery of God becomes revealed" (DBW 6, 69). Bonhoeffer describes the way traveled by this Mediator through time and the world, and the way God's love, embodied in the "fellow of sinners," stands like a signpost at the beginning and end of this way (ibid., 71). At the end of this credo to Christ, he writes, "Jesus is not just *a* man, but *the* man. What happens to him happens to man, happens to all, and therefore to us as well. The name of Jesus takes all of humanity and all of God into itself" (ibid., 710). These statements embody Bonhoeffer's interpretation of Christ in its purest form; they show par excellence that his understanding of Jesus can only be comprehended in a confession of Him as the Christ.

In his texts and letters from Tegel Prison, we find this confession in an even more intense form when he writes in one of his last known letters to Eberhard Bethge in August 1944: "Given that the earth was found worthy to bear the man Jesus Christ, and given that such a man as Jesus Christ once lived, then and only then does our life as human beings have meaning. Had Jesus not lived, our life would be—in spite of all the other men and women we know and revere and love—meaningless" (DBW 8, 573). For Bonhoeffer, his own life qualifies as a meaningful life only through the life of Jesus; without Him it would once and for all have no meaning at all. Jesus is the One who is the foreground and backdrop on the stage of life. Life for Bonhoeffer becomes conceivable first and only through this source.

One might think that God and Jesus Christ overlap perfectly for Bonhoeffer; at the very least, his thought is imbued with a Christ-centricity whose effect can be constricting rather than uniformly liberating. The reality of God and that of the world open themselves to him personally, in fact, only through Jesus Christ, and there is no doubt that this kind of exclusivity may strike one as Christ-monism or a Christ-monology. But for Bonhoeffer himself, it was neither monocratic nor monotonous to set Christ so absolutely in the center of being. For him, Christ was the "red-hot core" of all that is; in Him, he found the fulfillment of faith and life. The "*Solo Dios basta*"—"God alone suffices"—of Theresa of Avila, the Spanish Christian mystic of the sixteenth century, could be rephrased with regard to Bonhoeffer as "*Solo Christo basta.*"

But even so, Christ alone was not quite enough for Bonhoeffer. Faith shared with believers in Christ, the "communion of faith," as the third article of the credo states, was also one of Bonhoeffer's key themes.

8

The Holy Spirit—At Right
Angles to Reason and Logic

The Christian community is home to the great dawn
of joy for all human beings and the whole of
creation. Or it is not the Christian community.

Karl Barth

As we proceed through the three steps of the Christian credo in order
to approximate Dietrich Bonhoeffer's thought, we enter the realm
of what is commonly called "the Holy Spirit." The Spirit manifests
itself—often enough contrary to all appearances—in the existence of
the church. The last part of the credo speaks of the "communion of
those who are holy" ("unholy" as that "communion of the holy" has been
and still is on the whole, assuming that we understand "holy" as a sign of
quality). In biblical terms and in the early church, in contrast, "holy"
meant nothing other than "belonging to God." As a consequence, the
attribute "holy" was by no means a seal of quality or a certificate of perfection; rather, holy, or sanctified, originally designated "those who belong to God"; those who once and for all have become His, meaning
men and women who, while no better and no worse than others, are
better off than others because they have given God room in their lives
and have taken advantage of the promise of His love. The point is to say,
"I *believe* in the holy Christian church." The point is *not* to say, "I *see* the
holy Christian church." Bonhoeffer explains this situation more precisely, in a sermon he preached during his time in London: "The church
of the Reformation is never the visible 'community of the sanctified,' but
the church of sinners; it believes against all appearances in saving grace
and lives from it alone" (DBW 13, 401).

Even more than the first two articles of the credo, the last article is
one of hope: "I believe in . . ." means that I give myself over to something, I have hope of something, I trust in something, at times against all
reason and contrary to manifest reality. I build on the conviction that

"church" exists through the truly existent church on earth, in it and in spite of it. Those outside the church justly criticize it; and those within the church know only too well that by no means is everything that happens within the church "Church." What is more, they experience the fact that church can also take place outside the church. Nevertheless, the following remains true: church can become reality within the church as well. In another of his London sermons, we find a statement from Bonhoeffer that refers to the discrepancy between church as believed and church as experienced: "The church is the place of unshakeable hope" (DBW 13, 326).

Perhaps it would be helpful to speak of a "Communion of the Faithful" instead of a "Communion of the Holy." Bonhoeffer once contrasted—although in a completely different context—the ideal of becoming holy with the search for faith. He wrote to Eberhard Bethge, on July 21, 1944, the day after the attempt to assassinate Hitler had failed, "I remember a conversation I had thirteen years ago in America with a young French pastor. We had asked ourselves very simply what we wanted to achieve with our lives. He said, 'I want to be a holy man' (and I think it possible that he succeeded); that impressed me very much at the time. Nevertheless, I contradicted him and said more or less that I wanted to learn to believe. It took a long time for me to grasp the depth of this paradox" (DBW 8, 541–42).

This contrast also makes it clear that Communion of the Holy means "Communion of the Faithful"; a community of God's *children*, but also of *God's* children; the church as constituted by men and women bound together by faith—and failure. When Bonhoeffer wrote in one of his final examination papers in 1928, that for Luther the church "is nothing other than a signpost pointing to God, or to the cross and resurrection of Christ," he was indirectly describing his own understanding of the church as well (DBW 9, 482). But this "signpost pointing to God" cannot be overlooked, and in the life and thought of Bonhoeffer, Christian existence is coupled with the existence of the church, even when he himself in the end went beyond the well-worn—and aimless—paths traditionally traveled by Church and State in their relationship. The bond of the "living presence of Christ" with the church and vice versa is in his eyes the only chance, the true litmus test for Christian existence and the presence of church (DBW 4, 215). Only this bond constitutes the legitimation and life force of the church.

For Bonhoeffer, suffering because of the church *and* refusing to let go of the church are two sides of the same coin. The *communio sanctorum* as believed in and hoped for, this odd "Communion of the Holy," is already present here and now, even if it is in reality a very fragile and fragmentary communion. Clear-eyed and blind, splendid and picayune, strong and pitiable, human and inhuman, an erring community of believers, beset by failures, but nevertheless it is a community that holds fast to God and is held fast by Him, and this in spite of everything. The response rendered by the man or woman of faith to this God who holds him or her cannot take the form of individualistic self-isolation alone or of seeking refuge in one's own personalized faith. The Incarnation of God in Jesus Christ is matched on the one hand by the Incarnation of Christ in the community of believers and on the other by that community's embodiment of Christian faith. This means: Body of Christ. And that means: Christ existing as the community of believers.[1]

"Cannot, after all, every member of the church read the Bible on his or her own and pledge allegiance in silence to the community of believers, the unseen community of 'consciences,' of 'souls'? Why this fatal boredom of superficial gatherings where one is in danger of sitting before a preacher who has nothing to say and side by side with vacant faces?" (DBW 1, 155). This question, which was not merely a rhetorical formulation developed by Bonhoeffer in *Sanctorum Communio*, is another expression of his quite ambivalent attitude toward church services and church communities. But he would not have been Bonhoeffer had he not wholly rejected this doubting question. Faith evaporates when it is not anchored in the community of the faithful.

The practice of faith becomes real only when persons join together in it; it normally articulates itself in two areas of practical action: in the church service and in the pastoral care of souls; all other areas of practical action in the church community have their roots in these two. Bonhoeffer's personal unease is articulated with regard to both the church service (see above) and the care of souls. Self- and church-critically, he asked in 1932, in a letter he wrote from Berlin to his theologian friend Erwin Sutz in Switzerland, "We have again learned to preach, at least a very little bit; but what about the care of souls?" (DBW 11, 65). This skeptical protest is preceded by a short report on his worst experiences with visits to his parishioners in their homes: "I often (or even nearly always) stand there and think that I could really just as well have studied chemistry as pay such a visit. I often had the feeling that our work went for nothing because of our inadequacies in the care of souls" (ibid.). (It should be noted here, however, that Berlin was and is in any case a difficult place for the work of the church: "Nowhere was the 'ecclesiological vacuum' voiced more sharply than here."[2] This retrospective conclusion drawn by a modern bishop of Berlin applies equally to the decades after the Second World War, and Bonhoeffer was certainly brought up short by it no less than the young men and women in the service of the church there today.)

Later, in his "illegal" training of young theologians in the Confessing Church, Bonhoeffer gave high priority to homiletics, that is, to the theory of preaching, and to the pastoral care of souls; pastoral theology was one of his strengths anyway. In those days, at the beginning of the 1930s, however, he did not feel wholly at ease in his own church, as he wrote in another letter to Erwin Sutz in October of 1932; rather, he felt homeless in it, like an outsider, a foreigner. He expressed that a recent visit in Switzerland had been for him like a much-longed-for "*asylum* for a theologian with no home of his own," one he could only think back on with a pang while "in the cold loneliness here in the North" (DBW 11, 117). Shortly thereafter, toward the end of the letter, he wrote that he often thinks with dismay of the fact that they are both leading "existences somewhere on the outskirts of our church"[3] (ibid., 118).

Still, Bonhoeffer's faith remains incomprehensible without the dimension of "Church." Even in the years thereafter, when his critique of the church and his doubts about his faith intensified instead of diminishing, the church remained for him, in spite of everything, "God's abode in the world" (DBW 11, 244). However, the perspective from which he perceived this "abode" of God and wished it to be perceived, underwent a certain shift in the direction of the world; and his vision of an "open church of Jesus Christ, one that serves the world to the end," begins to shine through (DBW 6, 147). And finally, the *Ethics* introduces once and for all a view that will be taken up again in *Resistance and Surrender*, especially in the section entitled "Draft for a Paper": the vision of a church for the world, a church for others.[4] When "church" is an end in itself, a society for the preservation of spiritual—and concrete—inventory, it is no longer the church; rather, it has ceased to be the "church of God in the world," says Bonhoeffer curtly, as he sets priorities: "Therefore the first commission given to those who belong to the church of God is not to be there for themselves, by setting up a religious organization, for example, or by leading a pious life, but rather to be witnesses of Jesus Christ to the world" (DBW 6, 50).

At the end of the section of his *Ethics* entitled "The Commandment of God in the church," which he was working on just before his arrest, Bonhoeffer included a "punch list" of faults regarding a form of Christianity that calls itself "reformed" but fails to understand that "the end of the church in itself . . . is precisely to be there for the world" (DBW 6, 411). It is a list of faults that in some ways is astonishingly up-to-date: "The liturgical poverty and diffidence of our Evangelical divine services at present, . . . the complete inability of widest Evangelical circles to understand the meaning of disciplinary practices—spiritual exercises, for example, or asceticism, meditation, and contemplation, . . . the alarming lack of answers, or the presumptuousness . . . toward Christians who refuse the oath to Hitler or turn down military service" (ibid.). The manuscript breaks off abruptly a few sentences later.

"Church" was a topic Bonhoeffer grappled with from the beginning of his independent theological work to the end. His first major work, the dissertation *Sanctorum Communio,* focused only on this topic; and the course he taught in Christology in the summer semester of 1933[5] led to the question of the church, a church that "allows its sins to be forgiven" (DBW 12, 348). Finally, in his last "Draft for a Paper," which he sketched in his cell in Tegel Prison, the church is given a central role. It was in his "Draft" that Bonhoeffer formulated the sentence that would later be quoted so often: "The church then is only church when it is there for others" (DBW 8, 560). The continuation of the sentence, which sets the bar very high and—admittedly—also makes demands on the church that are not without risk, is quoted much less often: "Pastors must live only from the voluntary gifts of the church communities, and work at a 'worldly' job if necessary. The church must participate in the 'worldly' tasks of life in the human community, not giving orders to others but helping and serving. It must tell men and women in all walks of life what it is to live with Christ, and say what it means to 'be there for others' " (ibid.). This manuscript ends with the statement, "This is all a very rough summary. But I want to try for once simply and clearly to express certain things that we usually try not to think about. . . . I hope I can do the future of the church a service in doing so" (ibid., 561).

The Apostles' Creed, which sums up the faith of the so-called fathers—and mothers—of the church, has served here as a backdrop for offering a better look at Bonhoeffer's faith and a better understanding of it. Taking this tack implies using the credo's final three-step outline as our guideline: "forgiveness of sins, resurrection of the dead, and life everlasting." And in doing this we set foot upon the wide field known in theological terms as eschatology, the teachings about the Last Things. Bonhoeffer himself did not expound an explicit eschatology, nor was it for him—figuratively speaking—a separate "theological drawer in the filing cabinet" for the canon of disciplines of faith. In fact, for him, such "theological drawers," isolated one from the other, have no place in the realm of faith. Instead, each lays the groundwork for and establishes the conditions for the others. These change places constantly and overlap one another. One cannot teach about God *alongside of* Christology and vice versa, and both in turn are inconceivable without a teaching about the church, an ecclesiology. For

Bonhoeffer, this is also precisely the case with eschatology. Its hopes are woven into the basic hope that guided his thought and formed the foundation for his life: God's reality in Jesus Christ has imprinted it-self upon the reality of the world—once only, but then once and for all, for as long as the world and time exist—and in so doing has, so to speak, bound itself to it forever. The hope of God's forgiveness and of resurrection were matter-of-course for him, not in the sense of being commonly or constantly available and at hand, but in the sense of being intrinsic to his understanding of himself as part of the Christian's basic certitude (not basic knowledge!); as part of the "basic equipment" of Christian existence. In terms of an analogy with the oft-noted, uncomplicated faith of little children, one might say that this hope is what constitutes the basic trust of God's children.

However, Bonhoeffer also spoke clearly about the difference between the Last Things and the Nearly Last Things, most emphatically and extensively in the important *Ethics* text entitled "The Last and Next-to-Last Things."[6] He begins with a classic theological sentence from reformed theology: "The origins and essence of all Christian life are encompassed in the one event called by the Reformation 'justification of the sinner by faith alone' " (DBW 6, 137). Thereafter, however, he describes in nearly breathtaking fashion what it means to say that one is "found" by God: one becomes immediately aware of God's nearness; His reality becomes an overpowering certainty. It is as if knowing and experiencing become one for the believer. Finally, Bonhoeffer puts his finger on this experience of faith that renders the previous self invalid: "All of this happens when Christ comes to a human being. In Christ, all of this is truth and reality, and precisely because it is not a dream, the life of the person whom Christ's presence has touched becomes from this time forward not a lost life but rather one justified—justified by faith alone" (ibid., 138).

In the further course of the text, Bonhoeffer takes the position that such a "finality which cannot be encompassed by human existence, action, or suffering" (DBW 6, 137), a premonition of salvation so to speak, can only go hand in hand with openness to grace on the part of the one irrevocably caught by this grace. Prudently, Bonhoeffer locates the roots of this in the here and now: the Last Things and the Nearly Last Things are inseparably suspended in the force field that lies between Christ's "already here" and the "not yet" of the Christ who is to come. The man or woman of faith lives between the two, not only with the knowledge that he or she has been redeemed but also living in that redemption, according to the grace received, and doing his or her part to prepare the way for the coming of God. "But this preparation of the way is not simply an inner event; it is active, purposeful, and concrete to the utmost degree" (ibid., 153). It is a consequence of grace, of forgiveness; a consequence of what theology calls "justification." It is a consequence of God's love, independently of any service, unearned. The life of the believer in the time "after Christ" is no longer played out according to the pattern of crime and punishment. The freedom bestowed by God's love opens up new horizons for the believer because it shatters his or her previous criteria of living: no longer a balance sheet, now a cancellation of guilt.

Such a fundamental of contradiction of all human criteria and experiential values is matched by the Good News of the resurrection. This is a different version of the Good News of forgiveness. Both manifest what is basically unbelievable: the (unlimited) power of God, manifested strangely enough in the powerlessness of the cross. God does not abide by the normal rules of the game of existence: He does not give up on mankind. He does not allow death to have the last word. The proclamation of the cross and resurrection does not legitimize the status quo in which we must die, but is instead God's ultimate protest against the reality of death. God Himself takes death upon Himself in the death of the Nazarene; He Himself goes into death and in doing so renders it invalid.

This conviction—we note here only in passing[7]—is central, not peripheral, to Bonhoeffer's thought and faith. For him, there can be no mention of death without mention of the resurrection. As he states in *Creation and Fall,* God "annihilates nothingness" (DBW 3, 34). And as he wrote in *Sanctorum Communio,* "The resurrection of Jesus Christ reveals His death as the death of death, so that the boundaries of history set by death cease to exist" (DBW 1, 96). For Bonhoeffer, the search is for a Christian ethics that confronts man "with the issue of a *final* decision ['final' italicized here by this author], namely, with a decision for the reality we wish to live by: with the reality of God's word of revelation or with the so-called realities of life; with divine grace or with the imperfections of earthly life; with the resurrection or with death" (DBW 6, 33).

At another point in his *Ethics,* the *"Ecce homo"* motif, mentioned earlier, is incorporated into a statement that contains the core of Bonhoeffer's very specific faith: "God's love became the death of death and the life of mankind" (DBW 6, 78). He continues on, remarking that the miracle of resurrection and new life shines into the center of a world of death, making eternity appear on the horizon and bathing our world in new light. Then he writes,

The risen Christ carries within Himself the new mankind, God's final, glorious "Yes" to the new human nature. Mankind still lives, it is true, in its old ways, but has already left the old behind; man still lives, it is true, in a world of death, but has already left death behind; man still lives, it is true, in a world of sin, but has already left sin behind. The night is not yet past, but the day is already dawning. (ibid., 79)

Will this day come for the whole world? Does the witness of the Creed—to "forgiveness of sins, resurrection of the dead, and life everlasting"—constitute an exclusive preserve in which only a man or woman of faith may have hope? Does it not speak instead of privileges? To paraphrase Karl Marx, do we have here a form of "private property"—consisting not of a means of production but a "means of salvation"? Or may we instead have the hope of reconciliation for all, and the hope that all will be made new?

In theological terms, this is the question of the so-called *Apokatastasis panton*, often expressed as "Universalism," "*recapitulatio mundi*," or "*restitutio omnium*"; in German, the "*Wiederbringung aller Dinge*," that is, "making all things new." This question is as old as Christianity itself and has been a source of dispute since the time of the early church. Its most famous proponent was Origen, who was born toward the end of the second century and condemned in the sixth. A short, thought-provoking account has come down to us of the final encounter between Bonhoeffer and a theologian of Origen's persuasion—once again, Karl Barth. A tiny event that took place in May of 1942 reflects perhaps better than any other the theological proximity between Barth and Bonhoeffer, and this with regard to the theologically controversial issue of universal reconciliation. While Bonhoeffer was staying at a small hotel on Lake Geneva, he worked his way through Karl Barth's *Church Dogmatics,* which begins with a chapter entitled "Those Chosen by God's Grace,"[8] and he asked Barth whether or not he believed that all of creation will one day come back again: "Will it be—like Lake Geneva?" to which Karl Barth responded, "Yes! Like Lake Geneva!"[9]

The two were in honorable theological company, since in the history of the Christian church the idea of universal reconciliation has found "its advocates in every century, and not merely in heretical circles or among eccentrics";[10] an unambiguous affinity for the idea of universal reconciliation can be found in the Protestant tradition as well, in the nineteenth century, for example, in the thought of such diverse theologians as Daniel Friedrich Schleiermacher and Søren Kierkegaard. It was Karl Barth who no doubt preferred it most openly, but always—and this cannot be emphasized enough with reference to the *apokatastasis*—only as hope, never as doctrine. It is not well-suited to serve abstractly as "dogma" (a word that is in any case foreign to Protestantism) nor as accepted doctrine (not even in *Church Dogmatics*), that is, as a teaching declared to be a basic element of faith to which resource can be had as needed. The appropriate setting for *apokatastasis* is always only a *hope*, rather than a doctrine, of universal reconciliation in the personal process of faith.

This and nothing else, by the way, is what the Blumhardts, two theologians who lived in Germany's Württemberg area in the nineteenth century, meant when they said that Jesus had not after all come to put the world to death but rather to "put it to life"; that whoever doubts universal reconciliation is an ox, but whoever teaches it is an ass. This, and nothing other, is what Bonhoeffer had meant when he touched on the issue of *apokatastasis* in his dissertation, noting that it could be "at most the very last word in eschatological thought, but not a matter-of-course point of departure for a direction of dogmatic thought" (DBW 1, 111 note 29). He carries this same line of thought through to the end of his dissertation when he stresses "the intrinsic necessity of the idea of *apokatastasis*" and simultaneously emphasizes, "But here everything that is said is simply hope; none of it can be made into a system of thought" (ibid., 196). This is also the way a statement he makes toward the end of his professorial dissertation should be understood, when he says that most discussion of the *apokatastasis* is likely to be nothing more "than the sighs heard from theology when it must speak of belief and disbelief, election and rejection" (DBW 2, 160).

A comment Bonhoeffer makes at the beginning of *Discipleship*, in the context of "grace that costs little and is worth much,"[11] can be viewed analogously as the hope of universal reconciliation: "In order to understand everything here, it is important to employ actively the distinction between result and prerequisite. Luther's statement ['sin bravely!' (S.D.)] as prerequisite for a theology of grace is a proclamation of grace that costs little. But the correct understanding of Luther's statement is not as a beginning but only and exclusively as an end, as a result, as the capstone, as the very last word" (DBW 4, 39).

Bonhoeffer's own inner affinity for *apokatastasis*[12] is therefore not to be over-absolutized; nevertheless it is undeniably present and is, by the way, more than legitimized by the New Testament. This is also visible, for example, in the *Ethics*, especially in the opening texts, where Bonhoeffer emphasizes again and again "that God has reconciled in Christ the whole world to Himself," and that "all of mankind is included, and . . . the world is reconciled with God . . . Christ died for the world, and Christ is Christ only in the midst of the world" (DBW 6, 52–53). Bonhoeffer speaks of Jesus Christ as He who "atones for the world" (ibid., 68). The bottomless depths of God's love are great enough to "contain even the most bottomless Godlessness of the world" (ibid., 69–70). His basic thought is this: just as no sin, no godlessness, can be too much for God, so too no death can be mightier than God's reality. As a consequence, he formulates the following: "God takes the part of the godless; love takes the part of him who hates. . . . Now there is no godlessness, no hate, no sin that God has not taken upon Himself, suffered through, and made atonement for. Now there is no longer any reality, any world unreconciled or not at peace with God" (ibid., 70).

Finally, in his cell in Tegel Prison Bonhoeffer again wrote decisively on the subject of *apokatastasis*. Reflecting on a line from a church hymn, he wrote on the fourth Sunday in Advent in 1943, "What is the meaning of 'I make all things new'? It means that nothing is lost; all things are taken up into Christ and preserved, but also transformed. . . . The teaching that all things are made new, based on Eph 1:10, . . . is a splendid and deeply comforting thought" (DBW 8, 246). And after a few more reflections he again returns to the same line from the church hymn: "I believe that this thought is also very important when we are talking to men and women who ask us about their relationship to their deceased loved ones" (ibid., 248).

Indirectly, but no less persistently, Bonhoeffer's confidence in the *apokatastasis* is expressed in "Christians and Heathens," the most "headstrong" of his poems, which he sent to his friend Bethge at the beginning of July 1944 (DBW 8, 515–16). With a very sparing—but obviously very carefully polished—use of language, he describes the normal road traveled by man to God ("We go to God in our need"), the encounter with Him on the cross ("We go to God in His need"), and finally the road traveled by God to all men and women, a way which shatters all the normal criteria: "God goes to us all in our need, . . . dies the death of the cross for Christians and unbelievers, and forgives them both."[13]

One of Bonhoeffer's fellow prisoners, the Italian officer Gaetano Latmiral, reported years later that Bonhoeffer's extraordinarily composed, almost oddly serene and optimistic, attitude in prison, even during air raids, made a distinct and lasting impression: "One might have said he had nerves of steel. But in my opinion it was something else. I think he had such a strong hope that God through Christ will make everything new, will bring all to pass, that nothing will be lost. That, I think, is why he was so at peace."[14]

Isn't this the core of the New Testament message—". . . that nothing will be lost"? Isn't this the hope of a Christianity that is not out to clutch salvation anxiously and greedily to its own breast, but is instead rooted in Jesus Christ, in whom God Himself proclaims the salvation of the world? Or is this simply an over-interpretation of a message of salvation that has been misused in an inflationary manner? To be sure, the New Testament does not develop a *doctrine* of universal reconciliation, just as it does not develop any other doctrine. But it does indeed contain words of hope which cannot be overheard, of *apokatastasis panton*, the hope that all things will be made new. These words are clear and unambiguous, and are much too much in accordance with the true kerygma, the center of the New Testament proclamation, to be ignored as if they were moot, equivocal, or even marginal.[15] Full of intensity, they express the confidence of those whose lives are derived from Christ "that God is everything in all things" (1 Cor 15:28). That nothing will be lost: Bonhoeffer shared in this first—in both senses of the word—Christian hope.

The old Apostles' Creed has been used here as a guideline for understanding Dietrich Bonhoeffer's personal credo and situating the goalposts of his faith. But the lines of his thought ran not only between these goalposts but also and at the same time far beyond them.

9

Walking the Thin Line: *Sanctorum Communio* and *Act and Being*

Only one who has been alone with himself
can go out to others.

Martin Buber

As already indicated, Dietrich Bonhoeffer's thought is found both in his books and, perhaps even more extensively and comprehensively, in the many (and many-sided) writings preserved outside the body of his finished and planned books. As milestones along the road of his thought, two of his books will now be taken up individually, in order to sketch their characteristics and core ideas.

Two items catch our attention regarding Bonhoeffer and his books. First, he himself had quite mixed and indeed conflicting feelings about his own books, at least about those he was able to complete (the situation was different with the *Ethics*); "he never advertised his own books anywhere"[1] and very rarely drew on their contents. According to his biographer, he felt himself at a distance from them after their publication, but without publicly distancing himself from them.[2] Second, his books tend to have very concise titles, even though the short, descriptive main title of his academic writings is immediately followed by a subtitle that is all the more informative and/or complex. His doctoral dissertation is entitled *Sanctorum Communio;* its subtitle: *A Dogmatic Study of the Sociology of the Church.* The title of his professorial dissertation is *Act and Being;* its subtitle: *Transcendental Philosophy and Ontology in Systematic Theology.* (Since we are dealing here with his academic writings, this chapter will of necessity be more academic in character.)

Although there can be no doubt that Bonhoeffer's faith was unique to him, his thought was silhouetted by elements from completely different disciplines and fields of study. He moved through these areas with a sovereign ease bordering on the matter-of-course; this is astonishing, above all, in view of the fact that these scientific works were also his "younger works" (!): he wrote *Sanctorum Communio* in 1927 at the age of twenty-one; *Act and Being* two years later. The doctoral dissertation appeared in book form in 1930, the professorial dissertation in 1931.[3] Both are marked by the fact that he, as a theologian, delved into other, related sciences thoroughly, competently, and in an original manner. Bonhoeffer's doctoral dissertation—the subtitle says it in so many words—consciously stepped over the boundary with sociology and social philosophy; his professorial dissertation—here too, the subtitle makes it clear—crossed over in particular into the field of philosophy. Later, he characterized this phase of his life to a woman friend and colleague, in January of 1936, as follows: "I plunged into my work in a highly un-Christian and un-humble manner. A wild ambitiousness, which many have noted in me, made my life difficult and robbed me of the love and trust of those around me. I was terribly alone at that time, and was left to my own devices" (DBW 14, 112–13). Thus this time of ambition and aloneness was the time of the sociological investigations of a candidate in theology about the *Communion* of the *Sanctified*.

His works met with praise from his dissertation supervisor and the highest approbation of the faculty, but with no noteworthy echo after their publication. Recognition of them came only after Bonhoeffer's death. Barth's evaluation has already been mentioned in a different context.[4] The Evangelical theologian Ernst Wolf described them upon their republication, which he initiated in 1954, as "probably the most penetrating and perhaps the profoundest treatment of the issue of the structural nature of the church";[5] and not long thereafter, Bonhoeffer's work was even singled out in sociological circles as one of the few theological bodies of writing that perceived and dealt at all with (religio-)sociological issues. Dietrich Goldschmidt, a sociologist teaching in Berlin, wrote in 1959, "Even though we must say that his work has been superseded in many respects, in my opinion there is still nothing today that can match it."[6] And when *Sanctorum Communio* appeared as the first volume of *The Works of Dietrich Bonhoeffer,* its publisher, Joachim von Soosten, summed up the work as follows: "In an undertaking fully unique to that day and age, he starts from theology and attempts to establish a link to sociology."[7]

From a scientific point of view, Bonhoeffer did indeed enter virgin territory with this attempt. Up to that time there had not been the slightest dialogue between theology and the sociology of religion, not to mention sociology in general, and the question remains whether and to what extent the relationship has basically changed since that time. However, this much can be said: real dialogue was slow in developing on the part of theology in the second half of the twentieth century as well.

Even today, theology and the church still find it difficult to understand both the challenge and the opportunities presented by dialogue with socio-religious circles. What is at stake, after all, is nothing less than the debate about reality!

It is astonishing to see how circumspectly, and at the same time how surefootedly, Bonhoeffer ventures as a theologian—and he emphasizes at the beginning of his dissertation that he views himself as such—into the terrain of sociological and socio-philosophical issues and categories. What especially distinguishes his "border crossings," including excursions into the area of philosophy in his professorial dissertation, is the level of comprehensive knowledge he has in his own field of expertise as well as in the other disciplines *and* the clear maintenance of his own identity as a theologian and man of the church. Without falling into the fatal trap of either playing up to the other discipline or being arrogant, Bonhoeffer knew how to deal factually, respectfully, and self-confidently as a theologian with the insights and contemporary trends of other sciences, making them theologically fruitful without misrepresenting or misusing them.

At the beginning of *Sanctorum Communio* (DBW 1, 18), Bonhoeffer makes it clear that the issue at hand is a "socio-philosophical, sociological and structural, understanding of the reality of the church of Christ," adding immediately as a caveat, however, that the true nature of the church can be understood only from the inside outward, *with* wrath and affection, "but never by approaching it as a neutral observer" and therefore precisely not *sine ira et studio*, not without wrath and affection! Did he himself go into social philosophy and sociology *sine ira et studio*? In any case, he had familiarized himself thoroughly with the "grand old men" of sociology as well as sociological and historical philosophy; that is, with—to name only a few—Georg Simmel and Ferdinand Tönnies, Max Scheler and Theodor Litt, Alfred Vierkandt and Hans Freyer. He read Emil Durkheim, even at that time already a classic thinker in sociology and socio-philosophy, and above all Max Weber and Ernst Troeltsch. He read Eberhard Grisebach, the renowned philosopher of that time, and another Jewish religious philosopher who would not become famous until later, namely Martin Buber. He read a piece by Edith Stein, published in 1922, still very much a woman philosopher at the time and stamped by Edmund Husserl's phenomenological school. Like Bonhoeffer, Edith Stein would not survive the National Socialist system of terror; she was killed in 1942 in Auschwitz.

Bonhoeffer's attention in this doctoral dissertation (the topics of his later professorial dissertation are already perceivable here) focuses on ties between the person, the community, and God. To put it another way: he focuses on the individual as a social being, on God as the God of revelation, and on the community of the faithful as the church. In his own words, "Our understanding of 'person' and 'community' automatically defines our concept of 'God.' *The concepts of 'person,' 'community,' and 'God'* are indissolubly and essentially interrelated. Whenever an idea of 'God' is conceived, it is conceived in relationship to 'person' and to a 'community of persons' " (DBW 1, 19).

Bonhoeffer develops the Christian concept of "person" against a historical backdrop of philosophical reflections ranging from Aristotle and the Stoa, Democritus and Epicurus, Descartes and Kant, to Hegel and Fichte. He combines and counterbalances this concept with one of the central concepts of sociology, namely, that of the community, as well as with the central concept of theological thought, namely, that of God. He mentions in his dissertation not only his own personal theological instructors, Karl Holt and Reinhold Seeberg, but also such contrary theologians as Daniel Friedrich Schleiermacher and Søren Kierkegaard, Rudolf Bultmann and Karl Barth; and of course, in the most varied contexts and always with accurately focused citations, Martin Luther. It is significant, however, that the word "God" appears much less frequently in the course of *Sanctorum Communio* than the word "Christ."

First, last, and central in Bonhoeffer's thought is the rock-solid conviction that Christ is real in this world as the church, and the church as Christ. Again and again we read that Christ becomes reality in the church as Communion of the Faithful and as the church community, which is the "presence of Christ in the world" (DBW 1, 191). This also explains the phrase borrowed from Hegel and modified by Bonhoeffer: "Christ existing as community of the church." For Hegel, it was God existing as community of the church.[8] (The latent influence of Georg Friedrich Wilhelm Hegel on the thought of the young Bonhoeffer is manifest in his dissertation, but that "master philosopher of the spirit," as many call him even today, undergoes a startling transformation. Bonhoeffer also, by the way, conducted a seminar on Hegel's philosophy of religion in his final semester in Berlin, in the summer of 1933, from which a set of student notes has been preserved. At that time, his focus was clearly "what the critical theologian can learn from Hegel.")[9]

Later interpretations of Bonhoeffer's work have often regarded the expression "Christ existing as the community of the church" as formulaic. There is no doubt that the way was prepared for this by the fact that he himself, with only one exception, so characterized it this way (DBW 1, 142). It lights the way, for example, through the last two-thirds of the book like a signal lamp inasmuch as it is turned this way and that time and again. When first used, it is preceded by the statement that the church is the presence of Christ, in much the same way that Christ is the presence of God (ibid., 87). When used for the last time, it appears in connection with an eschatological image of hope that Bonhoeffer fashions at the end of the book and according to which—beyond the present time—*"the church will truly be 'Christ existing as community of the church'"* (ibid., 198).

What is specific to Bonhoeffer's understanding of the church crystallizes at this point, where Christ is "Christ existing as the community of the church": Bonhoeffer wishes to make clear the distinction between this and the familiar model expressed in the short formula "visible versus invisible church." He emphasizes that belief in the church does not mean belief in an unseen church, or in the kingdom of God *in* the church, but rather "that God has made the concrete, empirical church, in which word and sacrament are administered, His own community of the church . . . , in order that the working of God's Spirit may be seen in it according to the promise" (DBW 1, 191). This understanding of "church" implies above all two points worth noting: in all its shortcomings and fallibility, the church *is* God's church, and the church can be God's church *always and everywhere.* To put it in Bonhoeffer's words: "[The church] . . . is present wherever God's word is proclaimed in the world. Faith in the church is not in an unattainable, still to be completed ideal, but a present reality" (ibid.).

This is exactly where Bonhoeffer parts company with all sociophilosophically considered and sociologically experienced forms of society. On the other hand, he shares something basically in common with social philosophy and sociology, namely, the fundamental anthropological statement that man is a social being—Bonhoeffer speaks of the "sociality" of man—and that human beings basically constitute themselves as such by means of society. He adds to this view of man the theological insight that conventional conceptions of the person and the "I-you relationship" between human beings become different after encountering the personality of God. More precisely, Bonhoeffer contravenes these conventional views by arguing that God in person, namely, in Christ, intervenes for man, and that the concept of man as a person consequently becomes unique, genuinely Christian and Christ-like.

It is in this sense that Bonhoeffer writes: "The person in his or her concrete aliveness, wholeness, and uniqueness is the basic 'unit' desired by God. Social relationships must therefore be viewed as purely interpersonal and founded on the uniqueness and individuality of the persons involved" (DBW 1, 33). Stated more simply, every human being is raised by God, so to speak, to the status of nobility as His creation, as a

child of God, and lives in a personal relationship with God. In Bonhoeffer's terminology the result is: *"The basic social category is that of the I-
you relationship. The 'You' of the other human being is the divine 'You'"*
(ibid., 33–34). Or again more simply, when dealing with another person,
I am dealing with a child of God and therefore indirectly with God
Himself. Again in Bonhoeffer's words, the consequence is: *"But just as I
first become acquainted with God's 'I' in the revelation of His love, so also
with other human beings; here is where the concept of 'Church' must have its
origins"* (ibid., 34).

In *Sanctorum Communio*, Bonhoeffer arrives at his concept of the
church by linking his thoughts about Christ—that is, his Christology—
with his thoughts about the church, that is, his ecclesiology. For him the
latter is the testing ground for the former. The existence of the church is
to be seen as an analogy for God's becoming man in Christ. The church
is the "prolongation" of the Incarnation, in other words, the embodiment of Christ in the reality of the world, just as and because God has
entered the reality of the world. That means: Christ existing as community of the church. The church is a society because of the "society" God
Himself proclaimed in Christ with mankind. The early church's confession of Christ attempted to do justice to this Incarnation of God in the
world with the formulation "true man *and* true God"; and the really existing church is a model of another, but similarly constituted, theology
of two natures. It exists as the "Communion of Saints," of the sanctified.
It is full of abuses and defects, but of God nevertheless; living in guilt
and from love, marked by sin *and* by grace, between forgiveness and
promise.

So much for the theological aspects of the dissertation in summary
form. Its sociological aspects are no less interesting. Bonhoeffer defines
sociology with no "ifs, ands, or buts" as one of the humanities, as the
"science of empirical communal structures" (DBW 1, 16). In accordance
with this, its methods must be phenomenological and not, for example,
historical and/or genetic: Bonhoeffer expects to receive from it a minute
description of what exists and not an analysis of what has come about
in history as a result of social processes. (It is unfortunate that Bonhoeffer was unable to experience the critical social sciences and their
self-understanding that became widespread in Germany in the second
half of his century.)

At times, Bonhoeffer arrives at astonishingly independent conclusions. For example, in spite of all reservations about Ferdinand Tönnies,
Bonhoeffer remains true to Tönnies' basic definitions of communality
and society. He even dares to criticize Max Weber, the most distinguished sociologist of his day—and probably in German literature—an

author whom he greatly respected later in his life and in another context, namely, that of norms and ethics. He takes a similarly ambivalent position toward the seminal thought and conclusions of Ernst Troeltsch.

For Bonhoeffer, "*The church is a communal structure sui generis, one of a kind, a community of spirit and of love*" (DBW 1, 185). It unites and supersedes the basic sociological categories of "society," "community," and "upper and lower classes." Following a consistent line of argumentation, he formulates on this basis a conclusion that can only have come as a surprise to his readers: "Wherever God's word is proclaimed, it creates of itself a church community, no matter where this may be," (ibid., 187), and "The essence of *sanctorum communio* as a fact is to be acknowledged and regarded as genuine both in the Catholic Church and in sects" (ibid., 188). In his eyes, this insight also renders irrelevant the socio-religious distinction that Max Weber and Ernst Troeltsch make between churches and sects. For him, "church" means a community of spirit, of love, of will, of all classes, so that "there is no structure that is in and of itself sociologically holy," and thus "there is no structure that could completely block the way of the Word" (ibid., 187). For Bonhoeffer, as already mentioned, this holds true for the entire spectrum of "church" experienced by us—for both the Roman Catholic Church, which persists in calling itself "Mother Church," as well as for a church that calls itself, for example, "New Apostolic"—and all the more for a church that understands itself as the "Lutheran" church!

However, from both a theological and a sociological perspective, the critical question must be asked of Bonhoeffer whether or not he was too quick to hold the protective umbrella of forgiveness over defects and shortcomings of the church, this "Communion of the Sanctified," that sometimes truly cries out to heaven. (On the other hand, in *Discipleship* he himself warns against "cheap amnesty.") Bonhoeffer made it clear in *Sanctorum Communio* that faith in the church is not equivalent to faith in an unseen church; rather, he emphasized that God has made the concrete, actually constituted church His church as community. This empirical church, in which, as we say today in more senses than one, the word and the sacrament are "dispensed," is for him "Christ existing as community of the church." But precisely at the point where Bonhoeffer so enduringly identified this aspect, one feels that an answer or at least an acknowledgment of the—sociological *and* theological—issue of institutionalization is painfully absent. The dilemmas created by the institutionalization of the "Communion of Saints" are not only unavoidable in any case but also have an unending history, beginning with the early church through the church(es) of our time, and continuing on to Christianity of the future.

Still, Bonhoeffer's remarks on the church sometimes have a very liberating impact both sociologically and theologically, even today! "If we now ask," he writes in his dissertation, "where faith 'encounters the church' in its purest form, the answer is certainly not 'where people gather in the romantic solidarity of a peer group,' but rather where the only thing binding each one to the others is the community of the church; where Jew and Greek, Pietist and liberal bump up against one another in disagreement while nevertheless confessing their faith in unison, going to the Lord's Supper together, and interceding for one another in prayer" (DBW 1, 192, written in the year of the Lord 1927).

Two years later, Bonhoeffer wrote his professorial dissertation *Act and Being*. Like *Sanctorum Communio*, its diction is at times undeniably enigmatic and difficult to decipher, as voiced in clear-sighted and balanced fashion by the editors of a new edition of both works published more than 50 years later: "Although written by the same hand," they state in the Epilogue to *Sanctorum Communio*, "*Act and Being* has an enigmatic character all its own."[10] And the Epilogue to *Act and Being* opens with the sober conclusion that it is certainly among "the least known—and understood—of Dietrich Bonhoeffer's books,"[11] remarking delightfully and accurately later on that we, the readers, are being allowed to look over the shoulder of a young teaching assistant in Berlin who "attacks his recalcitrant material with a mixture of genius and chutzpah."[12] Later, Bonhoeffer himself was not on particularly friendly terms with his professorial dissertation, even though he was very pleased at the favorable echo it awakened, for example, on the part of his theological friend Erwin Sutz. Bonhoeffer wrote to him in February 1932: "That was the first serious response to my book, and I am so very grateful to you for it—even though you have praised the thing far too much. Meanwhile the product has come to arouse rather unfriendly feelings in me" (DBW 11, 63).

These two scientific works should not be viewed as a unit;[13] at the time, however, Bonhoeffer himself explicitly pointed out to the theologian Paul Althaus that there were major links between them in terms of their subject matter.[14] There is an inner connection between the two, and Bonhoeffer mentions this in *Act and Being*, if not *expressis verbis*, nevertheless in all clarity when he further elaborates the thesis developed in his first dissertation on faith: "The church is Christ present, 'Christ existing as community of the church' " (DBW 2, 108). In *Act and Being* too, we again hear the three-part harmony of Person, Togetherness, and God. The interplays within this three-part harmony constitutive of faith—interplays between Being and Act—can be explained summarily, if somewhat unfairly, as follows: Man's being as person is constituted by

God's being for man. God's being constitutes itself for man through God's being as person, since God exists "here" as a "You." This takes on reality in Jesus Christ, who is constitutive of togetherness—between God and man and between human beings.

It is of course impossible to describe or discuss Bonhoeffer's professorial dissertation in full here; and in any case detailed studies of it have been published even quite recently.[15] Rather, our purpose here will be to trace in outline form the intention behind *Act and Being*.

Even more than in *Sanctorum Communio*, Bonhoeffer ventures here into non-theological fields of study. In this case, it is philosophy which serves as the backdrop for unrolling the panorama of his own "existential theology."[16] Even today, Bonhoeffer's manner—"body and soul" a theologian, and not ashamed to admit it!—of dealing with philosophy can serve as a shining example to us. In his eyes, philosophy and theology are "emancipated," that is, equal in value and with equal rights. In his view, philosophy is no longer degraded, as it was under the domination of theology, when it was called the "handmaid of theology," during (hopefully) long and forever-gone times of the past. Rather, philosophy is the conversation partner from whom Bonhoeffer learns, the neighboring territory he is in the process of exploring. It has its own autonomous terrain whose borders he respects.

The areas of philosophy that interest Bonhoeffer most in *Act and Being* are the theory of knowledge and ontology, and with respect to the history of philosophy, Edmund Husserl's phenomenology, along with Martin Heidegger's existential philosophy. These are the age-old questions of theology *and* philosophy, and Bonhoeffer takes his very own approach in discussing them, reflecting upon them thoroughly and at the same time expressing what is nearly "un-thinkable": Is God a being? How is God? Is it possible to know God? How is it possible to know God? Does He exist only in faith? Does He exist outside me, the knower? Does God exist independently of man's faith? What is the connection between the existence of God and knowing Him, between the existence of man and man as a knower? What is contingency? What are the consequences in the context of revelation? These are the basic topics discussed in *Act and Being*.

The focus here, however, is on Bonhoeffer's cardinal interest: the reality of God. This reality remains irrelevant as long as man attempts to grasp it—in reality to escape it—by ignoring his own existence. God as a cosmic magnitude, as abstract, as a super-being existing only in and for Himself, with no relationship to man, is an empty God to whom we owe nothing, one who has little in common with the living God of the biblical Good News. A generally valid statement about a generally valid

God is, in the final analysis, an invalid statement, unless I find a connection between it and my own existence. One thing of course always remains valid: that God truly *is*, independently of whether or not I believe in Him. In other words, *extra me* as well, outside my faith. But also and above all, another truth also remains valid: God *truly* exists provided and because I believe in Him. God will be God *pro me*, for me, not (simply) in and of Himself. He is not a thing among other things; not one object of knowledge among others. But He is also not a "thing in itself" in the Kantian sense. So specific is the gravity of God's reality that it lies at ninety-degree angles to conventional human categories of knowledge.

God's reality consummates itself in His being as a living person with whom I interact, not as a higher being. He has no desire to be a mega-divinity whom we hold fast—but actually at arm's length—in remote worlds of understanding. Rather, He shares responsibility for us and desires that we share ourselves with Him. He is a personal God, who as a person addresses us as persons. And that is what the Bible and theology call "revelation." This is what Bonhoeffer wishes to express with a formulation in this professorial dissertation that often appeared in his later writings and is also quoted several times in this book. It may appear paradoxical at first glance, but is logical and consistent when viewed in the broader context of Bonhoeffer's thought: "Revelation can be categorized only in relation to persons. . . . The static concept of being, in other words, that something or someone 'exists,' takes on life in the social relationship of a person. God is not a God who 'is'; God 'is' in relation to persons, and His being is His being as person" (DBW 2, 112).

This last sentence is in fact the key statement made in *Act and Being* inasmuch as it expresses Bonhoeffer's understanding of God with unsurpassed conciseness and impact. However, his understanding of man and his personal understanding and processing of philosophical problems and basic insights are also expressed throughout *Act and Being*. Three examples illustrate this without the need to situate them in their broader respective contexts of thought.

The first topic is the theory of knowledge, as "the individual's attempt to understand himself" (DBW 2, 27). The second topic is Hegel, who wrote "a philosophy of angels, but not of human existence" (ibid., 35). The third topic is the predicates of being, which "precede consciousness just as conscious *being* precedes *conscious* being" (ibid., 59).

Act and Being is a treasure trove of philosophical and theological wordplay, as well as statements that are unorthodox, original, full of *esprit*, and often very sharply worded. Often, to be sure, they can be understood only as reminiscences from Bonhoeffer's time, and thus are often unduly apodictic or unnecessarily complicated. Are they fireworks of the spirit, impressive to be sure, but perhaps also many times "blinding" in more than one sense of the word? Nevertheless, even today *Act and Being* is a project well worth reflecting upon among the many attempts made in the history of the church to spell out the explosive issues and difficulties in the relationship between theology and philosophy, between faith and understanding.

How might we best follow the line of thought that undergirds Bonhoeffer's professorial dissertation? He begins by describing what is meant by "Act" and "Being." What interests him in this work is basically the "concreteness of the concept of God, along with a concept of knowledge that can adequately deal with the relationship between 'God's being' and the mental act by which this is comprehended. In other words, Bonhoeffer wishes to interpret theologically the meaning of 'God's being in revelation' and how it is known, and the relationship between faith as Act and revelation as Being" (DBW 2, 22–23). To this end he thus identifies more closely the essence of Act and Being: "Whereas the first concerns the relationships between the Infinite and the Extensive as bound together in *consciousness,* between discontinuity and existentiality (a concept used here not in the sense of 'the sphere of that which is,' but in the sense of the person as a potential, core event), the second concerns 'immanence,' the Infinite and Intensive, that which transcends consciousness, continuity" (ibid., 24). And he adds: "The manner whereby philosophy and theology concretize the understanding of both remains to be seen" (ibid.).

These introductory passages make it more than clear that in his professorial dissertation Bonhoeffer embarked on no small undertaking. In a classical three-step, Bonhoeffer gradually unveils his understanding of "act and being." In the first part he takes up the Act-Being problem in philosophy. In doing so, he identifies the two poles of tension that theology must always keep in view when dealing with the question of the existence of God—the dialectic of the *extra me* and the *pro me,* the reality of God and the reality of man. He writes, "God is reality above the world, transcending consciousness, Creator and Lord. This statement is unconditionally necessary in Christian theology. . . . However, in response to this it can *also* be stated that God exists only in and for the consciousness of man" (DBW 2, 51; italics by S.D.).

In the second part, Bonhoeffer casts light on the Act-Being problem in relation to revelation and the church, and—being wholly true to Martin Luther—goes into the thought of Rudolf Bultmann and, above all, that of Karl Barth, clearly following in his footsteps. We read there, for example, "God is forever the Lord, forever a subject, so that whoever thinks he can grasp Him as an object no longer has *Him;* He is forever the 'Coming' God, never the 'Already Arrived' God (Barth)" (DBW 2, 79). This God is not of this world, but He is indeed for this world. He binds and allies Himself in freedom with the world and the people in it. Brooking no objections, Bonhoeffer describes this single and final declaration of God's freedom by pointing to its ratification, completed in Christ and ever ongoing in the being of the church: "God is free—not from man, but for man. Christ is the word of God's freedom. God *is* present, not in the form of an eternal spirit but—provisory though the expressions are—'haveable,' 'graspable' in His word in the church" (ibid., 85). This description is one of the keys to understanding not only *Act and Being* but also Bonhoeffer himself. In a nutshell, it contains his understanding of God, Christ, and the church while, at the same time, documenting the affinity between *Sanctorum Communio* and *Act and Being*.[17]

During the course of his professorial dissertation, Bonhoeffer turns explicitly to the motifs presented in his doctoral dissertation by painting a picture of the community of the church in Christ in which the distinction between man and mankind, "act and being," is repealed. Quite unexpectedly in this work, which required the extensive use of scientific nomenclature, we find one of Bonhoeffer's most moving descriptions of the nature of the church. Nowhere else does he express with more empathy what the community and church of Christ meant to him than when he wrote, "I hear another person who truly proclaims the Gospel to me; He brings the sacrament to me: 'You are forgiven'; he and the community of the church pray for me, and I hear the Gospel. I join in this prayer and know in word, in sacrament, and in prayer, that I am one with them, with the new mankind; that they give me strength and I strengthen them in return, whether here or elsewhere. Here am I addressed: my whole historical humanity, as an individual and as mankind. I believe, that is, I know that I am held in good hands (classical Latin: *pati*). This is why I exist (*esse*), this is why my belief is active (*agere*). This is where the wheel comes round" (DBW 2, 118).

In the final part of his work, Bonhoeffer sets the Act-Being problem in relation to man; that is, to his old and his new being, his being "in Adam" and "in Christ." This part is much less systematic in character than the two that precede it and contains some explicitly eschatological elements,[18] as well as an affinity for emotional and visionary statements that are unusual in nature for a professorial dissertation, even a theological one, even today. At the end of *Act and Being*, he counterpoises "the unechoed cry of loneliness to the loneliness of the self," the "tortured awareness of the self as torn apart," with the person who comes to himself in the church, the community of Christ, and (again) finds his home there (DBW 2, 161).

Bonhoeffer had, from time to time, been intensely preoccupied with the theme of the child as a metaphor for man standing before God, and it becomes more and more crystalized in these concluding statements, reminding us that his original idea had been to write about the "problem of the child in theology."[19] This work, which he *never* wrote might have ended in much the same way as the one he did finish. In any case, it is indeed an unusual way for an Evangelical theologian to conclude a professorial dissertation in the year 1930. After all, he had been educated through the sternly rational school of Evangelical theology, which was ever mindful of its chosen duty to be "scientific"! He writes, "Here a new creation emerges in faith and is completed in contemplation: the new man of the future who no longer reflects on himself but looks only away from himself to the revelation of God—to Christ—and who is (re)born out of the confines of this world into the wideness of the heavens; who becomes, whatever he was or even never was before, a creature of God, a child" (ibid.).

At the end of July 1930, Bonhoeffer gave his inaugural university lecture, entitled "The Question of Man in Philosophy and Theology Today," in Berlin; in it, his many border-crossings between philosophy and theology find expression. He discusses Max Scheler and Martin Heidegger, Paul Tillich and Ernst Grisebach, Karl Barth and Rudolf Bultmann. At the end of the lecture, two themes again come to the surface. One is peripheral: that of the self that cries out and remains silent. It played a role at the end of his professorial dissertation (see above). Here, however, Bonhoeffer speaks of the cry that "echoes through the silent, subjugated world of the self" (DBW 10, 376). The other is the main theme from his dissertation: "The church is Christ hidden amongst us" (ibid., 377).

10

Documents of Lived Faith:
Discipleship and *Life Together*

> The goal is to find a truth which is truth for me; to
> find the idea for which I will live and die.
>
> *Søren Kierkegaard*

Worlds appear to lie between Bonhoeffer's first books—the academic, theological *Sanctorum Communio* and *Act and Being*—and the spiritual works of piety that followed, namely, *Discipleship* and *Life Together*. However, apart from the fact that there need essentially be no contradiction between academic works of theology and works of piety, since in the best case each will merely have its own specific orientation, in other words, a different form of dealing with the same contents and intentions, there is also a clear link between the two. Bonhoeffer's leitmotif in *Sanctorum Communio*, which also played a role in *Act and Being*, surfaces again in *Discipleship:* "The church is the presence of Christ Himself. In saying this, we regain a long-forgotten thought about the church" (DBW 4, 232). In *Life Together*, Bonhoeffer describes in full a concrete attempt to live the church, to realize Christian being not in isolation but together with others; an attempt to live in conformity with the *sanctorum communio*, the Communion of Saints, in the form of a Christian community.

Apart from this link, however, there is also a basic difference between Bonhoeffer's first two books and those that followed; namely, *Discipleship* and *Life Together* contain statements made by Bonhoeffer that are open neither to commentary nor to analysis, since they belong more properly in the realms of depth psychology and religion. Strictly speaking, as has already been emphasized in a different context, they are therefore also less appropriate as objects of study in rational discourse and argumentative discussion. Whereas *Sanctorum Communio* and *Act and Being* were rooted in other sciences—that is, they were oriented toward them and used them as a basis for opening up theological perspectives—*Discipleship* and *Life Together* are books of faith in the original sense of the word: written from faith, in faith, and for faith. They are not concerned with theology's compatibility with other sciences or its openness to dialogue with them, but with a return to the origins of New Testament thought, along with intra-theological certitude and existential self-reflection on the part of Christianity. In short, they are concerned with engendering faith and making it stronger.

These two books by Bonhoeffer have been widely read. *Life Together* was the book read most during his lifetime, and of the books published by Bonhoeffer himself *Discipleship* is the one with the most copies in print. Like the later *Ethics* and *Resistance and Surrender*, both have been translated into numerous languages since their (re-)appearance from the middle of the century on. Both books, of course, had their own histories and consequences in Bonhoeffer's own life.

Bonhoeffer mentions the topic of discipleship and, for him closely related to it, his first intense encounter with the Sermon on the Mount, in a somewhat despairing, lonely letter he wrote to Erwin Sutz from London, on April 28, 1934 (DBW 13, 128–29). In it he writes of his disappointment and apprehension regarding the church, particularly the church in National Socialist Germany: "You know, I really believe—you may be surprised by this—that the whole point of the Sermon on the Mount is decision. . . . *Being a disciple* of Christ—and I would like to know what that means—is not summed up by our concept of faith. I am working on a paper I would like to call 'The Exercises,' just as a working title." On January 14, 1935, he wrote again from London to his brother Karl-Friedrich:

> I think I know that I would really be inwardly clear and truly honest only if I were to begin taking the Sermon on the Mount seriously. This is where the one and only source of strength is to be found that can blow away all the 'magic,' all the illusions and superstition, in a fireworks that leave only a few charred cinders behind. The restoration of the church will certainly come from a new form of monastic life that has nothing in common with the old form, except an uncompromising life lived according to the Sermon on the Mount in the following of Christ. I believe it is time to gather people together for this. (ibid., 272–73)

Bonhoeffer then worked out *Discipleship* during 1935 and 1936, while lecturing and teaching at the Preaching Seminary of the Confessing Church in Zingst and Finkenwalde; after many attempts, he finally got the manuscript to the printer in 1937.[1] Of all his books, *Discipleship* is the one he later refers to many times, but always modestly, saying that he had only intimated certain thoughts in it "but never really developed their implications thereafter," as he wrote to Eberhard Bethge on December 5, 1943 (DBW 8, 226). His best-known comment about *Discipleship* is found in the now-famous letter he wrote on July 21, 1944, where he relates the story of his conversation thirteen years earlier with the French pastor Jean Lasserre and then states, "I thought I could learn faith by trying on my own to live something like a holy life. I think I wrote *Discipleship* to mark the end of this road. Today I see clearly the dangers of this book, while continuing to stand behind what I wrote there. My experience later and down to this present hour has been that we only learn faith by standing fully, and with both feet in this present life" (ibid., 542).

Bonhoeffer's ambivalent attitude toward *Discipleship*—which is also characteristic of his attitude toward his other books—is evident in a reminiscence reported by his biographer: in response to a proposal made by his curates that he revise *Discipleship* in view of critical objections to it, he laughed and merely remarked, in the words of Pilate, that he had written what he had written.[2] With regard to the topic of discipleship, Karl Barth commented in 1955, in his *Church Dogmatics*, that Bonhoeffer's *Discipleship* was "By far the best thing written on the subject."[3] Warmly and with unreserved respect, he discusses Bonhoeffer's book and the authenticity of his way of faith. In 1936, however, while Bonhoeffer was writing *Discipleship*, Barth had written to him, voicing skepticism concerning reports he had heard about the life, the rules of piety, and the unusual practices of faith in the Preaching Seminary in Finkenwalde; he could not help having the impression that "a difficult-to-define odor of monastic eros and pathos" was in the air (DBW 11, 253).

And Barth was not completely wrong. Bonhoeffer felt a conspicuous affinity in those years for monastic forms of life. During his time in England, he informed himself thoroughly and "on location" about communities of Anglican provenience that functioned along the lines of monastic orders. His repeated attempts to visit Gandhi's Ashram in India document the special magnetism any kind of *sanctorum communio* exerted on Bonhoeffer. The House of Brethren (German "Bruderhaus"), which was established in Finkenwalde during the time he was writing *Discipleship*, represented an effort to establish a life community of "brothers" in the Evangelical faith. His longing for Christian community, for a concretely practiced "society of Jesus" in the original sense of the term, was the definitive influence on both *Discipleship* and *Life Together*. However, these monastic tendencies had for Bonhoeffer a function eminently aimed at the world and designed to aid proclamation in the world. For him, paths inward were simultaneously paths outward: Bonhoeffer sought the former as a means of travelling the latter in more Christ-like fashion. As he explained in a letter of application, dated September 1935, written to church leaders on behalf of the young theologians at the Preaching Seminary in Finkenwalde, hoping to found the House of Brethren, "The aim is not monastic withdrawal but innermost concentration for outwardly-directed service" (DBW 14, 77).

The real focus of *Discipleship*, however, is neither the interior of man nor the exterior of the world, but the person of Jesus Christ, His image and example. *Discipleship* is Bonhoeffer's most Christ-centered book. Classically, and like his earlier books, it is made up of three parts, even though this is not immediately apparent. In reality, *Discipleship* is an exegesis of the Sermon on the Mount with a short, albeit very succinct and provocative, introduction and a longer closing section. It makes manifest what in retrospect appears as Bonhoeffer's key experience with the Christian Good News, in contrast to a merely theological type of encounter. As Carl Friedrich von Weizsäcker remarked in a lecture he presented in 1976, on what would have been Bonhoeffer's seventieth birthday, with remarkable empathy and great respect, "His breakthrough into the Bible was occasioned"—unlike Luther and Barth, we might add—"not by the highly intellectual text of the Letter to the Romans, but by the intolerable, merciful simplicity of the Sermon on the Mount"; he then emphasized that the theology of *Discipleship* speaks a "biblicistic language."[4]

From beginning to end, *Discipleship* does indeed represent an elucidation of basic New Testament themes and the traditional topics of Christian faith and life: justification, growth in holiness, grace and sin, cross and resurrection, discipleship and baptism, suffering and transfiguration. It follows the texts very closely, often nearly to the point of being indistinguishable from them, so that the reader who is less familiar with the Bible often cannot discern directly, for example, what is from Paul and what is from Bonhoeffer. And something else catches the eye: in addition to Martin Luther, another theologian is also very much present in *Discipleship*, one who also protested against the ossified church practices of his own time, namely, Søren Kierkegaard—notably through his work *The Individual and the Church: On Luther and Protestantism.*[5] According to an entry in Kierkegaard's diary, "Not 'discipleship,' but 'grace' is the place to begin; and then discipleship is to follow as a fruit of gratitude to the best of one's ability."[6]

Grace, one of Luther's favorite words, plays an important role in the first part of Bonhoeffer's *Discipleship*. Luther situated grace where it belongs from a New Testament point of view: in the center of Christian faith and beyond the reach of the intrigues and power of human beings, back in the hands of God. God is on our side *sola gratia*—"by grace alone." Not because we might have earned it through living a virtuous life, not even half-and-half, but only and for no other reason than that He loves us. This love is free and without strings—or it does not exist. It is meant wholly for us. And that means: justification of the sinner by grace alone. He takes part in this justification, this acceptance, just as he is, *sola fide*—"by faith alone."

In Bonhoeffer's eyes, the brilliance of this grace has faded because the church allowed it to degenerate into cheap grace. He describes in drastic language what has become of the splendid glad tidings of the grace of God: "it is brummagem" (DBW 4, 29) in a church of constant "everything-must-go" sales; it is to be had cheaply, because the supply is inexhaustible; it is of equal interest to all at all times, and therefore now disinteresting to all at all times. It is offered by the church at a low price, as a bargain. Because the church itself is indifferent? Or with full intention? Whatever the case, for Bonhoeffer, the Gospel has been watered down to "forgiveness and comfort at dirt-cheap prices": When grace is peddled "as a theory, a principle, a system," and "forgiveness of sins as a general truth, . . . and God's love as merely a Christian idea of God," then grace is transmogrified under the counter into cheap grace, thus becoming and for this reason a "denial of the living word of God, a denial of the Incarnation of the Word of God" (ibid.). Cheapening grace automatically implies justification, not of the sinner, but of sin. It overlooks how rare and valuable God's love is: "Grace is costly: it is the Incarnation of God" (ibid., 31).

God paid for it, not the church. The latter acknowledges the grace of God in person—that is, in the person of Jesus Christ—and is its caretaker, but fails to practice the discipleship of Jesus Christ: "Grace that was costly has become cheap grace, without discipleship" (DBW 4, 36). But in so acting, the church has done neither itself nor us a favor; for it has frittered away its greatest capital in the form of small investments. Bonhoeffer asks two provocative and simultaneously rhetorical questions: "But are we also aware that this cheap grace has been utterly unmerciful toward us? Is the price we must pay today, in the breakdown of the institutional churches, anything other than a necessary consequence of grace too easily acquired?" (ibid., 40). He responds to these questions immediately with a caustic balance sheet of a people's church, whose relevance for the present day is open to discussion. He writes, "It [the church] has cheapened the Good News and the sacraments; it has baptized, confirmed, and absolved a whole nation without question and without setting conditions, . . . rivers of grace without end have been dispensed, but the call to rigorous discipleship of Christ is heard less and less often" (ibid.).

Precisely because of God's love for man, it is Bonhoeffer's intention to prevent costly grace from being perverted into an object found at a bargain sale; he does not wish, for example, to formulate a new law of works or discipleship. He wants to prevent costly grace from becoming watered down into a cheap, dogmatic dictum, and—here the same thing holds true as discussed earlier in the context of universal reconciliation[7]—he wishes to point out the intrinsic danger of viewing "grace as a principle," as a building block firmly embedded in doctrine and systems, as an item purchasable at any time independent of the cost of discipleship (DBW 4, 39). (The English title of one translation of the book, by the way, is *The Cost of Discipleship*). Bonhoeffer is not trying to say here that grace is to be earned through discipleship, but rather that grace reaches fullness in discipleship. Otherwise costly grace mutates into cheap grace. Speaking realistically from today's perspective, however, it must be noted that the question of God's grace and man's justification, existentially so crucial for St. Paul, Luther, Bonhoeffer, and many others both within and outside the history of Christianity, is viewed as utterly irrelevant by most people of our time. The question as to whether or not God shows man mercy has long since given way to the question of whether or not God exists at all—and in our time, in the eyes of many, even this question has become obsolete. For many, as a fact God no longer *is,* nor as a question, certainly not as an answer, and most certainly not as a question concerning a God of mercy. Interest is aroused neither by the topic of God as love nor, corresponding to it, that of the "freedom of a Christian" (Luther) or the "Discipleship of Jesus Christ" (Bonhoeffer). The question whether or not God exists at all has become largely irrelevant. His reality is no longer even recognized as a possibility. There is no sense in bemoaning this situation. But in spite of all this, does it perhaps indeed make sense to bear witness to God's reality and dare to risk the discipleship of Jesus Christ?

This made sense to Bonhoeffer. In the first part of *Discipleship,* he traces Luther's way from the world into the cloister and back again to the world, and applies this indirectly to the challenges of being a Christian, which he senses in his own day: "Now it was necessary to live out discipleship of Jesus in the midst of the world . . . the world could no longer avoid confrontation with the Christian. It was a battle fought in the trenches" (DBW 4, 35). Without going here into specific problems with Bonhoeffer's conception of the world, problems that lie at the roots of *Discipleship,* it must nevertheless be emphasized that, for him, the discipleship of Christ is of course realized *in* the world[8]—or not at all; not in flight from the world, not in a world divided into, for example, a (good) interior side and a (bad) exterior side. Bonhoeffer makes this clear: "With the very first step, the substance of the Gospels requires an action that affects the whole of life" (ibid., 53). This literally total demand, in which the discipleship of Jesus has it origins and its claim on each disciple, is what Bonhoeffer refers to in the statement that is usually quoted as *the* basic statement of his *Discipleship:* "*Only he who believes is obedient,* and *only he who is obedient is a believer*" (ibid., 52). He himself avers concerning this key statement, which thereafter takes a variety of different forms, that both of its parts are equally true. It results in readiness to suffer, not at any price or under all conditions, but only under conditions appointed by God alone: "Discipleship is a bond with the suffering Christ" (ibid., 82).

At that time, Bonhoeffer's involvement in conspiracy and imprisonment still lay far in the future; but for us looking back, it already appears on the horizon when he makes the statement quoted earlier, "An outcast in suffering, scorned, and abandoned by all, . . . this essential characteristic of suffering on the cross is incomprehensible to a Christian mentality incapable of distinguishing between civil and Christian existence" (DBW 4, 80). The extent to which Christian existence had mutated into civil-Christian existence, and done its best to wipe from memory the characteristic traits of life lived in discipleship of the One from whom it takes its name—all of this was as clear to Bonhoeffer as it was to another existential theologian who lived a hundred years earlier, one whose name we have already mentioned often, namely, Søren Kierkegaard. For both men, the cross of Christ stands in opposition to a powerful and lackluster church. For them, the cross of Christ is the symbol for God's suffering because of and in the world; it is diametrically opposed to a Christian mentality that distances itself from such suffering in order to come to an understanding with the world. Later in *Discipleship* Bonhoeffer writes: "*Passio* (classical Latin, 'suffering') as part of Jesus' love on the cross—this is what is 'extra-ordinary' about Christian existence" (ibid., 148). When discipleship is put to the final test, it means discipleship unto the cross and unto death.

First, however, Bonhoeffer spells out discipleship in Jesus Christ in the language of the Sermon on the Mount. Bonhoeffer had found his new, very direct understanding of this text probably at the beginning of the 1930s (see above). During his year of study in New York, he met for the first time the French theologian Jean Lasserre, whose radicality and acceptance of consequences fascinated him. He seems to have learned from Lasserre not only to read the Sermon on the Mount with new eyes but also to become aware of the spirit of pacifism in the New Testament.[9] In *Discipleship,* Bonhoeffer interprets the text thoroughly and persuasively, but *not* particularly objectively. He does not render it powerless through theological hair-splitting or banal references to a world of reality in which it could not exist. Rather, he takes it at its word and considers its promises—as well as unabashed challenges—in all seriousness. He understands its statements less as demands than as badges of Christianity. It is for him the Magna Carta of discipleship in Christ, a program which is to be put into practice in the everyday world, in the existing reality of life. He believes that it is really not difficult to understand the Sermon on the Mount—provided we wish to. It speaks in clear, uncomplicated, and unambiguous language. Likewise, Bonhoeffer's language here is clear, uncomplicated, and unambiguous.

In the final part of the book, he confronts the actual being of the church of Jesus Christ with the discipleship of Jesus Christ, by drawing from the depths of the New Testament letters, especially—but not only—the Letters to the Romans and Corinthians. He combines these two texts into a tapestry of promise and challenge, merging his own statements so intimately with them in the process that—as already mentioned earlier in discussing *Discipleship*—the difference between them is sometimes unrecognizable, at least for the theologically unschooled reader. The book's final chapter, the section Bonhoeffer entitled "The Image of Christ," is characterized by mystic and eschatological, if not ecstatic, tones rarely found in such intensity in Bonhoeffer's other writings.[10] These are the deep tones of the mysticism of suffering, like that found earlier—in the developmental stages of Christian mysticism—in the writings of Theresa of Avila and John of the Cross, and later in Edith Stein and Simone Weil, who were both contemporaries of Bonhoeffer.[11] As Bonhoeffer voiced, "Whoever wishes to carry in his person the transfigured image of Jesus must already have carried in the world the battered image of the One who was Crucified" (DBW 4, 300). Christ Himself wishes to "become apparent in us"; we are to "take on" his appearance (ibid., 301).

Although Bonhoeffer does not speak of becoming one with Christ or of a mystical union as such, his statement that the image of the believer and disciple must be identical with that of Christ is reminiscent of the witness borne by those who have experienced *unio mystica,* that is, the mystical union—or at least a form of mystical experience—linked with the figure of Christ and normally described as a mystical experience of Christ. Those who have testified about their mystical experiences speak remarkably often about stations and stages in their experience of God, and of visitations by God.[12] In connection with the image of Christ, Bonhoeffer says that "the splendor of Jesus Christ will shine through us while we are still on this earth"; there is a "progression from awareness to awareness, from clarity to clarity, and on to ever more perfect identity with the image of the Son of God" (DBW 4, 302). He calls this process the "indwelling of Jesus Christ in our hearts": "The life of Jesus Christ has not yet come to an end on this earth. Christ lives on in the lives of his followers. . . . He who became man, was crucified and transfigured, enters into me and lives my life" (ibid., 303).

The question as to whether or not we are hearing an echo of mystical experience in this text, which is entitled "The Image of Christ" and concludes *Discipleship*, must remain an open one. The text contains many elements that are reminiscent of attempts undertaken by individuals in the past to describe mystic experiences in words. Such experiences—let it be said in passing here—have little or nothing to do with a motherhood-and-apple-pie, New-Age sort of mysticism. Rather, they plunge the individual into turmoil far more than they edify him; they are anything but a melody of spirituality gently wafted on the breeze of the Spirit. In their final consequences, they do not bear the individual upward into the music of the spheres but downward into the hard realities of this world, a world in which God wishes to play a role. For Bonhoeffer as well, and in particular, the immediate experience of Christ bears completely concrete consequences for man. From his perspective, since such an experience can result only from the Incarnation of Christ, he can say, "In the Incarnation of Christ the whole of mankind is restored to the dignity of being made in God's image. Now, whoever does wrong to the least of mankind does wrong to Christ. . . . He who became man makes his disciples brothers of all mankind" (DBW 4, 301). Love for man, the "philanthropy of God," says Bonhoeffer, "revealed in the Incarnation of Christ, gives rise to the brotherly love Christians have for all who are called 'man' on earth" (ibid.).

The title of Bonhoeffer's book, *Discipleship*, is reminiscent of another book with a similar title, the *Imitation of Christ*, a Middle-Age compilation of mystic texts attributed to Thomas à Kempis. Bonhoeffer was well acquainted with this book, and he closes his own *Discipleship* with an indirect reference to this *Imitatio* and a quote from Eph 5:1: "The follower of Jesus is the imitator of God. Be you now followers as beloved children" (DBW 4, 304). We remember: Bonhoeffer's *Act and Being* also ended with the image of a child.

Bonhoeffer's *Life Together* reads like the unbroken continuation of *Discipleship*. Once again we encounter Thomas à Kempis and Martin Luther, and once again nuances stemming from the New and, now, the Old Testament as well. Where *Discipleship* contained the theological foundation stones, *Life Together* now presents the concrete form of an attempt to live a Christ-like life. The two and one-half years he practiced a *vita communis* in the Preaching Seminary of the Confessing Church in Zingst and Finkenwalde, especially in the House of Brethren at the seminary in Finkenwalde, provided the necessary experiential basis for Bonhoeffer to write this book, seemingly at a single sitting in the autumn of 1937, after the State Secret Police closed the preaching seminary. He missed the life he lived there very deeply, and *Life Together* was, so to speak, its swan song, as Bonhoeffer was to write later in 1941, in a letter to Eberhard Bethge from Cloister Ettal (DBW 16, 128).

It comes as no surprise that Bonhoeffer thought back to life lived in community with others precisely when he was in the Benedictine Abbey of Ettal. *Ora et labora*—prayer and work—this was the motto of Benedict of Nursia, which later came to typify life in all Christian monastic communities. Bonhoeffer composed variations on it in *Life Together*. Prayer and work are two different things, but their unity becomes visible precisely when the two are clearly distinguished one from another. The cloister and the world, Finkenwalde and Berlin, were not separate places for Bonhoeffer; rather, Christian existence was lived in both. Up to this time, Bonhoeffer had not given his candidates very much that was already familiar to them: ". . . a regular daily routine, a liturgy of prayer, and a modest knock on the door of the immeasurable realm of experience available through meditation";[13] only in this way could they participate in what Bonhoeffer had already experienced in his own life, namely, "that Christian life can be more worldly only when it is more spiritual, and more spiritual only when it is more worldly."[14]

Bonhoeffer's preliminary remark, that this was not something for private circles but rather a task for the church, is decisive in order to situate *Life Together* properly within the chain of his works (DBW 5, 14). *Life Together* presents a balance sheet, a call, and encouragement to undertake the project of living life together in the Spirit and in the world; not to be thought of as just another project conceived by individuals along their road of life experiments, but rather as a binding personal commitment, an infectious example for the future of the church. For those who journey into this future, in Bonhoeffer's view at that time, Christian brotherhood is both the basis *and* the final consequence of life lived in following Jesus. This conviction appears to have remained with him to the end of his life, albeit in somewhat different form. Just before his death, in a message he uttered to an English fellow prisoner, to be passed on to his friend in England, Bishop Bell, Bonhoeffer expressed the conviction shared "with him that the foundation stone is our universal Christian brotherhood, which supersedes all national feelings of hatred" (DBW 16, 468).

Bonhoeffer's most immediate interest, however, was concrete Christian brotherhood: a community of dwelling, working, and living together, or at least living together for a time. *Life Together* documents the everyday life of such communities. From an evangelical point of view, they are not only unusual in form but even downright suspect: their characteristics smack of the classical religious orders, even though these have not been incorporated lock, stock, and barrel. For example, there were no vows of poverty, chastity, and obedience in the House of Brethren; but there was indeed a high degree of (self-)discipline; there was a sharing of possessions, and there was certainly the practice of celibacy, if only for a time. While no mention was made of a commitment to remain unmarried, Bonhoeffer's above-mentioned partiality for the monastic way of life became evident when he himself broke off a—possibly—promising friendship with a woman theologian, stating that, at least at the moment, it was not the right time for him to bind himself and live for a family. The decisive factor in this decision, however, was probably the ever-increasing pressure put upon the Confessing Church by the machinery of the State.[15]

In *Life Together,* Bonhoeffer speaks of rules that form the foundation for Christian community and promises that will be experienced as reality when they are fulfilled. "Life together" is a life of both discipline *and* fulfillment. At its center, there is neither religious vanity nor spiritual ambitiousness; rather, the center is Christ, the sole mediator, who is constitutive of the lives of individual brothers living in togetherness: "Christ in our hearts is not as strong as Christ in the words of a brother; the former is diffident; the latter is confident" (DBW 5, 20). This confidence mutually conditions both faith and life lived in togetherness with others, resulting in a triangle that is not at all "magical" but an absolutely everyday reality—but only for a time. "We have one another only through Christ, but through Christ we really and truly *have* each other, we have all of us forever," writes Bonhoeffer (ibid., 22). Christian brotherhood is not an ideal but a divine reality; he draws an important distinction here between pneumatic and psychic reality. Pneumatic reality is an experience of togetherness that is rooted in the Spirit of God; psychic reality on the other hand arises from one's own psychic efforts. God is "not a God of feelings, but the God of truth" (ibid., 23).

Bonhoeffer's concern is with sobriety of thought, not with religious ecstasy; with watchfulness, not with spiritual numbness. At issue for him is not a dream of Christian togetherness, but its reality. Thus he summarizes his viewpoint, "Where the early morning fog with its dreamy forms dissipates, that is where the bright day of Christian togetherness begins," and warns against spiritual narcissism: "Just as the Christian should not attempt constantly to check the pulse of his own spiritual life, so also Christian life lived in togetherness with God is not given to us in order that we constantly measure its temperature" (DBW 5, 25–26). The experience of God in and through all members is not the goal, but the fruit of Christian life lived in this togetherness. It may, if God wills it, be absent at times. It will not be felt in grandiose theatrical productions on the part of an individual or group, but in the hard crust of working on oneself and in the promise of forgiveness. For this reason, Bonhoeffer arrives at apparently contradictory statements. At the end of the first chapter of *Life Together* he writes, "We are bound together in faith, not in our common experience" (ibid., 34); and in the final chapter, entitled "Confession and the Lord's Supper," he concludes, "Whoever confesses his sins to his brother knows he is no longer here all by himself, and he experiences in the reality of the other the presence of God" (ibid., 97).

It would appear that Bonhoeffer's faith and thought constantly—his whole life long—revolved around the question of the presence of God. And it would also appear that he experienced it most directly in the life of togetherness in the House of Brethren in Finkenwalde.

11

The Book of His Life: The *Ethics*

I do not claim to have found some sort of new
principle or a new teaching. I have simply
tried in my own way to apply eternal verities
to our daily life and its problems.

Mahatma Gandhi

The book that we know as Bonhoeffer's *Ethics* stands midway between his academic books and his unabashed books of faith—not "midway" in a chronological sense, but in terms of language, ease of understanding, and the breadth of its content. His diction does not bear so much the stamp of scientific, philosophical, or socio-philosophical thought, as is the case in *Sanctorum Communio* and *Act and Being;* nevertheless, the *Ethics* contains and unfolds a panoply of issues from the fields of theology, anthropology, historical and literary studies, social studies, and the history of thought. Although we do not find in it the sternness and spirituality of *Discipleship* and *Life Together,* the core of his *Ethics* is Christ. The book shares Bonhoeffer's basic ideas that are found in all the books he had written before, and molds them into one question: given that the reality of God became concrete in Jesus Christ, how does it become concrete in our world? This was the basic thought and question that his later reflections in prison revolved around as well.

In contrast to his other writings, we note here a special, emotional bond Bonhoeffer felt with regard to his *Ethics:* he was attached to this book. Even in his very last months, he was aware that his work on the *Ethics* had not been work on just one more publication, but that it came from the core of his being. His friend and biographer reports that Bonhoeffer had long had a feeling, which he also expressed to others, that his life's work and—even more—his principal mission in life consisted in producing a theological *Ethics.*[1] He worked long and hard on it, and even in the manuscripts completed by the time of his arrest there were passages he considered by no means polished or finalized. On November 18, 1943, Bonhoeffer wrote that he had reproached himself when first in prison for not having finished the book (DBW 8, 188). Moreover, it had been confiscated. He felt, however, soothed by the fact that he had already communicated "the essentials" to Bethge, but added, "Then too, my thoughts were still unfinished" (ibid.). A month later, on December 15, 1943, he disclosed to his friend his worries over his own future in a way that was very open, fearful, and almost resigned (ibid., 237). This fear included fear for the future of his—hoped-for—marriage to Maria von Wedemeyer: "I often think [I] may now actually have my life more or less behind me and now need only finish my *Ethics*. But you know, at such moments I am gripped by an indescribable longing to have a child and not go without leaving a trace. . . . " Such self-descriptive statements express not only his longing for a future but also the extraordinarily high value he placed on the *Ethics*.

As a curate abroad, Bonhoeffer delivered a talk to his congregation in Barcelona in February 1929 entitled "The Basic Questions of a Christian Ethics." It reads like an early prelude to the themes later expressed in his *Ethics,* although in the course of the later work their instrumental setting changed. It already exhibits the resentment he felt toward inflexible ethics, which act only as a handmaid whose task is to help fulfill and defend ironclad principles. Bonhoeffer's response is a clear rejection of any hope of arriving at generally valid, quasi-eternal norms; that is, fixed Christian keynote ideas that are set once and for all, or absolutely fixed moral principles. Any attempt to describe such principles is like an attempt "to sketch a bird on the fly" (DBW 10, 323). He takes a different approach: ethical acts in Christian life take place between two poles that cause tension but also give them power. The poles are, in wholly New Testament language, freedom and love: ethical acts have their source in love—and can even be described basically "as love"—that becomes creative in freedom (ibid., 329). Augustine's command applies very well to this understanding of ethics: Love, and do what you will! For Bonhoeffer as well as for Augustine, "lawlessness"—that is, freedom from the Law as proclaimed in the New Testament—is not a *carte blanche* for ethical anarchy but something unique that opens the way for us to accept the gift of freedom: it puts us on our own feet. "The Christian," Bonhoeffer reasons, "stands free, all bridges burnt behind him, before God and the world; upon his shoulders rests full responsibility for how he deals with the gift of freedom" (ibid., 331).

This does not mean that a Christian's situation is easy, for with this freedom he also accepts the risk of isolation and the loss of ethical handrails. There is no rock-solid, timeless scaffolding of principles where he can move self-assuredly and surefootedly from rung to rung. "An ethical decision leads us into deepest aloneness," says Bonhoeffer emphatically

(DBW 10, 331–32), that is, into the aloneness of one who stands before the living God, upon whom he must fall back in concrete situations; he must act responsibly in the concrete situation toward Him and toward himself, without a pole star to point him toward eternal good or eternal evil. What is important in each case is to probe and redefine the criteria of ethical action, in order to rediscover them in the new situation. But the question arises, doesn't this open the door for arbitrariness? Does it not result in decisions drawn from the (arbitrary) depths of an (arbitrary) space? Is there not a danger of succumbing to arbitrariness in the free fall act of decision? "No," Bonhoeffer would respond, for "One must subordinate oneself in ethical decisions to the will of God, must see one's own actions *sub specie aeternitatis,* in the light of eternity, and then no matter what course is taken, it will be the right one" (ibid., 333).

Bonhoeffer's certainty, which borders on the obstinate, that the profile of his ethical action will certainly correspond to God's will if he simply subordinates his decisions completely to Him, appears to lie between naiveté and arrogance. But this is not the case. There is a precondition that protects against arbitrariness and this is, namely, love. Bonhoeffer had no doubts about this even when he was in Barcelona in 1929. Similarly, he had no doubts about it in London, when he said in a sermon he preached on October 28, 1934 on *the* New Testament chapter concerning love, chapter 13 of First Corinthians, that where there is love, we are not the ones who act purely of our own volition, but it is God Himself who acts in love through us: "Since love is therefore God Himself and His will, . . . it can never go wrong; that is why it stays on course, that is why it travels along that course with absolute certainty" (DBW 13, 394). And this deepest of convictions about the dependable networking of love and ethics, of freedom and responsibility, of God's single-minded will and man's multitudinous decisions, is the basis of the work that Bonhoeffer began to write in the autumn of 1940: his *Ethics.*

He wrote his *Ethics* in troubled times. He was able to carry out his real assignment at that time, the training and counseling of candidates for ministry in the Confessing Church, only in rudimentary fashion. The Gestapo had closed and sealed Sigurdshof, the home of the last "Group Vicariate," in the spring of 1940. Bonhoeffer continued to write open letters to his "pupils." He traveled through Eastern Prussia to make so-called visitations in the name of the Council of Brethren, the directing body of the Confessing Church, and was also commissioned by that same body to write academically—about a theological ethics of the church.

It was at this time, in the autumn of 1940, after months of loose contact and passive insider knowledge, that Bonhoeffer also took the decisive and irrevocable step of allying himself with those who opposed the National Socialist system of oppression. He joined the resistance group that formed within the military. Its leader: Admiral Canaris. Bonhoeffer's contact: Hans von Dohnanyi, his own brother-in-law. The plan: to bring down the government, if necessary by assassinating Adolf Hitler. The means: sending secret information abroad and laying the groundwork for a new political start in Germany. Bonhoeffer's life during this time was kaleidoscopic and distracting: he moved between the small towns of Klein-Krössin and Schlawe in Northeast Germany, Berlin, the capital, and Cloister Ettal near Munich, where he was able several times to find a refuge from the outer world and carry on his theological work for months at a time. His life became fully restless the moment he began to travel abroad as a conspirator in early 1941. His work on the *Ethics* was both inwardly and outwardly the fixed pole in his life during these years. At the moment of his arrest he was working on the final pages, which lay prominently on his desk in order to help camouflage his other, secret activities.

The individual sections that survived the war were first published in loosely arranged, preliminary form by Eberhard Bethge in 1949. As Bethge pointed out from the very beginning, however, this book, entitled *Ethics* and published posthumously, was by no means the finalized version Bonhoeffer originally envisioned. It consists of very disparate elements. Some of these are systematic, thoroughly developed and for the most part complete treatises; others are only preliminary drafts that are in any case unfinished passages of text. The overall composition he had planned for his book is visible in its basic outline, but what has come down to us is in the final analysis only a group of individual parts; some portions leave the impression of being relatively finished both in content and in format, while others have only a fragmentary character. A separate chapter would be required to describe in detail the minute detective work required to decipher Bonhoeffer's handwriting, analyze his many notes on scraps of paper, painstakingly number and bundle his manuscript pages, and count the number of times it was necessary to start over again, in order to reconstruct plausibly the interior order of the individual sections of what we now usually call the *Ethics* of Dietrich Bonhoeffer.[2]

During his research for this book from 1939 on, Bonhoeffer acquired as far as possible every book of "ethics" he could find, as well as everything written theologically and philosophically on the subject, particularly from second-hand booksellers. These publications influenced his manuscripts during the following years to such a great extent that only a few can be mentioned here. Whether influenced by them or distancing himself from them, whether taking up what they contained or contrasting his ideas with them, Bonhoeffer grappled with them in various ways, developed their ideas further, or set himself apart from them. For instance, either directly or indirectly in his writings we encounter Immanuel Kant and Friedrich Nietzsche, Max Scheler and Karl Jaspers, Jacques Maritain and Romano Guardini, Max Weber, the pedagogue Hermann Nohl, Augustine and Thomas Aquinas, and of course Martin Luther, Karl Barth, and many contemporary theologians. We meet (Georg C.) Lichtenberg and (Gotthold Ephraim) Lessing, Tolstoy and Dostoyevsky, even Don Quixote.

Bonhoeffer's *Ethics* is distinguished by an unmistakable inner dialectic, a broad spectrum of thought that provides entrance into argumentation and dialogue. At the same time, it proceeds from a basic viewpoint that embraces the whole of human existence and knowledge. This basis is unambiguous and, for its author, irreplaceable. It is the conviction that the reality of God has not been done away with by man's diverse attempts either to kill Him or pronounce Him dead; it is a conviction that this reality has opened itself to man by the power of its own witness (theologically speaking, through revelation). As a result, this basic viewpoint means that the origin and reality of Christian ethics consists neither in recognizing man's unremitting effort to be good nor in his pitiable, often catastrophic failures, but only in the reality of God in Jesus Christ, in the church *and* in the world, for both are inseparably intertwined; neither can or should be separated from the other. As Bonhoeffer expresses his viewpoint in the *Ethics*, reality is undivided and subject to the one will of God, a will that is, however, "nothing other than Christ's reality become real amongst us and in our world" (DBW 6, 60–61). In outlining what is possible and what is impossible for man, the goal of ethics in an era after Christ is to share in Him.

Gospel spirituals sing of the Christ event: "He's got the whole world in His hand." In the manuscript section of Bonhoeffer's *Ethics* entitled "Ethics as Creation" (DBW 6, 69), the Christ event is described in the following (core) statement as a world event: "Whoever sees Jesus Christ actually sees God and the world in one; he can no longer see God without the world nor the world without God" (DBW 6, 69). Bonhoeffer then develops this thought in one of his most compact *and* broad texts: a key text for grasping Bonhoeffer's thought, his faith, his conception of ethics, his own concrete activity, his understanding of Christian life and existence as a whole, and the road traveled by him through this world. It reflects something of his real life—this life of bits and pieces and reconciliation. It has the sound of a hymn to Christ and touches on many of the same themes as the New Testament Letter to the Philippians. It contains not only the Gospel in sum but also an Evangelical ethics in sum and in purest form, and Bonhoeffer's *Ethics* in miniature.

We are referring here to the passage already mentioned, which introduces the *Ecce homo* sections. It will be quoted here in full because of its importance, its multidimensionality, and its linguistic impressiveness:

> *Ecce homo*—Behold, what a man! In Him, reconciliation of the world with God was made perfect. The world is not overcome through demolition but through reconciliation. Not ideals, programs of action, not conscience, duty, responsibility, virtue, but simply and only the consummate love of God is capable of encountering reality and overcoming it. Nor is it a generalized idea of love, but God's love truly lived in Jesus Christ, which accomplishes this. This—God's love for the world—does not withdraw itself from reality in a rapture of noble souls foreign to the world, but instead experiences and suffers the reality of the world in all its harshness. The world does its worst to the body of Jesus Christ. But He who was martyred forgives the world its sins. This brings about reconciliation. *Ecce homo.* (DBW 6, 69)

According to Bonhoeffer, Christian ethics is full of surprises. Its intention is always to be full of the Spirit and fully other than normally supposed, for it does not draw its life from norms or "shoulds" but from the spirit of love. It does not proceed on the basis of eternal truths and values, but begins with a concrete situation. The Good Samaritan, who has gone down in history as the prototype for a Christian ethos, is scorned; he is one who does what is good for others without first asking about rigid rules or checking for small-printed directives of action in each respective situation. Christian ethics moves consciously between the pitfalls of formalism and casuistry. It avoids the pitfall of turning to stone as part of a petrified system of norms that derives its laws "from above," whatever that is taken to mean. But it also avoids the pitfall of a minute, persnickety "from case-to-case" type of ethics in which it would fall apart.

Bonhoeffer also describes the nature of Christian ethics succinctly and clearly in the manuscript "Ethics as Creation," where he makes it clear that Christ was not the founder of a system that hovers over all worlds; He did not establish an abstract, eternal ethics that He wanted to see implemented at any cost. He was not a lawgiver, but a true man; therefore we too can act as true human beings and not as sallow advocates of a doctrinal system. "Christ did not love—as the ethicist does—a theory of the Good; rather, He loved real men and women," writes Bonhoeffer (DBW 6, 86), while alluding to Immanuel Kant in what follows. Christ was not concerned with anything like the "categorical imperative" of Kant, the philosopher from Königsberg, Germany, who posited that the maxims of my will and my actions may also serve at all times as the basic principle for a generalized set of laws. Nor was Christ concerned with a philosophically motivated interest in generalities. Rather, He was interested in "whether my action of the moment has helped my neighbor to be a human being before God. We do not say that God became an idea, a principle, a program of action, a generality, a law; but that God became man" (ibid.).

Once again, it becomes clear that the final part of the prologue to the Gospel of John—"and the Word became flesh and dwelt amongst us"—is, for Bonhoeffer, the beginning and end of all theological thought. Theology for him is always automatically Christology, just as Christology on closer view is inseparably linked to ecclesiology.[3] The relationship between Christology and ethics is almost the same, which perhaps can best be described as follows: for Bonhoeffer, theology is consummated only in Christology, and his Christology in turn is the foundation for his understanding of the church and ethics. This makes his conclusion plausible when, based on the realization that Christ is true man and the guarantor of all human reality, he characterizes the nature of Christian ethics as follows: "We are thus turned aside from every form of abstract ethics toward a concrete ethics. Not that what is good once and for all can and should be put into words, but rather *how Christ takes shape among us here and today*" (DBW 6, 86–87).

With this, Bonhoeffer himself formulated the most meaningful possible description of his own *Ethics* and his understanding of Christian ethics: it is a *concrete* ethics. Concrete ethics has nothing to do with casuistry nor with literal "value(s)-lessness" in the sense of a mere accommodation to circumstances. In order to avoid misunderstanding and acquire an accurate sense of the "Sitz im Leben" of his ethics, it is necessary to heed his own further characterizations. He describes ethics as requiring courage and demands that its statements be neither abstract nor casuistic but rather fully concrete (DBW 6, 89). In another section of his *Ethics*, "The Ethical and the Christian," he emphasizes that ethical statements cannot be made "in a vacuum, that is, in the abstract, but only in a concrete context," and he continues, "Ethical statements are not a system of principles that are in and of themselves true and applicable to anyone, at any time, in any place; rather, by their very nature they are linked to specific persons, times and places" (ibid., 374).

The core of this concrete link is God's commandment. This is the force that correctly centers Christian ethics, a force without which Christian ethics has no handhold, no consequences, no inner life. Christian ethics is concrete always and every day, and refuses to dissipate into relativism or abstractions. Bonhoeffer describes this indispensable connection with Christian ethics, very much along Barthian lines, as follows: "God's commandment can never be found or known apart from a specific time and place; rather, it is to be *heard* only in connection with time and place. God's commandment is either emphatic, clear, and concrete to the last detail, or it is not God's commandment" (DBW 6, 382). Christian ethics as a concrete ethics shuns sublime directives written high on the heaven of ideals. Rather, it attempts to perceive God's commandment in concrete situations and to respond accordingly. Concrete ethics is unprincipled in the sense that it does not look first and foremost for guiding principles in every situation. But it also does not stagger from situation to situation without being oriented toward God.

In relating Bonhoeffer's understanding of ethics to more conventional ethical conceptions, it is helpful to refer to the distinction made by Max Weber in "Politics as Profession," his famous 1919 lecture, between an ethics of attitude and one of responsibility. Although discussed very little in Evangelical theology between the two World Wars,[4] Weber's distinction was certainly known to Bonhoeffer. There are many indications of this. Bonhoeffer had already studied the works of this universal thinker and universally educated sociologist while preparing his dissertation, and he had also dealt with Max Weber in various contexts.[5] His familiarity with the terms "responsibility" and "ethics of attitude" as Weber uses them is reflected, among other things, in a passage in *Discipleship* (DBW 4, 89) as well as in a text written in 1942, in Bonhoeffer's year-end report to friends in the conspiracy (DBW 8, 29) and also in a passage in the *Ethics* itself (DBW 6, 37). In his *Ethics*, Bonhoeffer refers explicitly to Max Weber, whose name appears in connection with the concept of one's profession in life and again in connection with the concept of responsibility (ibid., 209). As Bonhoeffer notes, "responsibility" has connotations that are not normally ascribed to it in everyday use, not even when it becomes—as it does, for example, in the writings of Max Weber—a "magnitude with highest ethical qualifications" (ibid., 254).

The analogies between Bonhoeffer's concrete ethics and what Max Weber classified as "Ethics of Responsibility"—in contrast to an "Ethics of Attitude"—are evident above all in the two versions of the manuscript section entitled "History and the Good." The most salient examples are Bonhoeffer's reflections in the first version (DBW 6, 224ff.)

concerning the consequences of one's own actions—reflections which are then carried fully to their logical conclusion in the second version (ibid., 275), where he ends by saying that a structure of responsible action cannot exist without *"readiness to take responsibility for one's misdeeds and freedom."* (The explosiveness of this conclusion for the concrete situation in which Bonhoeffer lived at that time is noted here only in passing. It will later be the topic of a more detailed discussion.)[6]

In the first version of "History and the Good," Bonhoeffer elucidates—not explicitly but only implicitly—one of the main differences between an ethics of attitude and an ethics of responsibility. Responsible action may never be carried out blindly, may never shut its eyes to the consequences of its own deeds. Moreover, it is aware of the impossibility of being perfect and completely just. In contrast to ideological action, says Bonhoeffer, it is carried out with trust in God's forgiving grace: "Whereas ideological action is always justified by its own principles, responsible action foregoes certitude of its ultimate rightness" (DBW 6, 224). He who acts ideologically, on the other hand, brooks no queries about the consequences of his actions and has no doubt of the Good. A further and central element of responsible action is love. Love is the force that orients Christian ethics. Bonhoeffer writes, "Because God's love for man is Jesus Christ become man, He is not a proclaimer of abstract ethical ideologies but rather the concrete executor of God's love. Our call is not to the practice of ethical ideals but to life in God's love, and that means—in reality" (ibid., 231). Christian ethics is concrete ethics because reality is concrete. It extends between the poles of God's love on the one hand and man's responsibility on the other. Its life springs forth from freedom, and it accepts the risk of guilt.

To what extent are there points in common between such a profoundly theological ethics and the type of ethics Max Weber designated as an "ethics of responsibility"? Weber assumed that there are basically two contrary maxims of ethical action: the one of ethical attitude, the other of ethical responsibility. These conceptual postulates, according to Weber, do not imply that an ethics of attitude is synonymous with an absence of responsibility or that an ethics of responsibility is synonymous with an absence of attitude; rather, with regard to the consequences of one's own action, the dichotomy between the two is "a yawning abyss."[7] The ethics of attitude—or, as Weber also says, "absolute ethics"—does not ask about consequences; rather, its primary concern is that the goal of attaining the good is given its due. It is concerned with upholding the principle, with the "flame of pure attitude,"[8] whereas an ethics of responsibility also accepts the concrete results of its actions and for this reason weighs, decides, and consciously accepts guilt in case of doubt.

And that means: making free decisions in concrete situations and taking responsibility for one's own ethical actions.

This brief sketch of the typology of ethics as worked out by Max Weber makes it clear that there is not *one* set of ethics and not *one* Christian ethic ("ethic" here is singular rather than plural), but that there are in fact different types of Christian ethics. Christian ethics can in fact correspond to either the attitudinal variant or that of ethical responsibility. What remains constant, however, is that the understanding of Christian ethics upon which Bonhoeffer's thought was based and documented in his *Ethics*—but not only there!—best corresponds to the ethics of responsibility described by Max Weber. Nevertheless, ethics as understood by Bonhoeffer does not lose itself in what Max Weber called the "ethics of responsibility." Rather, it is consciously impelled and sustained by a basic current which differs from that of, for example, philosophical ethics and gives it a specific stamp of its very own (DBW 6, 254): "This life lived in response to the life of Jesus Christ . . . we call it *responsibility.*"

This intonation of the concept of responsibility in Bonhoeffer's writings prompts a further attempt to categorize his ethics. A fully different tack than that based on Max Weber, for example, is taken by a well-known type of categorization that asks how an ethics is to be grounded: is it to be derived from elsewhere, from a law found outside ourselves, in other words, from a divine law of morals? If so, we speak of "heteronomous" ethics. Or, do we find the grounds of our actions within ourselves, so that we can speak of an inner law and an "autonomous" ethics? Bonhoeffer himself provided the answer to this question. We discover it in a footnote on one of the last pages of the *Ethics* (DBW 6, 406), in the final manuscript entitled "The Concrete Commandment and the Divine Mandate." There, Bonhoeffer points out that the antitheses of heteronomy and autonomy are subsumed into a higher unity that might be named "Christonomy," the law of Christ. This footnote offers further confirmation that Bonhoeffer's *Ethics* in the final analysis is probably to be understood only dialectically, that is, as "a theologically grounded ethics of the autonomy of the believer."[9]

Much, much more could and should be said about Bonhoeffer's *Ethics*. It contains electrifying trains of thought of a unique clarity; and it contains many passages whose complicated and involuted character may have emanated from the necessity to camouflage their meaning under prevailing circumstances: government censorship was becoming massive in Bonhoeffer's life during the period when he worked on his book of ethics: the last house of the Preaching Seminary was closed in March 1940; he was forbidden to speak in public on the grounds of so-called "activities corruptive of the people" in August of 1940. He was placed under obligation to report his whereabouts regularly in Schlawe, Bonhoeffer's official place of residence, in September 1940; in March 1941 the Chamber of Written Works forbade him to print or publish his writings. Factually, this was equivalent to prohibiting Bonhoeffer from practicing his profession; it stripped him of any chance to exert public influence in the form of publications or any other means.

However, it should not be overlooked that Bonhoeffer's *Ethics* also contains some questionable passages: in the manuscript section entitled "The 'Ethical' and the 'Christian,'" for example, when he writes that the license to speak ethically is grounded in certain already existing structures of authority and emphasizes the existence of a "*tendency from above downwards*" which he believes, offensive as it may be to modern tastes, is intrinsic to the nature of ethical thought and action (DBW 6, 375). Or when he (ibid.) matter-of-factly interprets "sociological relationships of authority"—meaning *social* relationships of authority—as intrinsic elements of ethical thought and action and finally arrives at the apodictic statement: "There is no getting around the fact that ethical thought and action require clarity concerning the relationship of Higher to Lower" (ibid., 377). Or when, in his manuscript "The Natural Life," he defends the view—popular not only in his own time—that life is its own physician, warding off whatever is unnatural, that is, whatever seeks by its very nature to destroy life. Only when this principle ceases to be effective do "the destructive forces of the Unnatural carry the day" (ibid., 169). Nevertheless, in spite of all reservations regarding such ideologically burdened postulates, it must always be borne in mind that human beings are after all historical beings, and that Bonhoeffer too—like each of us—was a child of his time and the world in which he lived.

But it is precisely in the manuscript section entitled "The Natural Life," on the other hand, that Bonhoeffer thematizes issues of his own and our time in an almost un-contemporary manner, making the original outline of his thought succinctly apparent. It is a manner that was not customary for the society of that time, particularly by theological and ecclesiastical standards. Above and beyond that, even today, his themes and conclusions are (still, or again?) dramatically, alarmingly up-to-date. Bonhoeffer discusses them with a mixture of nuanced insights and concise demands, of unambiguous answers and ideas left floating in the air. This can be demonstrated through two examples: man's bodily existence and the issue of euthanasia. (A possible third example in this context, which we will not address here, however, would be his reflections on the issue of suicide.)[10]

With respect to the first example, in the chapter on "The Right to Bodily Life," Bonhoeffer's basic premise is—for him—the sacrosanct assumption that human life is life in a body and bears within itself the right to be preserved for man's own sake. He vehemently contradicts the view of the body as the prison of an immortal soul and comes to an opposite view when he says, "Every human being is a being with a body and remains so eternally. To be a body and to be a human being are inseparable" (DBW 6, 180). He interprets bodily being as the form of existence wished by God—a view that for the theological anthropology of his time was absolutely not a self-evident fact. On the basis of this premise, Bonhoeffer goes on to unfold indirectly a canon of fundamental human rights.[11] He speaks of the right to happiness, of the joys of the body—but not without providing biblical corroboration—and of the things of this life, of that which is necessary for the body and for life, of that which brings pleasure to the body and joy to life: of the place where one dwells and the area around it, of eating and drinking, of clothing and gathering new strength, of games and sexuality.

For Bonhoeffer, the appropriate context for the last topic is in marriage alone, although it is "not only a means of procreation, but also contributes its own joy within marriage, independently of its utilitarian purpose, in the love two human beings have for one another" (DBW 6, 182). But even in marriage there is never the right to control the body of the other person. Bonhoeffer writes unmistakably of the rights over one's own body, rights that have much to do with the preservation of distance and the experience of identity: "The body is always 'my' body; even in marriage, it can never belong to another in the same way as to me" (ibid.). Man's being as a body cannot and must not be ignored theologically. It cannot and also must not be interpreted as a burdensome accessory of human existence. Bonhoeffer broke away from clear concepts here: existence as a body is the first thing that constitutes one's existence as a human being, as a unique person distinguished from others. (How would this line of thought look when transposed into today's matrix of views on bodily existence and sexuality?)

By way of a second example, we consider Bonhoeffer's comments on euthanasia. These take on particular relevance in light of the systematic murder in his own day of persons who had particular illnesses, handicaps, and health care requirements under the completely misrepresentative euphemism of "euthanasia," meaning soft, liberating death, by order of the State, legitimized by distinguishing between a life worth living and one not worth living. Bonhoeffer says categorically that before God there is no life that is not worth living; even the most miserable life before Him is worth living. This "before God" implies for

Bonhoeffer simultaneously, however, that such life is not simply *perhaps* but *therefore* and precisely then worth living before others as well. He describes the immanent consequences of using "life not worth living" as a criterion: "sooner or later, it destroys life itself" (DBW 6, 189).

Bonhoeffer also analyzes the so-called cost factor that was cynically popular to introduce into the public debate over euthanasia in his day (and, in other disguises, today as well). He comments laconically, "The expenditures of a people for the care of those with such illnesses have never in the least matched those for luxury articles" (DBW 6, 190). Almost as if writing today, Bonhoeffer uncloaks the propagation of so-called euthanasia methods as an attempt on the part of man to declare human society a distress-free zone. Long before prenascent prophylaxis was perverted into precautionary elimination of the "genetically challenged"—to use the kind of terminology preferred today—and long before prenatal diagnostics threatened to degenerate into a genetic form of population allocation and became established as prenatal technology, Bonhoeffer came, in the context of euthanasia, to the following short and succinct conclusion: "People think a new and healthy humanity can be built by rational means" (ibid., 91).

All manuscript sections of the *Ethics* make it clear that Bonhoeffer was not concerned with erecting an edifice of thought that was in harmony with itself in all respects, and certainly not with giving us a perfect set of ethical precepts. He was concerned neither with a stringent system of argumentation nor with eternal truths. Nevertheless, his aims were anything but negligible. In accordance with his view that truth is always concrete, he called for a concrete ethics that addresses the question, *"How does Christ take on concrete shape here and now among us?"* (DBW 6, 87). On the other hand, he was also aware that we are not searching continuously and everywhere for ethical orientation, but that each of us is "a mortal creature living in a finite and fragile world; we are not in and of ourselves, and exclusively, students of ethics" (ibid., 367).

According to Bonhoeffer, it cannot be the intention and task of ethics to produce a compendium of ethical values and universal directives for action; nor is it the intention and task of an ethicist to burst forth as an authoritative source of theological truth. The limits of both the ethicist and a set of ethics are clearly defined. He emphasizes how easy it is to say what does *not* constitute an ethics and an ethicist: "Ethics cannot be a book that defines what everything in the world by rights should be, but unfortunately is not; and an ethicist cannot be one who invariably knows better than others what and how things are to be done; . . . an ethics cannot be a laboratory beaker in which ideal ethical behavior and Christian human beings are produced, and the ethicist cannot be the embodiment or ideal representative of a basically moral life" (DBW 6, 372).

These words indirectly describe his own *Ethics*. They also contain a warning by Bonhoeffer against overestimating oneself and others— a warning *we too* should hear clearly with respect to *his* person. Bonhoeffer himself intended with his *Ethics* nothing more than to help us "*learn to live with others*" in a world he loved (DBW 6, 372), and this in spite of and in that world's atrocities, in spite of and in the shortcomings of its inhabitants.

12

Amor Mundi

> The world is wonderful. The world is terrible.
>
> *Helmut Gollwitzer*

Amor mundi—love of the world—was a definitive element of Bonhoeffer's thought, to a degree that was rare in Evangelical theology, the church, and personal faith before his time. In his case, this love did not derive from any form of "natural theology" that might exist outside the mainstream of Christian revelation. Nor was it rooted in any subordinate component of life, unconnected with faith, that might simply have been appended to his Christian faith. On the contrary, for him, love for the world springs from the midst of this faith. It is the basis for Christian existence in the here and now of the world. It embraces the person as a whole. From it come the understanding and practice of a worldly Christian existence, one that is fully in accordance with Bonhoeffer's own way. It is almost the very core of his thought that love for the world is grounded in the Christ event—and even more—it only comes into being in Him. In Christ, assent to the worldliness of the world becomes definitive. This is God's love, His word of life expressed to mankind, that opens up to us the possibilities—but not always the answers!—to the question, How are we to live?

Although emphasized to varying degrees, all of Bonhoeffer's books revolve around this question. In particular, learning to live together responsibly with other human beings is the central focus of his *Ethics*. And the whole of his ethics, together with this purposeful learning process, is neither a peripheral nor drearily moralistic piece of homework, but belongs at the heart of Christian existence. For Bonhoeffer, Christian existence does not mean spending a winter of discontent grinding our teeth in the dreary here and now of the world, until liberation comes in a better world beyond this one, whether this takes the form of an individual other world that follows on the heels of one's own death or a universal other world that dawns with the kingdom of God. Thus for him, Christian ethics is not an externally imposed exercise for dealing with the world as a necessary evil; it is not a burdensome piece of home-work along the way to true existence. For him, Christian existence is more than existence in transit: it is a form of homage to this world.

Thus it is no coincidence that Bonhoeffer formulates his thought in a way that reflects his interpretation of Christian faith and Christian life as expressed, in particular, in his *Ethics,* more specifically, in the last section of the final manuscript entitled "The Commandment of God in the church": "The world in its worldliness has received its final signature once and for all through the cross of Christ. . . . The cross of reconciliation frees us to live a life before God in the midst of a God-less world; it frees us to live a life in true worldliness" (DBW 6, 404).

What is decisive for Bonhoeffer is that such a life is not lived along-side Christian proclamation, and certainly not in contradiction to it: it is inextricably and undeniably interwoven with it. What is decisive for him is the fact "*that true worldliness exists precisely and only due to the proclamation of the cross of Jesus Christ*" (ibid., 405).

The worldly Christian, both as self-evident and as a self-imposed goal, is the *one* unifying theme that spans his entire *Ethics,* from the first to the last manuscript sections. Above all, this theme implies God's love for the world. Fondness for the world receives its legitimation from the fact that God intends to mediate Himself to the human beings of this world through Christ, and He has committed Himself to this world without reserve. In the very first manuscript section of his *Ethics,* Bonhoeffer rejects clearly and curtly all theories of the existence of two worlds, in whatever guise they may appear. For him, the prototypes for a worldly dualism that calls itself "Christian" are the monk and the cultural Protestant of the nineteenth century; above and beyond these two typically basic orientations, he also addresses the attempt to have Christ without the world or the world without Christ. In either case we deceive ourselves. Moreover, it is a disavowal of God's revelation in Jesus Christ to aim at being a Christian without being worldly—and vice versa. Bonhoeffer summarizes his thought here as follows: "Therefore there are not two worlds, but rather only *the one world of the reality of Christ,* in which God and the reality of the world are one" (DBW 6, 43).

Reality for Bonhoeffer is one, and any attempt to divide consciousness or reality into Christian and worldly domains is absurd. The reality of the world is mirrored in Jesus Christ. For one captivated by Him, there can be no dividing line in the sense of "Christian life here, worldly life there." As expressed by Bonhoeffer, "The Christian's worldliness does not separate him from Christ, nor does his Christ-likeness separate him from the world" (DBW 6, 48). Thus Bonhoeffer never devalues the world, nor can he do so, for this world is God's world. Just how, in particular, can Christian life withdraw from it? Why should thought that is explicitly Christian discriminate against it? Animosity toward the world and contempt for the world appear in all the colors of the rainbow and are not always immediately and unambiguously identifiable. But they are certainly not Christian. Bonhoeffer's dictum, already cited from the first *Ethics* manuscript ("Christ, the Reality and the Good"), describes precisely the special relationship between Christ and the world: "Christ died for the world, and Christ is Christ only in the midst of the world" (DBW 6, 53).

In Bonhoeffer's personal life, this theology of worldliness found expression in his decision to become a conspirator. It took on ever sharper and more systematic contours in the writings and letters he later wrote in prison. But was it also perhaps present prior to the period of the *Ethics*? Is it not a fact that Bonhoeffer's relationship with the world was very reserved—indeed previously even at odds with the world—especially when he wrote *Discipleship* and *Life Together*? Is it not also true that the "this-worldliness" of human existence and Christian faith come to the foreground of his thought more as a matter of course only later, from about 1939 on?

Over the years, various responses to these questions of interpretation have been given, both directly and indirectly. Inasmuch as the cardinal emphases laid down in *Discipleship* and *Life Together* have been ignored whenever possible, for the sake of a myopic, truncated "political theology" that recognizes only Bonhoeffer's openness to the world and his accentuation of the "this-worldliness" of Christian faith, the question has been answered indirectly; also answered, moreover, inasmuch as even the latter was ignored, so that Bonhoeffer was interpreted as an Evangelical "church father." On the other hand, the question has been answered directly, for example, by portraying his theological development as a series of qualitative leaps and viewing his final openness to the world as a consequence of the christological pairing of *Discipleship* with *Life Together*.

From both a theological and a secular point of view, all that needs to be said about these variegated and, for the most part, reductive interpretations has been written long ago. Both points of view arrive at the same conclusion: from a theological perspective, "The way through discipleship 'back' into the world does not mean retracing a wrong way in order to find the right way from which one has strayed, but rather a continuation along the path taken in discipleship";[1] from a secular perspective, "His life was to plumb the depths of the experience that Christian life can only become more worldly by becoming more spiritual, more spiritual only by becoming more worldly."[2] In the same tradition of interpretation, the growing intensity of the dimension "world" for Bonhoeffer in prison is explicitly recognized in the Afterword to the most recent edition of *Resistance and Surrender,* which points out that he always held fast to the thought "that God cannot be understood without the world nor the world without the God who has entered it in Jesus Christ."[3] When read, for example, under these aspects of world and worldliness, the last poem Bonhoeffer wrote during his imprisonment—and one occasionally misused to promote shallow edification—*By Goodly Powers Wondrously Sustained* allows this to appear in a new light.

Without question, faith and openness to the world permeate the length and breadth of Bonhoeffer's life and thought as two sides of *one and the same* coin. For example, even in *Discipleship*—where one might least expect it—there are statements such as "This is God's temple: He prepares for Himself His dwelling, His temple, in the midst of the world" (DBW 4, 269–70). And in *Creation and Fall*, written at the beginning of the 1930s, we find him saying, "In the midst of the world, on the wood of the cross, the wellspring of life breaks forth" (DBW 3, 135). Indeed it was in his earlier years that Bonhoeffer completed the essential turn toward the world that made his later, original theology of the world and his concrete activity in this world possible! Different though the diction and pathos doubtless were, and in spite of his subsequent development, a very real congruence nevertheless appears indisputably between Bonhoeffer's earlier and later perception of the world.

In a sermon he preached in 1928 entitled "Carpe Diem," he says laconically that eternity can be had only in time, and God only in the world. He stressed this point by employing the metaphor of painting, as it were, a picture of the radiance contained in each moment of time. In every moment there is something of eternity. Thus he concluded that "Whoever flees the present flees God's hours; he who flees time flees God" (DBW 10, 514). For Bonhoeffer, it is important that one not desire to bypass the metamorphoses of one's own life, but rather to live out in these whatever it is that makes them what they are. The point is to be a child fully, to be an adolescent fully, to be a man fully, to be a woman fully: "Be full human beings, with wills of your own, with your passions, your cares; your joys and your needs, your seriousness and your foolishness, your celebrations and your sorrows" (ibid., 516). God wants human beings, not bodiless specters who shun the ground; for He loves the earth and made us from it. In this same sermon, Bonhoeffer refers to one of his favorite characters from Greek mythology. Antaeus became vincible only when he lost physical contact with the earth. The wisdom we gain from this example: "Only he who plants both feet on the ground, he who is and remains fully a child of the earth, . . . makes the fullest use of time and thus of eternity" (ibid.).

The connotations found later by Bonhoeffer in the concept of "this-worldliness" were for the young Bonhoeffer simply: earth. He had spoken of the earth as the mother of us all in the sermon he wrote in 1928, entitled "Carpe Diem." He again spoke of the earth, for example, in a lecture he presented in 1932 entitled "Your Kingdom Come! The Prayer of the Faithful for God's Kingdom on Earth"; in this sermon Nietzsche functions as a latent "antipode," just as he does later in the *Ethics*.[4] Bonhoeffer warns in his sermon against two fatal alternatives: other-worldliness and secularism. Christian existence must avoid losing itself in either the one or the other. Other-worldliness means shutting out the world under the illusion that one thus loves God, and illusionary "Christian secularism" attempts to bring about God's kingdom by its own efforts. Bonhoeffer rejects both. Only he "who loves the earth and God as one" has faith in God's kingdom (DBW 12, 265).

It is un-worldly and un-Christian to bypass the present and despise the earth. Christ does not lead us into other-worlds of religious escape from this earth: He gives us back to the earth. If we try to avoid it, we do not find God but only a shadow world; "never the world of God, the one which dawns upon this world" (DBW 12, 267). Leaving room for God only in the shadow of this world means ignoring God in the world. The same is true, in reverse, of Christian secularism, which abstracts God out of the world and has its own pious scenario for pulling the kingdom of God out of a hat. It is not unusual for such secularism to become entangled with the world in ungodly mimicry. Bonhoeffer describes dialectically how both of these treacherous pseudo-responses to the question of Christian existence can be surmounted: "One who loves God loves Him as Lord of the earth as it is; one who loves the earth loves it as God's earth. One who loves God's kingdom loves it fully as *God's* kingdom, but also fully as God's *kingdom on earth*" (ibid., 267–68). Bonhoeffer's love for the world was of this sort.

It thus set itself apart from love of the world as found in the philosophy of Life Affirmation, a philosophy that did not leave Bonhoeffer otherwise unmoved—quite the contrary! The similarities between Bonhoeffer's thinking and understanding of the world and those of Life Affirmation philosophy are unmistakable. However, the latter seems to have made an ambivalent impression on Bonhoeffer. Although the affinity he felt for it was deep, he also maintained a certain distance from it and/or relativized it for theological reasons; perhaps also for reasons of rationality. Although a statement such as "We can only live life, and not define it" (DBW 6, 248) bears a genuinely philosophical stamp,

Bonhoeffer reverses its poles, so to speak, by following up immediately with the theological position that the question, *what* is life? has been transformed—through Christ's word that He is life—into *who* is life?

Much could be said about the manifold influences of Life Affirmation philosophy on Bonhoeffer's own philosophy of life; here, however, we can only touch on them.[5] This philosophical trend was widespread from the end of the nineteenth century through the first third of the twentieth century. Its points of crystallization were the concepts of "world," "this-worldliness," and "life," expressed or latently articulated in philosophy and literature, pedagogics, and sociology. Friedrich Nietzsche and Wilhelm Dilthey are generally regarded as the founding fathers of Life Affirmation philosophy, and there is no doubt that both exerted great influence on Bonhoeffer's thought.

Although one might hesitate to call Nietzsche the founder of Life Affirmation philosophy, he was in fact instrumental in shaping it. Bonhoeffer studied him with lasting effect not only in the 1920s; Nietzsche's presence, as already mentioned, was detectable even in his *Ethics.* Almost no one in theology at that time took Zarathustra's (i.e., Nietzsche's) dictum "be true to the earth . . . !" as seriously and perceptively as Bonhoeffer. He made no attempt to "weasel his way out" of Nietzsche's brutally frank critique of Christianity, and, with his intimate knowledge of Nietzsche's desperately cynical analysis, often enough saw clearly how justified it was in light of church history and the history of theology. Indeed Nietzsche's importance remained decisive in the development of Bonhoeffer's so-called Tegel Prison theology, which we will discuss in the last part of this book.

A unique aspect of Life Affirmation philosophy is that it cannot be squeezed into the category of an orientation, a body of teachings, or a school of thought; rather, among the schools of philosophy it occupies a more or less marginal niche. Vastly disparate thinkers are ascribed to it; their lowest common denominator can only be determined from case to case. Even though not fanatically iconoclastic, Life Affirmation philosophy was characterized at one extreme by a fanatical contempt for life and irrationalism; it thus offered fruitful ground for the National Socialistic ideology of Blood-and-Soil and promptly became its willing tool. At the other, truly thought-provoking extreme of Life Affirmation philosophy we find integrity; not only intellectually honest but also highly gifted and influential thinkers who would either have been immune to a "Volks"-ideology of life had they experienced it or were in fact immune to it. Among them, for example, were the educator Hermann Nohl, the sociologist Simmel, and the philosopher Wilhelm Dilthey with his pupil Theodor Litt, each of whom became important to Bonhoeffer in his own way at various times.

The last two examples alone well illustrate Bonhoeffer's affinity for the direction taken by Life Affirmation philosophy. Bonhoeffer felt "a surprising inner resonance" with the educator and philosopher Theodor Litt.[6] This led Bonhoeffer to write to him in 1939 in order to call his attention, in spite of—or perhaps even better, because of—his admiration, to a gap that he, the theologian, believed he had found in Litt's most recent writings. His correction was intended not to exclude but to supplement. Although there are many reasons, for Bonhoeffer, why personal commitment to the world—that is, to "the work of building this world"—is certainly obligatory for Christians, the decisive reason remains "the fact of God's having become man" (DBW 15, 113). His proof: "Only because God became a destitute, miserable, unknown failure of a man and because God will now let Himself be found only in this destitution—in the cross—for this reason alone we can never be separate from the world, and for this reason we love our brothers" (ibid.). For Bonhoeffer, the this world/other world pattern shatters at the point where it intersects the cross; only at this place in the world does the believer find "God and man in one, and now love of God and love of brother are inseparably joined as one" (ibid.). Loyalty to the earth—again, Nietzsche's familiar motif—is one aspect, but not all. Christians, says Bonhoeffer, long for the future of a new heaven and a new earth. The present earth "can be taken so seriously . . . with its dignity, its splendor, and its accursedness" precisely because the past, present, and future earth is God's one earth on which the cross of Christ has stood (ibid., 114)!

A line extends from the category of the "world" in Bonhoeffer's thought until it meets the category of the "world come of age," one of the key categories in his prison theology, which became part of his thought for the most part through his thorough study of Dilthey. Research into Bonhoeffer's thought demonstrated decades ago that it was Dilthey more than Kant who was godfather to the "world come of age" he refers to in his letters from Berlin's Tegel Prison.[7] Clearly, Bonhoeffer studied Dilthey with particular intensity in his Tegel Prison cell. But he had also referred to him in his professorial dissertation, where he explicitly mentioned Dilthey's "totality of life" (DBW 2, 66), singling out his attempt to rise above the idealistic theory of knowledge "in favor of a historically conditioned philosophy of life" as his special merit (ibid., 49, note 26). Dilthey's work was therefore "of decisive importance for the philosophy of history in its most recent form, which has just now influenced theology as well" (ibid.).

Although Bonhoeffer's thought had roots in Life Affirmation philosophy, this did not lead him (astray) to the point of ascribing to life a "totalitarian" totality, which could only come to an end through becoming inimical to life and mankind. True, Bonhoeffer's love of the world was in its own way a complete, undivided love. It was a passion for God *and* for the world. And it was love undivided in yet another sense. It was love of the counterpoints of existence, the smile and the blackness of the world. He did not paint a flattering, false picture but clearly perceived its trampled-down countenance. Bonhoeffer's affirmation of the world and life are documented in early texts that must be viewed first and foremost as spoken texts and—as we will see later—in the letters he wrote from prison. Most of all, however, his affirmation appears in the manuscripts he wrote for his *Ethics,* written with full awareness and consciousness of the meaning of the "world" in war and state-organized terror. He also understood, however, the *Ethics* precisely as his book for a Christian existence in the time to come—for the day after—for the world that would come after the National Socialist system of dictatorship. Even apart from this special historico-political aspect, however, Bonhoeffer's love for the world was not blurred by a naive optimism seeking to sidestep the dark side. He knew that the world can be both breathtakingly beautiful *and* senseless, full of radiance *and* a home to disfigured life. Here too, the Christ event is the magnifying glass of reality; the star and the "Place of the Skull"; the birth of a child and the cry of the Crucified.

In the letters he wrote from prison to his friend Eberhard Bethge, Bonhoeffer uses the image of polyphony to express the ambivalences of life. He perceives double ambivalence: the ambivalence immanent in love and the ambivalence in suffering and knowing happiness. Erotic love *and* love of God are part of the spectrum of human love. While he always affirms that erotic passion has its own justification, it is love of God that constitutes the *cantus firmus* of life: "Life first becomes a whole when we stand in this polyphony," he writes in the spring of 1944 (DBW 8, 442). The other level of meaning in his image of polyphony— "excuse this fascination with my little discovery!" (ibid., 445)—consists in the fact that "pain and joy are also part of the polyphony of all life, and can of course exist side by side" (ibid., 444).

Bonhoeffer lived with the awareness that all dimensions of human existence are interwoven with the reality of God. Even wounded life is life from God and life on the way to God. Even in the experience of suffering, God remains God for us. In December 1944, in the basement of the Gestapo prison on Prinz-Albrecht Street in Berlin, Bonhoeffer wrote the poem that expresses his certitude that God's presence in this world—and through and through this world—shines forth, *By Goodly*

Powers Wondrously Sustained (*Von guten Mächten wunderbar geborgen*) (DBW 8, 607–8). He wrote this poem in a world of annihilation, one that contained the seeds of his own annihilation. Nevertheless, sitting in the eye of the storm of the world, on that day his thoughts breathed the same spirit as lines written nearly 2,000 years earlier by the Apostle Paul to the Christians in Rome. At the end of the eighth chapter of the Letter to the Romans the apostle writes, "I am certain that neither death nor life, neither angels nor powers that be, neither that which is nor that which is to come, neither higher nor nether forces nor any other thing in the world can separate us from the love of God which is in Christ Jesus our Lord."

Bonhoeffer's love for the world was not a blind addiction to the world, making the world itself a god, nor was it a brittle affirmation of the world indebted to theological insights. It was not a theorem; rather, it manifested itself through a personal love of life, an unreserved orientation toward life on this earth *as* God's earth. Infatuated with this world, his love for the world nevertheless acknowledged the world beyond. This love of the world drew life from the assurance that, instead of shattering at the borders of the world, God's love promises us that this world is part of God's larger reality. We encounter in this world the reality of God, but—and this hope became a certainty for Bonhoeffer—the reality of God does not confine itself to the world. God is a God who has committed Himself to the world; but He would not be God if he were identical with the world. He enters into it, but He does not lose Himself in it. He surpasses and overcomes it, but only *because* He loves it. God's love for the world is the constitutive element in man's love for, and life in, this world.

13

The Whole Man, in the Here and Now

Give us teachers who praise the Here and Now.
Rainer Maria Rilke

Bonhoeffer's love of life never dwindled to a one-dimensional glorification of life. It drew its power from the love of life which God has
provided, which subsumes both our life and our death, and is infinitely
more than the life of this world. But here and now, on this side of eternity,
life is to be lived out and loved, not with qualms of "Christian" conscience,
but in rejoicing, with open eyes and ears; lived without desperately cling-
ing to what appears to be the one and only, finite life, but in awareness of
the reality of God, which embues the present realm of existence with ra-
diant color. This is the here and now Bonhoeffer discovered for himself
and, without knowing it, for Evangelical theology and an understanding
of Christian faith in a future far removed from his own time.

"He loved life in all its fullness," reports Albrecht Schönherr, one
of his students who later became a bishop.[1] In a sermon Bonhoeffer
preached in London in April 1934, he told a story about the Italian
poet Petrarch, who greatly influenced the Renaissance. Once, when
gazing from the summit of a mountain at the indescribably beautiful
landscape below, Petrarch was overcome by the feeling, "O God, how
beautiful, how beautiful this world is—but then immediately he made
the sign of the cross and took up his breviary in order to draw prayer
from it" (DBW 13, 352).

Bonhoeffer understood Petrarch's response to the beauty of this
world only too well. But he instinctively drew back from Petrarch's response, which he viewed as the antithesis of the Christian who can give
himself up to the beauty and fullness of the world; the antithesis of one
who lives consciously and gladly, and whose enthusiasm for the world is
not promptly "sicklied o'er with a pale cast of thought" about God, to
borrow a phrase from Shakespeare's Hamlet (Act 3, Scene 1).

Nevertheless, Bonhoeffer appears to have been inwardly quite close to Petrarch, at least once in his life. While in prison, he described to Maria von Wedemeyer an experience he had in Cuba that caused him to feel curiously similar to what Petrarch felt on the summit of Mt. Venoux in southern France. For Bonhoeffer, it was the sun that held him enthralled with fascination, almost to the point of helplessness. This was so much the case that years earlier, he nearly fell victim "to the cult of the sun" in Cuba (*Love Letters from Cell 92*, 42) and hardly knew thereafter how and what he could preach in his sermons. His confession was that "For me, the sun is not an astronomical body but something like a living force that I both love and fear" (ibid.). From prison, he also wrote to Eberhard Bethge about the sensuality of experiencing the sun. In June 1944, he described a truly physical sense of homesickness for sunshine; he would like to "really feel it once again in all its might when it burns on the skin and gradually brings the whole body to a glow, and we know again that our existence is a bodily one" (DBW 8, 501).

A broken, fragmented existence. Mirrored in the letters is a longing that can only remain a dream: a longing for "real life" (*Love Letters from Cell 92*, 152), for the immediacy of sensation, and the opportunity to live a true, a whole life. Bonhoeffer also remembers having suffered earlier from the feeling of a bankrupt life. When Maria von Wedemeyer became twenty years old in the spring of 1944, he wrote to her of his own experience of life at the age of twenty and his hopes for her: "You will not write books, thank goodness. Rather, you are a doer, a knower, an experiencer; what I thought was life was only a dream; you fill it up with true life" (ibid., 167). In her, knowing, willing, doing, sensing, and suffering were not fragmented; for him, she was the embodiment of "wholeness, undivided" (ibid., 169), something he longed for his whole life.[2] During the same period he also wrote to his friend Eberhard Bethge of his longing to directly touch "something of real life" through his encounters with Maria (DBW 8, 375).

It is as if the motif of the wholeness of life was more immediate for Bonhoeffer during his imprisonment. Observing the reactions of his fellow prisoners, who were completely helpless to protect themselves during air raids, in Tegel Prison, he had the growing impression that they—like many others of his time—"were missing out on the fullness of life and the totality of their own individual existence" (DBW 8, 453). So few people are able to accommodate many things simultaneously within themselves. In a letter he wrote at the end of May 1944, he said that "Christianity on the other hand situates us in many different life dimensions simultaneously" (ibid.); he then continues boldly, "God and the whole world, so to speak, find room within ourselves."

But one cannot exist without the other: we cannot have God without the world, nor the world without God! This finite and infinite interplay of words and thought is echoed in the often-quoted, sibylline passage he wrote in a letter dated April 4, 1944, which marks the beginning of his Tegel Prison theology: "God is in the midst of our life beyond it" (DBW 8, 408). This statement is consistent with the demand Bonhoeffer made in a letter he wrote on May 29, 1944: "God must be recognized not just when our strength gives out, but in the midst of life" (ibid., 455); that is, not *just* when we die, not *just* when we suffer! God wishes to be discovered by us in the here and now of human existence. It is possible that Bonhoeffer perceived and grasped the meaning of this here and now nowhere else as directly, nowhere else as immediately, as in his cell in Tegel Prison.

The here and now for Bonhoeffer is not a kind of second-class dimension to be endured or overcome: it is an elementary part of the world. And it is also an elementary part of Christian faith that is grounded in the glad tidings that God became man in the here and now of the world. The *proprium*, the very core of Christian faith, is that God comes to meet us in the here and now of the world, not—and not just—in the "there and then." This is why the here and now is not a truncated, "insipid, banal Here and Now" (DBW 8, 541), as he wrote on July 21, 1944; he realizes that he learned only in the previous few years for the first time to see more and more deeply "the profound here and now of Christianity" (ibid.), and "to believe in the fully here and now of life" (ibid., 542).

It seems almost a painful irony of fate that this here and now seemed to become more intensely apparent to Bonhoeffer during his imprisonment, that is, during the extreme situation that implied the end of his own physical existence (and he knew this—at the latest—after the attempt to assassinate Hitler failed on July 20, 1944), a situation which also mirrored the here and now of life in its most inhumanly distorted forms. This and nothing else is what he meant when he used the term "earthly," which today is (linguistically) out of style. For Bonhoeffer, there are two biblical motifs that especially encompass all that is earthly: the Song of Solomon in the Old Testament and Jesus' cry of abandonment on the cross in the New.

This cry seems to have seared itself deeply within him, for he refers to it often. Thus on June 30, 1944, he stated as a requirement that a Christian must (not simply "can"!) taste earthly life to the full, in analogy to Christ Himself and in contrast to so-called religions and myths of liberation. Here he explicitly quoted Mark 15:34: "My God, why have you forsaken me?" The crucified and risen One is with a Christian only if he also does this. Bonhoeffer continued, "The Here and Now cannot be brought to an end before its time has come" (DBW 8, 501).

He often varied this thought, for example, in voicing his apprehensiveness to Maria von Wedemeyer, "that Christians who timidly stand with only one foot on earth will also stand with only one foot in heaven" (*Love Letters from Cell 92*, 38). Or in his warning against dreaming this earthly life away in thoughts of heaven: "There is a type of quite godless homesickness for the other world that will certainly never be allowed to find its way home," he wrote (DBW 15, 530) in the comprehensive exegesis of Psalm 119, his favorite psalm, written in the winter of 1939–1940.

It is not only Jesus' cry of abandonment that echoes through this world, but also Solomon's song of love. Both bear witness to the profound here and now of biblical faith. Solomon's Song of Songs has often enough been played down with panache in the history of Christian theology, which long regarded the human body as an enemy to be conquered. The Song of Songs is a unique collection of love lyrics traditionally (re-)interpreted allegorically as an expression of man's love for God; Solomon's song of the body became a song sung of pure love in the Court of God. The Song of Songs of love, of the erotic, bodily love which is self-evidently at the heart of God's creation was transposed into a song of spiritual, intellectual, and disembodied love and thus— perverted. Bonhoeffer on the contrary wanted to view it "as in fact an earthly song of love," as he wrote to his friend at the beginning of June 1944 (DBW 8, 460), but not without adding the very fine theological distinction that this is "probably the best 'Christological' interpretation" (!) and that "No love can conceivably be more passionate, more sensual, more glowing" than that of which the Song of Songs sings, and it is "truly a good thing that it stands in the Bible, contradicting all those who see Christianity as a cold bath for the passions," as he had written to the same friend earlier in a letter dated May 20, 1944 (DBW 8, 441). Likewise and very much in the same sense, he declared categorically in a letter he wrote on December 12, 1943, that "it is bad taste, to put it mildly, and certainly not God's will to say that a man lying in the arms of his wife should be longing for the other world" (DBW 8, 244). On the contrary, Bonhoeffer rejected an exaggeratedly zealous, "pious," religiously overheated and allegedly Christian type of thinking that pours vinegar into the happiness of man on this earth (thus the term "earthly happiness"). In so doing, such thinking interferes in the affairs of a God who not only does not begrudge us such happiness but has in fact intended it to be for us! To be human can and may mean pursuing happiness rather than encountering it with shame or the allegedly Christian

mentality that happiness must occasion pangs of conscience. From today's perspective it may be difficult to realize what a liberating effect this
love of life, which was so much a part of Bonhoeffer, had on later
generations of theologians of both genders.

Max Weber demonstrated the connection between the capitalist
spirit and the Protestant ethos, that is, the key role played by the Reformation Movement's intrinsic tendency toward an inner worldly asceticism. But even outside this context, a certain inner worldly asceticism
had established itself in Protestantism: an un-Christian "Christian" form
of setting little store by the world and perceiving the beauty of life only
in watered-down fashion. Bonhoeffer, on the other hand, emboldened
others to make no bones about their love of life in a pseudo-Christian
fashion. He made it clear that being in love with the beauty of life as a
whole and with the earthly light of the world is not contrary to God's
intention but very much in accordance with it; and this without hesitation and misgivings, without gnawing guilt feelings, wholeheartedly and
undividedly. For example, Bonhoeffer loved a certain beauty in the fine
arts, which he said in a letter dated March 25, 1944, is "unmitigatedly
earthly and has its very own justification" (DBW 8, 367). He loved the
beauty of music; it acted as yeast without which his life would not have
been the same. Certain landscapes and cities had become part of his life-
blood and fascinated him for the rest of his life. Rome was one of these,
"the place on earth that I so love" (ibid., 365). One of the protagonists in
the novel he attempted to write in prison says, "If there is one result, one
lesson to be learned from history, I would say that it is . . . the love of life
as it really is" (DBW 7, 178).

Corresponding to his single-minded affirmation of the world and
life, Bonhoeffer also viewed man as an undivided whole. In accordance
with the Bible, his interest focused on the *whole* man, for whom he used
the Greek expression *anthropos teleios.* The prevailing, dualistic anthropology of his time, which even today is far from vanquished and deems
itself "Christian," has a long history. Hopefully its future will not be
nearly as long! At any rate, the notion of man as a conglomerate *of parts*
is not "Christian" in the original sense of being "Christ-like"—and certainly not in the biblical sense either. Man cannot be clinically separated
into a body and a soul without atomizing him in the truest sense of the
word. There is in fact no separation of body and soul (or spirit), no division into outer and inner; these categories exist—and indeed, very stubbornly—only in the mind of post-biblical man. "The Bible has no
concept for our distinction between the outer and inner man. And why
should it? The Bible is always interested only in . . . the *whole* person,"
states Bonhoeffer in his letter dated July 8, 1944 (DBW 8, 511).

It was Pinchas Lapide, the influential Jewish philosopher of religion, who called attention, with astonishment and emphasis, to the parallels between Bonhoeffer's view of man and the Jewish view: "Any partition into above and below, sacred and secular, mundane and ethereal, is a purely human view, an invention"; the Jew, and Bonhoeffer in full congruence with him—at the latest from 1942 on—sees "no rent between nature and man, body and soul, the Greek *sarx* and *pneuma*, no matter what all the dualists and Manicheans may aver."[3] However, Lapide erred on one point, secondary though it may be: Bonhoeffer saw the *anthropos* as *teleios,* man as a whole, even *before* 1942. This can be demonstrated with a few examples.

In his dissertation, he underscores the New Testament tendency "to see the church as 'visible,' as a community of persons, body and soul; not a communion of souls or a community consisting of those of like mind, but rather a loving community of whole persons" (DBW 1, 156). Elsewhere, he emphasizes that "Soul and body are bound together into an indissoluble unity in the Christian person" (ibid., 195). He formulates this even more pointedly in *Creation and Fall,* his lectures from the Berlin period: "It is not the case that man 'has' a soul, but rather that he 'is' body and soul" (DBW 3, 71). Borrowing the notion of the earth as the mother of all men from the apocryphal book of Sirach, he interprets Gen 2:7 during the winter semester of 1932–1933 as follows: "The gravity of human existence is its tie to mother earth, its existence as a body" (ibid., 72).

In *Discipleship,* he comments on the "bodiliness" of man from a christological perspective: "Man with his whole, living bodily life belongs to Him who took on human body for man's sake" (DBW 4, 248). And in *Life Together,* he mentions the "bodiliness" of man (that is, "Man is created as [a] body") in the same breath as Christ's bodiliness, which manifested itself in His coming and resurrection, continues to manifest itself in His presence in the sacrament, will manifest itself finally in the resurrection of the dead, and will bring about "the final and perfect communion of God's soul-body creatures" (DBW 5, 17).

In discussing the *Ethics,* we have already called attention to a basic tone heard in particular throughout the manuscript entitled "The Natural Life": the bodily existence of man is of essential importance in Bonhoeffer's anthropology.[4] For him, the bodiliness of human existence is neither irritating nor troublesome, as it was in earlier centuries, nor is it central to a body cult that abstracts from man as a *whole* and thus isolates itself, as in our own time. Rather, the body is a matter-of-course, constituent element of Bonhoeffer's anthropology, which views itself—and for him there is no question about this—as a theological anthropology.

Bodiliness is as much a part of man as breathing, death, and love. The body of man is not simply a vessel or outer shell. It is not merely a secondary factor of human existence. Violence done to the body of a human being violates the whole person. Bonhoeffer developed this thesis under various aspects in the section of his *Ethics* entitled "The Natural Life," along with the corresponding significance of violating the dignity of the body. Such violence is never "merely" a bodily violation but always violates the dignity of the whole human being to the very depths. Bonhoeffer developed this using the example of "deliberately inflicted physical torment," which he understood in general as "physical pain administered arbitrarily and violently under the aegis of prevailing power structures, particularly with the aim of wringing admissions or statements from others as desired" (DBW 6, 214–15).

The thought of physical abuse and torture, inflicted with the goal of "squeezing out"—in the truest sense of the word—information, occupied his thoughts and those of his fellows in the Resistance of necessity and with particular intensity, as Eberhard Bethge emphasized in personal discussions. Bonhoeffer was not the only one to make a clear-eyed, existential decision in favor of suicide as a last, acceptable option for ending his own life, should it come to the worst case of torture. For him, torture meant the "misuse of a body by others, thus dishonoring it, exclusively in order to reach their own goals, such as satisfying the greed for power or acquiring certain information" (DBW 6, 215).

Quite independently of the extreme, borderline situation of torture, this definition makes it unmistakably clear that Bonhoeffer's characterization of "deliberately inflicted physical torment" encompasses what we refer to today as "abuse." He summarized his position at that time as follows: every form of deliberately inflicted physical torment is equivalent to doing "the worst possible dishonor to a human being" (ibid.). In the same manuscript, "The Natural Life," Bonhoeffer speaks of man's right to happiness and, *expressis verbis,* even of his "right to the delights of the body" (DBW 6, 180), which represent the promised joy of being in the immediate presence of God. Such theological justification of this "right to the delights of the body" is truly "a great rarity in Evangelical ethics and proclamations during the first half of the twentieth century."[5]

Was there anything like it in Evangelical theology up to that time? It was not common in those days to view and take seriously man as a soul *and* body. On the contrary, theological anthropology at that time was shot through with contempt for the body; the Christian was viewed as a disembodied being living in the thin air of sublime spirituality. Not only was the physical existence of man ignored, it was viewed as unfortunate. The suppression was perfect: whatever could not be affirmed must be demonized. Bonhoeffer not only rendered obsolete Protestantism's traditional contempt for the body, but also replaced it by making the reality, the rightness, and the joy of bodily existence unmistakably explicit. For him, it was not simply permissible; it was God-given terrain. Physical existence is the manner of being given to us by God; it is inseparable from our existential condition, the *condition humaine* itself, and there is no reason to look down upon it with contempt, much less deny it wholly.

Bonhoeffer opened the way for this insight and gave it a theological foundation. He made the point most successfully with a quote from Friedrich Christoph Oetinger, Germany's eighteenth-century theosophic theologian from the province of Württemberg, whom he was fond of quoting and had apparently become aware of through his friend and colleague, Elisabeth Zinn. In *Creation and Fall,* Bonhoeffer used it to introduce his exegesis of Gen 3:7: "The road traveled by God ends in a human body" (DBW 3, 114).[6]

Bonhoeffer put man as a *whole* at the center of his anthropology—*anthropos teleios*! Here again we see his indivisible faith, corresponding to his view of man as indivisible. This appears in various contexts in the *Ethics,* and not merely in the context of immediate bodiliness: man is an indivisible whole—if not before men, then at least before God! As he states at the end of the manuscript entitled "The Love of God and the Fall of the World": "We are loved by God in Christ and reconciled with Him as whole human beings, as men and women of thought and action. It is as whole human beings, with thought and action, that we love God and our brother" (DBW 6, 341). In the first part of his manuscript "Christ, the Reality and the Good," Bonhoeffer emphasizes: *"Man is an indivisible whole not only as an individual in his person and works, but also as a member of the community of men and creatures* in which he exists" (DBW 6, 38).

In a different context in this manuscript, by the way, he attacks the attempt to split human beings into multiple roles: "the worker, the spouse, the vassal" (DBW 6, 59). Instead of man thus being alienated and defined by roles attributed to him and played by him, Bonhoeffer depicts man as a whole, "standing before the whole of earthly and eternal reality" (ibid.).

It is only a short step from this image of man presented in the *Ethics* to a letter Bonhoeffer wrote from prison at the end of January 1944, when he once again speaks to his friend Eberhard Bethge about man as a whole, the *anthropos teleios,* and formulates his understanding as follows: "None of us is complete in himself alone, but only together with others" (DBW 8, 304). Whether man likes it or not, he is a social being. Even as a hermit, he is always defined by his togetherness with or separation from other human beings. There is no human existence without a human body, just as there is none outside the *polis.*

14

Political Existence and Awareness

In this twentieth century world it is no longer
possible for me to build my life outside society, like a
schlemiel, like the lord of a dream world.

Hannah Arendt

Bonhoeffer's commitment to the *polis,* that is, his political views, were not rooted in any kind of basic orientation but in his theologically grounded attitude toward the world. According to today's criteria, he did not develop a decidedly political ethics; nevertheless his ethics were involuntarily an ethics of the individual *and* society. Political theology was the implicit consequence of his theology. Although neither a corresponding system of political theology nor a full-blown theology of social action can be found in Bonhoeffer's *Ethics,* his theology and its resulting ethical thought led to personal, politico-social commitment. His love for the world as a whole and its human existence in physical form—his "Yes" to the here and now of life—were elements of his faith that corresponded to God's entry into this world in Jesus Christ. And worldly Christian existence was for Bonhoeffer man's response. For him, "worldly" meant, among other things, not leaving political affairs to their own devices but making them a part of faith. And that meant taking political action when and because faith calls us to do so.

But even though the motivation and foundation of Bonhoeffer's political thought were primarily theological, it is only natural to ask about the nature of his political thought: Was there, or is there, a specific tendency that characterizes it? Is it conservative? Progressive? National-Socialistic? Liberal? Socialistic? Authoritarian? Democratic? The answers are difficult to find without forcing Bonhoeffer into one of the conventional coordinate systems of right and left, black and white—and, depending on the spectacles through which we view the world—into right or wrong, good or bad. We are confronted, in fact, with the fact that Bonhoeffer was basically a relatively apolitical person—"apolitical" at least in the sense that he did not explicitly support any specific set of political views nor was he continuously involved in the events of daily, or party, politics. It is therefore difficult today to assign him to a precise political movement. On the other hand, he was naturally preconditioned ideologically like each and every one of us: but in what sense?

And what was the relationship between his political thought and consciousness on the one hand, and his political action and existence on the other? Perhaps we can sum up tentatively as follows: Bonhoeffer was more political, more politically effective, and more progressive in his actions than in his thought. In practice, he was politically ahead of his own political categories; his political consciousness limped, to a certain extent, behind his political existence.

He was stamped to the core with everything that is understood by the term "middle class," including all its strengths and weaknesses. (This is neither a criticism nor a reproach, but only a statement of fact that may be seen one way or the other—how could it be otherwise?) This makes Bonhoeffer's politico-social behavior all the more astonishing, from his work with young people, which he also viewed as social work, and his pacifist phase to his first vehement protests against the National Socialist power coups in the year 1933 and his active involvement in the opposition and resistance.

When we investigate the political Bonhoeffer, we discover that it was very much a part of his political/apolitical awareness that in the final analysis there is no such thing as an "apolitical" human existence. It is the Christian above all who cannot and will not live in a house in the clouds. Speaking to Helmut Rößler, a friend and colleague, in 1932, Bonhoeffer used the term "frivolous" to describe his earlier disinterest in the political relevance of church positions (DBW 12, 41). In the diary he kept of his journey to America in 1939, he described the dubious value of an illusionary abstention from politics on both the individual and church levels: "The admonition to 'stay out of politics' is only a way of saying that the church should concentrate on its 'religious mission'— a mission that interests no one. I always have difficulty understanding how the basic principle of the separation of church and state can be compatible with the social, economic, communal, and political effectiveness of the church in actual practice" (DBW 15, 236).

It is fiction to think that we can be and remain politically neutral. Even non-intervention is a form of taking sides; at least it does not remain without consequences. Political abstinence, "arrangement," and personal political commitment always represent a position, whether passively or actively. To take no position politically is already to have taken a position politically.

Here we come across another fact that Bonhoeffer was painfully honest about: the price of acting responsibly is guilt consciously incurred.[1] There are situations where we (must) incur guilt regarding human beings—for the sake of other human beings. It is exactly here that the risk of participation in the world lies. To take only a few examples from Bonhoeffer's coordinate system of political thought and political ethics, we cite the requirement of obedience, or at least neutrality, toward so-called authorities—but at what price? Or the absolute validity of the biblical prohibition against killing—but at what price? Do I not directly and indirectly support a regime of terror through my neutrality and obedience? Is not violent resistance to those who stand for a reign of force the inescapable *ultima ratio*, the final remedy?

"Sorry, but I can't sell it for less": Keeping this statement by Bonhoeffer in mind, we now trace a few of the main aspects of his political being and consciousness and their major nuances (DBW 8, 510).

The key to his familial and political socialization has already been mentioned: the middle-class way of life. Bonhoeffer grew up in a tradition of liberalism and tolerance, of discipline and middle-of-the-road thinking: a middle-class way of life based in the most fundamental sense on conservative values. It was characterized by an alliance—not always matter-of-course—between humanistic education and humanity of thought. Even those who formed the Resistance circle, whom he felt drawn to, had their roots in the middle class.[2] Bonhoeffer's development as a person cannot be understood apart from the atmosphere and standards, the worldview and sense of self-worth, held by the educated middle class of his time. Thus at first glance, it is all the more surprising to read the statements made by his dissertation supervisor, Reinhold Seeberg, with respect to *Sanctorum Communio*. Regarding the political views and criticism of church practices expressed there by his young professorial candidate, Seeberg viewed Bonhoeffer's "(overly) optimistic hopes regarding the proletariat and low opinion of the middle class" as subjective value judgments and thus as superfluous (DBW 1, 3). We may put aside the question whether and to what extent Bonhoeffer was attempting in this fledgling work to liberate his thought from the hegemony of the middle-class way of life. The final texts of his life, on the other hand—especially his letters from Tegel Prison and the unfinished biographical and belletristic work subsequently known and published as *Fragments from Tegel Prison*—document in elementary fashion his affinity for a civil frame of mind and existence. In a letter he wrote to Eberhard Bethge in November 1943, he himself characterized his attempts to write a novel as a "rehabilitation of the middle class as we have known it in our families, precisely from the Christian point of view" (DBW 8, 189).

Bonhoeffer was very conscious of his personal affinity for the middle class from which he came. But between the beginning and the end of his theologico-political journey, that is, between *Sanctorum Communio* and *Resistance and Surrender,* a certain ambivalence surfaced time and again in his attitude toward the middle-class way of life that he himself experienced.

On the one hand, he appears to have assimilated Kierkegaard's passionate rejection of middle-class attitudes on the basis of Christianity. Thus in a lecture he presented in Sweden in 1936, he voiced his opinion that it was no longer possible in the modern world to lead a Christian existence in the midst of civil existence as in earlier times.[3] And in *Discipleship* he expressed an almost intuitive premonition of his own—un-middle-class—path through life: "To be cast out in suffering, despised and abandoned by others, . . . this basic and characteristic trait of suffering on the cross cannot be comprehended by a Christian mentality that is incapable of distinguishing between civil and Christian existence"[4] (DBW 4, 80). On the other hand, many passages in his literary attempts at drama and a novel, written in Tegel Prison, almost pay homage to the middle class; this becomes more understandable if these *Fragments from Tegel Prison* are viewed as attempts to preserve, and not lose, his own identity in a traumatic and traumatizing situation. It is almost as if Bonhoeffer wanted to keep at bay the danger of psychic fragmentation that insidiously threatened to overtake him under the extreme conditions of incarceration.

For Bonhoeffer's parents and family, in his upbringing and worldview, and therefore *also* in all of his own later thought and existence, the middle-class way of life had immense importance. There is no question that his social origins and the network of social relationships he later constructed solidified and reflected his roots that were firmly planted in the educated Prussian and Protestant middle class. Sociologically he was, as one writer observed, "An especially reflective representative of the thought- and life-form that he himself called the 'Prussian-Protestant world.' "[5] Bonhoeffer learned his humanity in a middle-class family, he studied theology "at the dividing line of the middle-class epoch"[6]—and finally he broke with civil culture by breaking his ties with academic theology, with the collaborative church, and with the State. In prison, the failure of civil resistance brought him to the "consciousness of a post-middle-class, 'unreligious' world,"[7] as one theological study of Bonhoeffer's middle-class roots described the framework within which his theologico-political existence was lived out.

The fact is that this framework for life was one of a kind. Bon-hoeffer's political thought cannot be assigned to any specific category. On the contrary, it is crucial to avoid labels in his case. After all, such categories run the risk of simply being projections of one's own horizon of thought! Bonhoeffer's political consciousness was anything but an er-ratic, albeit unified, whole: it exhibited cracks, breaks, and contradic-tions. But these not only make it authentic and vulnerable to criticism on the one hand, but also alive and unique on the other. In studying Bonhoeffer we find very diverse, sometimes even contradictory, utter-ances and views concerning politico-social realities. This should serve as a warning against trying to put him into an ideological box. The essence of his political self-understanding is precisely (1) that it was theological in character; (2) that it was not tied to any particular political standards; and (3) that it varied widely during the course of his life, without falling into any of the categories so often described in clichés favored by their respective observers. In short, his political thought—to use an expres-sion from Bonhoeffer himself—"doesn't fit the system," no matter which system we may be thinking of (DBW 1, 196).

The result for us is that we must respect this dialectic without attempting any form of retrospective, ideological, and biographical (re-) construction: "We need merely designate any given situation as willed by God, created by God, promptly to view it as forever just. That man-kind is rent apart into conflicting nationalities, that there is war among nations, that there are class differences, that the weak are exploited by the strong, that money creates life-and-death competition: nothing is easier than to see all this and sanction it as God's will—because, after all, it is the status quo" (DBW 11, 336). In writing these words in 1932, Bonhoeffer was rejecting stolid submission to any so-called order of cre-ation! But as he also remarked in his *Ethics,* "The problem of rich and poor will never be solved in any way other than by remaining unre-solved" (DBW 6, 357). Both tendencies were and are present in Bonhoeffer's political consciousness: one that questioned, criticized, and was indignant about the traditional "orders" of this world; the other that accepted, defended, and sought to prolong them.

Even though the latter side of his character is at times difficult for us to understand today, no panoramic view of his thought may gloss over it. Secondary literature has at times gone too far in discussing it, whether in terms of polemical exaggeration or nearly breathless admiration.[8] Eberhard Bethge, who kept both feet on the ground, often vehemently referred to Bonhoeffer's natural immunity to patriotic, reactionary, or even chauvinistic ideas, which he acquired in childhood and early adoles-cence.[9] But at the same time he also referred to "awful sentences"[10] uttered by Bonhoeffer, for example, when he was a young curate in Barcelona at the end of the 1920s and wrote in his lecture entitled "Basic Questions of a Christian Ethics" that "God gave me to my mother and my countrymen; whatever I have I owe to these countrymen; whatever I am, I am because of my country. Therefore whatever I have shall belong to this country; that is the divine order, for God created nations" (DBW 10, 337). The basic tone here reflects the spirit of the times and was expressed again in the same lecture when he spoke of power, might, and victory; of youth and strength; of growth and development; and when he expressed that the peoples of the earth are like individual human beings—"they are immature and need guidance" (DBW 10, 339).

It is as if political developments in Germany at the beginning of the 1930s had sobered Bonhoeffer and taken his breath away so much that he began to grapple critically with the concepts of leadership and leaders. On February 1, 1933, just after Adolf Hitler was named the new Chancellor of the German Reich, Bonhoeffer gave a radio talk entitled "The Leader and the Individual in the Younger Generation." Hardly by accident, the radio station broke off this talk in the middle of a sentence while he was speaking of limitations imposed on leaders, and the dangers and responsibility incurred by them. His voice was abruptly cut off as he declared that "the image of the leader then changes gradually into that of the seducer" (DBW 12, 257).

A few years later, when Bonhoeffer was working on the manuscript for his *Ethics,* these earlier themes—the relationship to authority and the order found among living things—returned in modified form in his comments, together with a certain nostalgia for Western culture. At this stage of his life he viewed secularization as a loss; later, in his letters from Tegel Prison, he saw it as a gain. In the years before his arrest, he still viewed the gradual wasting away of the once matter-of-course religious foundation of thought in European history and the final, quite manifest breakdown of the Western world's self-identification as "Christian" as a catastrophe, rather than an opportunity for the future of this very same Europe. He had not yet begun to see it as an opportunity for the development of a Christian mentality "beyond religion."[11]

Few have dared to question the structure of political thought that clearly emerges, embedded in categories of authority and deep-rooted conservatism, in many passages of Bonhoeffer's *Ethics.* Three descriptions of Bonhoeffer's position are quoted here, in order to illustrate different ways of viewing what might be called—to borrow from the title of a book written by Tiemo Rainer Peters on the subject—the "presence of conservatism in the theology of Dietrich Bonhoeffer." His biographer, Bethge, observed in retrospect in the 1970s that "Some of the passages—for example his comments on State and Society—seem to be, in light of today's problems concerning the redistribution of power, records of a forgotten conservatism."[12] Another Bonhoeffer interpreter, namely the above-mentioned Peters, came to a somewhat milder and certainly more approving judgment when he affirmed that in his *Ethics,* Bonhoeffer "chose the path of constructive dialectic in accordance with the conservative heritage of his time."[13] A third and much harsher point of view, on the other hand, is voiced by the critic Klaus Kodalle, who concluded that "Bonhoeffer's loud-mouthed authoritarianism" is most clearly evident in his *Ethics.*[14]

Certain authoritarian and conservative traits are indeed quite undeniably present in his political consciousness; they surface above all in some of his earlier lectures, in his *Ethics,* and in many of his letters; most saliently, however, in the literary fragments from Tegel Prison. It would be wrong to ignore these elements in Bonhoeffer's thought. They are prominent, for example, in the *Ethics* manuscript entitled "The 'Ethical' and the 'Christian,'" where he deals with order and authority in politics, society, history, and the family, and describes under the key word "authorization, as already mentioned, a *tendency from above downwards* that is anathema for modern feelings, but is part and parcel of the very inmost nature of ethical thought and action" (DBW 6, 375).

We again find the categories of above and below in the manuscript section entitled "The Concrete Commandment and the Divine Mandates": God's commandment is always so designed that we encounter it "in an earthly relationship with authority, that is, in an order established by a clear Above and Below" (DBW 6, 395–96). In good Lutheran tradition, Bonhoeffer understands mandates as the different works, tasks, or areas of life instituted by God. The number of such mandates differs in his writings. Among them are the church, marriage and the family, work and culture, and the State or the "Authorities." Although he took up the classical Christian teachings on mandates in the manuscript section entitled "Christ, the Reality and the Good," his accent there is quite different: namely, that these teachings have the purpose of "confronting mankind with the *one,* the whole reality, revealed to us in Jesus Christ" (ibid., 60).

In his *Ethics,* we abruptly come up against a legitimation of war. This is unexpected, since Bonhoeffer adopted a basic attitude of pacifism years earlier.[15] When cataloguing the basic rights of man in his manuscript "The Natural Life," he omits "killing the enemy in war" from the acts of arbitrary killing against which every person must be protected (DBW 6, 183). Can it be, we must ask, that Bonhoeffer did this in order to protect himself during a time when he and his writings were under surveillance? In the same context, he also provides the justification for "killing the criminal who has taken the life of another" (ibid.). For many, including Bonhoeffer, fundamental contempt for the death penalty was absolutely not a self-evident tenet of Christian ethics in the early 1940s. (We may add that even today, Christianity on the whole does not find it self-evident that the death penalty is an absolutely un-Christian option.)

A further example of conservatism in Bonhoeffer's thought is found in his vision of the future, developed in his cell in Tegel Prison during May of 1944. His *Baptismal Day Thoughts for D.W.R.*, written for the son of Eberhard and Renate Bethge (who was Bonhoeffer's niece) reveals an almost elitist, at the very least pre-democratic, understanding of the State. He writes of the possibility of an "aristocratic order" in a future society, where "a new elite" might possibly claim for itself "the right to strong leadership" (DBW 8, 434). Similar thoughts are found in passages of "The Last 10 Years," a report he wrote for his friends in the Resistance at the turn of the year 1942. It must be added, however, that this text also contained reflections of a much different sort.[16]

The conservative and patriarchal elements in Bonhoeffer's political and social thought were not at all unusual for his time, his family, his social circles, and his church, especially in light of his theological profession. But what is indeed unusual is that Bonhoeffer arrived, in spite of this basically conservative orientation, at a point where political consequences literally and radically transcended this conservatism and rendered it powerless. And he developed, both with and in spite of this basically conservative orientation, a fully new understanding of Christian existence as worldly Christian existence. We learn from Bonhoeffer that theological existence is invariably, by its very nature, also political existence; that Protestantism comes from the word "protest," and this is not to be understood as an insult but as a unique and honorable title; that there is a Christian-motivated and Christian-required solidarity with those who dwell in the shadowy byways of our "brave new world." Bonhoeffer often referred back to the passage from Prov 31:8 "Open your mouth for those who cannot speak!"—and this not in word alone but also in deed.

Even in the mid-1930s, he had already propounded to his students in the Preaching Seminary in Finkenwalde that a separation of politics and the church in modern times is no longer possible, "since in this day and age there is no longer any area that might be viewed as un-politicized": "When political aspects are presented to us, we must call injustice by its name" (DBW 14, 579). He adds a further, very telling sentence: "The possibility of appearing reactionary is inconsequential for us; we have no fear of it" (ibid.). That Bonhoeffer himself linked these statements together demonstrates in the clearest possible way the heterogeneity of his political thought and his unique freedom from fear, as well as the best possible response to any—always problematic— attempt to stereotype and include him in one camp or another!

Any classification of his basic political stance can only go awry inasmuch as Bonhoeffer's political ethics (a term to be used with caution, since strictly speaking it does not exist in his case) is a genuinely theological ethics. This constitutes the soul of his ethics as a whole and also determines the place of his ethics in his theology. In *Discipleship*, when playing on the identical title of a book written by a contemporary theologian, Friedrich Gogarten, in 1932, he remarked about political ethics that the "political" character of the church as a community is indispensable if it is to be made holy (DBW 4, 277). The church as a whole is the *polis*, "the city on the mountain founded by God Himself on this earth," and it must publicly proclaim God's claim on the entire world. Its political character thus consists in the fact that it must proclaim to the entire world that "the earth and all that is in it is the Lord's" (ibid., 278).

For Bonhoeffer, political protest and confrontation result from the fact that God lays claim to the whole world; that on the whole, God takes the side of man. To protest in God's name *for* His creation—that is, to "pro-testare"—means, as is well known, to bear witness to and/or take sides for a thing or person; to protest *against* inhumanity is one of the consequences of Christian faith. Our solidarity with those whose existence and right to existence are destroyed by others grows out of God's solidarity with us, as witnessed and experienced in Jesus Christ. Opposition and confrontation, personal commitment and protest, in the *polis* are a part of Christian existence "for God's sake" and the sake of others.

The contours of opposition and confrontation, of personal commitment and protest, in Bonhoeffer were manifold in form. In, with, and among his written works and activities he mirrored the politico-social realities of his time, responding to them not only in word but also in deed. (The concretizing of his political ethics regarding war and peace, church and resistance, will be taken up later, along with his attitude toward the persecution of Jews.)

His unconditionality and longing for a solidarity of existence not in word alone is indeed striking. No less striking, however, is his sober realism on the one hand and his pathos that borders on being apolitical on the other. Moreover, his utterances are at times as relevant for our own day, as if everything we refer to as social or political progress has made only snail's progress in the decades since his time. This includes working conditions, the economy, poverty, and war, as well as other areas.

As a curate in Barcelona, Bonhoeffer began for the first time to experience work as a responsibility; work that is important. For him personally, work as a dimension of life possessed substantial importance for as long as he lived. In a letter he wrote to Helmut Rößler in August 1928, he expressed the hope that, for him, work would be the key to a fulfilled, unalienated life; it was for him "a very singular experience to see work and life actually flow into one another . . . so that one truly lives only *one* life, not two—or, to put it better, one-half of one" (DBW 10, 90). At the beginning of 1932, during the worst time of mass unemployment in Germany, he gave a lecture at the Technical University of Berlin entitled "The Right to Self-Assertion." His opening remarks sarcastically declared how terribly replaceable those in the work force are, how it is a matter of utter and terrible indifference where they find themselves in that process, and that entire groups of human beings are given the feeling of being "too much," that is, of being superfluous examples of the species of mankind. Bonhoeffer sketches a normal morning in a normal city: "And what resident of the big city has not experienced this feeling of emptiness and meaninglessness at 7:30 a.m. on the streets or in the streetcars, when thousands stream to their jobs, to earn their bread, being one member of a condemned, patient, replaceable mass? There is something infinitely dreary and monotonous about it; but also something that arouses anger and indignation" (DBW 11, 216).

It was during this time that Bonhoeffer came face to face with social misery. In addition to his teaching duties, he took on the task of giving confirmation instructions to a group of fifty boys, a problem group, as we would call them today, in the Wedding suburb of Berlin. The area was, as we would say today, a social cauldron. Bonhoeffer was not satisfied with meeting this challenge in a conventional pastoral manner. He rented a room in the area so he could not only visit the boys but also be available to them at any time. He also leased a little plot of ground with a barracks on it in the northern part of Berlin—a container in today's terminology—in order to give the boys a place for sports and recreational activities. He thus practiced experiential pedagogy in miniature.

This project in Berlin is vividly described in Bethge's biography, along with another Bonhoeffer project from the same time period: the Charlottenburg Boy's Club.[17] This was a social education project, expressly inter-confessional and unaffiliated, for unemployed youths of all races and worldviews. It was initiated and financed by young women from the circle of Bonhoeffer's friends and relatives. Although he himself participated in building up the project and setting it in motion, the step-by-step establishment of the National Socialist system of oppression at the beginning of 1933 quickly terminated it.

Bonhoeffer's inspiration to participate in projects involving concrete social and personal commitment came, among other things, from his encounter with the Social Gospel movement during his year of study in New York from 1930 to 1931. Confronted there with the abysmal misery of the Great Depression, he searched for solid answers on the part of Christianity. The Social Gospel was one of these. The "unwavering conviction felt by Christians here regarding this very real social distress and the felt obligation to do something about it" fascinated him in spite of certain theological objections and, as he himself said, made a lasting impression on him (DBW 12, 210). Bonhoeffer was fascinated above all during this time by the practices and church services of the black communities in Harlem, which he attended regularly. It was there that he *really* heard the Gospel preached!

During the remainder of his professional life, it was a matter-of-course for him to see to it that material help was gladly and generously given to other human beings: in the community in London, in the Preaching Seminary, and during his dangerous travels as a "messenger" agent of the Resistance. Here only one small episode among many need be told: in his London community he built up an extensive system of assistance for fugitives from Germany. In a letter he wrote to a banker who had apparently already rendered frequent aid as a "sponsor" with funds for this work with fugitives, Bonhoeffer again asked him to help penniless fugitives, admitting that his own attempts to render aid had reduced his personal bank account "as of today, completely to zero" (DBW 13, 274).

The conviction that Christian faith cannot stand by passively before the misery of the world was one of the essentials in Bonhoeffer's thought. The motif of Christ-like solidarity surfaces in his sermons, books, and letters time and again: a solidarity that goes beyond mere declarations. As early as 1928, Bonhoeffer stated in his sermon "Carpe Diem": "Do not attempt to shrug off the events of our modern world; all of us bear responsibility for the guilt and misery of all. It is our task to learn once more to understand the *meaning of solidarity within the human race*" (DBW 10, 515). While in London in 1934, he reported to his friend, the theologian Erwin Sutz, that he had visited Jean Lasserre in northern France. During his year of study in New York, Bonhoeffer had encountered in Jean Lasserre a "radical" Protestantism whose core was the Sermon on the Mount, and he had extraordinary admiration for the work Lasserre did in extremely poor industrial areas. He wrote, "This was the first time that I truly saw a *completely* proletarian community. The area around the battlefields of World War I, the war cemeteries, and the terrible poverty of these mining communities provided a dark background for the preaching of the Gospel" (DBW 13, 204). And later on in this letter, when commenting on the political situation in Germany at that time, Bonhoeffer again made one of his frequent references to Prov 31:8: "It is high time to stop this theologically justified reticence regarding the actions of the State—which is after all nothing but cowardice. 'Open your mouth for those who cannot speak': Where can we find someone within the church who knows that this is the minimum the Bible requires in such times?" (ibid., 204).

Bonhoeffer also quotes this proverb in *Discipleship*, when emphasizing Gal 3:28: for their brother's sake, "whether he be Jew or Greek, slave or freeman," Christians will not make common cause with a world that rejects justice and clothes itself in lies (DBW 4, 253). Elsewhere in *Discipleship* he says that the community of those who believe in Jesus must examine its own conscience to see "whether it has given a sign of Jesus' love to those who are disowned and dishonored by society, a love that wishes to maintain life, to uphold it, to protect it" (ibid., 125). And in prison in May 1944, Bonhoeffer wrote in *Baptismal Day Thoughts for D.W.R.* a line that would later be quoted again and again: ". . . our Christian existence today can consist only of two things: in praying and in doing what is just among men" (DBW 8, 435). The question for us, of course, is: What about today? And what is "just"? We have no other choice if we truly wish to brave the experiment of Christian existence: to find out what is just among men here and now, and to do it, we must ever seek the answers anew, ever with our gaze fixed on that peculiar wandering preacherman from Nazareth.

This is precisely the task of a political ethics whose absence within Bonhoeffer's *Ethics* is glaring, but undeniable. How so? In *Discipleship*, Bonhoeffer was still setting the terms "political" and "political ethics" in quotation marks; but in the *Ethics* he no longer does so, even speaking at one point about "the individual question of political ethics, which will be discussed later" (DBW 6, 243). This "later" never came. Nevertheless, we see the outlines of his political ethics everywhere in the *Ethics*. Bonhoeffer's whole political being opens up, for example, in a statement such as the following: "To understand Jesus Christ as God's love for the real world with its real history, its politics and so forth; to recognize, in other words, real human beings, circumstances, movements, the real world in Jesus Christ and Jesus Christ in the real world: this gives us the freedom to act responsibly in a way that influences the world and history" (DBW 6, 243). This statement is concretized directly and indirectly in many passages in his *Ethics*, in a way that is at times surprising in its up-to-dateness.

At the end of his manuscript entitled "The Natural Life," Bonhoeffer takes up the subject of "exploitation of the human body," using language that is directly antithetical to the political correctness of his time to discuss the tableau of man's domination over man (DBW 6, 213). He uses examples from history, as well as his own time, to illustrate the numerous open and—no less numerous—hidden ways in which relationships of dependency, of contempt and scorn, of degradation and debasement are used to instrumentalize and enslave human beings. In his manuscript "On the Possibility of a Meaningful Word from the Church to the World," he writes: "For example, certain economic and/or social attitudes and situations are a hindrance to faith in Christ, and thus have a destructive effect on human beings at their core and on the world. The question is, for example, whether capitalism or socialism or collectivism are among these economic entities that hinder faith" (ibid., 363).

The manuscript "Heritage and Decline" contains socio-critical reflections that cast doubt on the honor of our present television world as well: "We let nothing cling to us, nothing weigh us down. We immediately erase the film of events and its ending from memory: a sign of the profound forgetfulness of this age. Events of significance on the stage of world history, along with the most outrageous crimes, leave no trace behind on our forgetful souls. We play with the future. Lotteries and wagers . . . are our ways of seeking nothing but unlikely opportunities in the future" (DBW 6, 120). No less up-to-date in this day of body cults and the science of ready-made human beings, of embryonic spare parts and cost-benefit balance sheets that calculate how we are to function, is his remark in the manuscript "Ethics as Creation": "The glad tidings that God became man goes directly to the heart of an age in which . . . both contempt for human beings and adulation of them are the best that our wisdom has to offer" (ibid., 72). Or his remark on success as a god: "The figure of the One condemned and crucified remains foreign and at best pitiable to a world in which success is the Alpha and Omega and the justification of all things" (ibid., 75).

The manuscript section entitled "The Last and Next-to-Last Things" sums up with particular succinctness what is specific to Bonhoeffer's political ethics under the heading of "Preparing the Way."[18] For him, it is undeniable and understandable that belief in God's righteousness and goodness is almost too much to expect from a human being struck down "in the depths of disgrace, abandonment, destitution, and helplessness" (DBW 6, 154). Thus it is all the more important to witness to such a one, that it is "precisely the disenfranchised, the abased, and the exploited who are closest to the justice and mercy of God" *and* to make every effort to help them (ibid., 155). To allow those who hunger to go on hungering "would be a blasphemy toward God and one's neighbor"; to give them bread is "to prepare the way for the coming of mercy" (ibid.).

For Bonhoeffer, preparing God's way meant two things: to proclaim faith in God's reality in the world, and to (trans)form the world or at least situations in this world as a result of, in conformity with, and as an implication of this faith. He sometimes intentionally used understatement to express this viewpoint in a way that almost smacked of a politics of realism (very much so in Max Weber's sense, by the way). For example, he writes in *History and the Good* that "The task can only be, not to move the world but to see things realistically and do—really do— what is concretely necessary in our own place and time" (DBW 6, 224; also 267). It was this understanding that lay behind the statement—and appeal!—made by the young Bonhoeffer, with a mixture of moderation and idealism, in 1932, at an international Youth Peace Conference in Ciernohorské Kúpele in the former Czechoslovakia: "We cannot reconstitute the creation, but we should indeed shape the world toward goodness, as commanded by God, just as the God who commands us today will Himself one day in the future shape the New Creation in Christ. Herein lies the full burden of the divine commandment" (DBW 11, 342).

Through the Sermon on the Mount, Bonhoeffer arrived at the certainty that peace and not war is part of such a world, and that the peace of God is truly "peace on earth," truly "higher than all understanding." His mission was to shout this out over the "City on the Mountain" mentioned in the Sermon on the Mount and in *Discipleship*—over the rooftops of the *polis*.

15

Pax Christi!

Stay at your post and help with your call;
and if they throttle you,
stay at your post and help with your silence.

Seneca

Pax Christi, the peace of Christ, is not for the inner world of individual piety alone; it asserts its claim likewise on the outer, political world of society and must become reality in that world. Bonhoeffer unearthed this position through a new interpretation of the Sermon on the Mount he developed at the beginning of the 1930s, triggered in particular by his year of study in New York and his conversations with the French theologian Jean Lasserre. This view was unconditional and theologically radical to a degree that was foreign to him before that time. It was through Lasserre that he arrived at the unswerving understanding of the Sermon on the Mount that was the decisive turning point on his journey of faith. One of its best-known consequences was *Discipleship.*

For Bonhoeffer, this encounter with the Sermon on the Mount was a key experience. With it came a dawning consciousness that was unique for him. This resonates with a comment he made in a letter he wrote to his brother Karl-Friedrich, from London at the beginning of 1935: "The fact is that there are things which are worth standing up for without compromise. And I think peace and social justice, actually Christ, is one such thing" (DBW 13, 273). The enduring traces of this key experience also appear in another letter written a year later, in January 1936, to his friend and fellow theologian Elisabeth Zinn; there too he explicitly mentions his encounter with the Sermon on the Mount and its implications for him: "Christian pacifism, which I fought bitterly against . . . only a short time ago, suddenly became self-evident for me. And this change continued step by step. My views and thoughts revolved around nothing else" (DBW 14, 113). This pacifism was out of step with the times and went largely unnoticed in his day.

Moreover, it was a pacifism with no support whatever within the church. It did, however, strike a chord with later generations. For example, the heated discussion in postwar German Protestantism regarding issues such as rearmament of the Federal Republic and conscientious objection to military service, and the shape taken by the peace movement in the church during the 1980s in Germany, would have been unthinkable without Bonhoeffer's pacifism.

Bonhoeffer did not reject every form of force. His oppositional attitude toward the National Socialist system of oppression led him indirectly to participate in plans for a coup. Of necessity, these plans rejected non-violence as a universal principle and consciously accepted force as a means for their implementation.[1] To this extent, his pacifism was relative rather than absolute. However, in comparison with the unreflective affirmation of war that was common during his time and widespread within his own church, not to mention its intense form of the glorification of war, Bonhoeffer's pacifism represented a radical questioning of worldviews, and in particular a questioning of theological bastions that before him had only been the provenience of so-called zealots and utopians: it went to the very heart of Christian faith.

Numerous monographs have studied Bonhoeffer's path to pacifism, the specifics of his pacifism, and its later relevance.[2] One recent, broad-based study even set itself the goal of presenting the history of a twentieth-century theologian "in light of his perceptions concerning the realities of war and peace while also describing his theological reflections upon these perceptions, and how he put them into practice in his battles within the church and politically."[3]

The issue of war and peace in Bonhoeffer's thought will be examined here only briefly. The change in his attitude toward war and peace that took place over the course of his life can be reduced to a simple denominator: as much as it was basically a matter of course for him that war is a—murderous—fact of life, and that the Christian "naturally" must "serve" in war in order to fulfill his duty as a Christian and a citizen of the State, so also the conviction grew within him from the early 1930s on, that war cannot be God's will, that Christianity must oppose it, and that he himself—to the extent that his person was involved—could not respond as a Christian in any way other than by adopting a pacifist position.

As a young theologian, Bonhoeffer still saw it as a necessary evil that the peoples of the world must live with—or perhaps more precisely, at odds with—one another. This appears, for example, in a short passage concerning the history of theology, found in his dissertation, where he accurately summed up the generally prevalent spirit of his time, and with meek patriotism made approving use of categories such as "People," "War," and "History": God's will may serve as a command-ment for a people to fulfill its mission in the history of peoples—"war in that case is no longer murder," and the Christian will not and may not abstain (DBW 1, 74). He must immerse himself fully in the ambiva-lence of human action.

In his lecture entitled "Basic Questions of Christian Ethics," deliv-ered in Barcelona in 1929, Bonhoeffer firmly deals with the customary Christian justification for war; he begins rhetorically by asking how it is at all possible for Christians to justify killing in war, and then, making an about-face in his arguments, voices precisely the traditional Christian legitimation for war, in involuntary conformity with the nationalistic Protestant ethos. The context of this passage contains the pathetic words already quoted in the previous chapter, concerning the mother and the people to whom one has been given by God and the divine order (DBW 10, 337). Bonhoeffer at that time was manifestly unaware that this attitude merely served to justify a specific societal order. He con-cludes by stating that performing atrocities is a necessity, since "love for my people will sanctify murder and war" (ibid., 338). Even in the *Ethics* (DBW 6, 183) there is a passage that justifies killing the enemy. How-ever, this was possibly intended as camouflage for his role as a conspira-tor.[4] Interspersed among all these statements, however, are Bonhoeffer's calls to action, his lectures, and memoranda in which he publicly and unmistakably said "No!" to war.

Forerunners of this "No!" are found in his "Lecture on the Subject of 'War,' " written during his year of study (1930–1931) in New York. He probably delivered it more than once to various religious groups there, at the invitation of the International Alliance for Reconciliation. A prominent founder of this organization, which was one of the most prominent ecumenical pacifistic organizations, was the German theolo-gian Friedrich Siegmund-Schultze. Bonhoeffer would later have exten-sive contact with this man during his ecumenical work. At the end of the above-named lecture Bonhoeffer sketched a (wishful?) picture of a flourishing work for peace: "With deep religious feeling we recognized every people as brothers, as children of God" (DBW 10, 651). Germany, after the frightful First World War and the dissolution of the empire: a land with major pacifist alliances of workers, a land with an absolutely pacifist youth movement, a land with a functional peace movement whose motivation came from various sources, all resting upon the work-ing class, the middle class, the Christians! He sums up as follows: ". . . the peace movement in Germany is an enormous force," and he makes the demand: "May it never again happen that one Christian people wages war on another, brother against brother, since both have the same Father" (ibid.). He speaks of the international work of the churches and of the one Christian church, of the prejudices among the nations and the will to wage war, which must be overcome.

This picture has little in common with a realistic analysis of the situation in Germany between the wars; it cannot be doubted that Bonhoeffer's overly optimistic view of the peace movement under the Weimar Republic did not correspond to facts.[5] But it also cannot be doubted that a new idea is heard in Bonhoeffer's remarks about war and peace here, and this increases in frequency, realism, *and* intensity in the years immediately following. Between 1931 and 1934, Bonhoeffer developed an ethics of peace whose applications and intentions he worked out above all in the context of the ecumenical movement. (In order to avoid misunderstandings of terminology: the terms "ecumenism" and "ecumenical movement" were applied at that time to the work of institutions seeking to bring the many Christian churches of the world, especially the Protestant churches of North America and Europe, closer together and ultimately unite them. After 1945 this movement took on a new, more global and effective dimension; except for the Roman Catholic Church, nearly all Christian groups have since joined the World Council of Churches.[6])

In those years, Bonhoeffer defended his ethics of peace vehemently at ecumenical meetings: at Ciernohorské Kúpele in Czechoslovakia, at Gland in Switzerland, and at Fanø in Denmark; his defense was tentative at first, still in process, but basically unambiguous at the first two meetings, held in 1932, and more emphatically at the third in 1934. In Cambridge in 1931, Bonhoeffer was elected as one of three Secretaries for Youth in Europe of the World Council for Friendship and Collaboration of the Churches. He delivered a speech at the International Youth Peace Conference in Ciernohorské Kúpele entitled "On the Theological Foundations of the World Council's Work." It was published by the pacifist-leaning magazine *Die Eiche* (*The Oak Tree*), whose editor was the above-mentioned theologian Friedrich Siegmund-Schultze.

In the last part of this lecture, Bonhoeffer spoke at length about the issues of war and peace. He prefaced his remarks with a clear and curt statement: "To establish an order of *international peace* is God's commandment for us today" (DBW 11, 338); no more and no less. But he also qualifies this thesis by remarking that peace is not to be understood as an end in itself, nor merely in a formal way as the highest good. Peace according to Bonhoeffer must be "filled," so to speak, with truth and justice; the price of peace must not be a reign of lies and injustice. He also distinguishes the category of armed force from that of war: "The peace of a community is always to be forcefully interrupted whenever any group endangers or stifles the truth and justice inherent in peace, and then men must be called into battle" (ibid., 339). However, this cannot serve as a justification for war or armed force, for war today "has become a totally different entity" (ibid., 341). If in earlier times it was still possible to interpret war as part of the order of preservation established by God in preparation for revelation, it can no longer be justified in this way, because war today "means certain self-annihilation for both warring parties" (ibid.) and in this respect it differs fundamentally from earlier wars.

Bonhoeffer characterized this substantial change in the nature and consequences of war—and this in the year 1932!—by emphasizing its quasi-total aspect: the annihilating power of war today extends to the inner and outer man, to body and soul. He therefore demands, "Because we cannot under any circumstances understand war as part of God's order of preservation or as God's command, and because war derives its life from being idealized and idolized, war today, any next war, must be *banned* by the church. . . . And we must not shy away here from the word 'pacifism' " (DBW 11, 341).

Bonhoeffer's clear-sighted conclusions regarding war and peace stand out not only because he recognized the character of—later, so-called (and practiced)—"modern" war, whose implications and results include the annihilation of all participants, but also because he saw through the ideological ecstasy upon which war is dependent. Moreover, he is not concerned with a "look back in anger" which condemns wars of the past but not those of the future, preferring to turn a blind eye to the subject or to paint it in rosy colors that distort it ideologically. Bonhoeffer was not concerned with a cheap pacifism in principle that is hastily forgotten in the next best—that is, the worst—instance of war. For him the issue is not to be "against" it but rather to be against *it*, against the concrete, next war!

Bonhoeffer experienced the First World War from the perspective of a child. He was never to know the full extent of the Second World War's fury of destruction, nor the development of military high technology in the second half of his own century, which perfected the mastery over space and time which is at the heart of weapons systems now known as ABC weapons and their apparently innocuous offshoots, a technology in which war has attained a never-before achieved capability for quantitative and qualitative escalation. But in the summer of 1932, Bonhoeffer declared as a young theologian at an international youth conference in a country that would be occupied only a few years later by his own country's army, that modern war ends only in absurdity, and

Christian faith can no longer function as a justification of war. He declared that war is dependent both upon this faith, and upon other forms
of justification, and that both prepare the way for war and prolong it. He
declared that it is the duty of the church to reject war here and now—
without beating around the bush and without falling victim to mental
strategies of defense. What Bonhoeffer demanded in the summer of
1932 was very much up to date at the turn of the twentieth century. We
need mention only the Gulf war and others elsewhere.

Bonhoeffer delivered another, similarly explosive talk in 1932 at an
ecumenical and international youth conference in Gland, on Lake
Geneva in Switzerland. This speech moves through the same structure of
argumentation as—and is identical in many passages with—his lecture
entitled "On the Theological Foundations of the World Council's Work."
But it is more unequivocal, more vivid. His description of the world in
which he lives is almost exactly the same as our world today: "Events are
coming to a head today more terribly than ever before—*millions of hungering human beings* whose desires meet with feeble promises or go un-
fulfilled, desperate human beings who have nothing more to lose, except
their lives, and who in losing them lose nothing; *humiliated and dishonored
peoples, . . . political extremes fighting other political extremes, fanaticized humans against fanaticized humans,* idols against idols—and behind all this
a world whose gaze is transfixed as never before by weapons, a world
that arms itself feverishly in order to guarantee peace by arms" (DBW
11, 354–55)! He continues concisely and stubbornly: "Today there must
be no more war—the cross does not want it. . . . The church refuses to
obey when called upon to sanction war. The church of Christ stands
against war and for peace among men, among peoples, classes, and
races" (ibid., 356).

In the winter of that year, Bonhoeffer spoke to students in an ecumenical work group in Berlin about "Christ and Peace." He based his
opening remarks on the Sermon on the Mount, stating that understanding it is very easy: "For the unreflective reader, the Sermon on the
Mount says fully incomprehensible things" (DBW 12, 232). One thing
is certain: the issue is not to eliminate war; that does not lie within the
power of Christianity. But "bearing witness to peace" is undeniably part
of a life lived in discipleship (ibid., 233). The Old Testament commandment not to kill and the New Testament command to love one's enemy
require, according to Bonhoeffer, nothing other than "uncomplicated
obedience" (ibid., 234). His definitive conclusion is therefore: "All forms
of war service, except for field medicine, along with everything that
lays the groundwork for war, are forbidden to the Christian" (ibid.).
The decisive element of this Christian witness to peace is that peace be

established within Christianity, which otherwise has no right to speak of peace to the nations.

Bonhoeffer's manifesto for peace reached its climax in "The Church and a World of Peoples," a talk he presented in the summer of 1934, during a world conference convened on the Danish island of Fanø. In this talk, he presents his view of pacifism without qualifications or circumlocutory interpretations. Rarely did Bonhoeffer speak to a more important audience and rarely as electrifyingly, with so much conviction *and* persuasiveness, as in Fanø. His demands: to be truly ecumenical, the World Council must proclaim to the peoples that God wants peace, not war. It must avoid watering this down in any way; war and peace cannot be bandied about in the form of an open question; rather, Christ made the issue of "peace on earth" unavoidable. Christians cannot do otherwise than to take Him at His word. Unfortunately, the seductive question "Has God then told you . . . ?" in the narrative of the Fall in Genesis leads human beings time and again in the most varied forms into temptation:

> Must not God have understood human nature better and known that wars occur in this world as part of natural law? Must not God have meant that while we are certainly to speak of peace we must not take it so literally in practice? Must not God have said we should indeed work for peace but to be on the safe side we should also have our tanks and poison gases at the ready? (DBW 13, 299)

For Bonhoeffer, the most fundamental characteristic and task of the ecumenical churches is to break down the fences that separate races, nations, and the classes of society—and not to be ashamed of Christ's work but to identify itself fearlessly with it, to confront the world for the sake of peace among the nations, and not to satisfy itself with allegedly reliable assurances of peace. Bonhoeffer asks: "How does peace come? Through a system of political agreements? Through the investment of international capital in the different countries, that is, through the banks of the world; through money? Or even through universal, peaceful armament with the intention of ensuring peace?" (ibid., 300). In his eyes, these are the wrong paths to peace, since they equate peace with security—a fateful error. He advances the categorical thesis that peace must be dared, that it is "the one great daring venture" and "the opposite of a guarantee of security" (ibid.).

Who then calls us to peace if not the whole of Christianity? *How* then does it do so, and if at all possible, to the joy of the peoples? Bonhoeffer's response, made basically in his own interest as well, is that a Christian cannot achieve this alone; true, he can raise his voice for peace in the midst of general silence. "But the powers of this world can step over him without a word, and move on" (ibid., 301). No one church can effectively intervene on behalf of peace—"Would that it would do so!"—and even suffer for it if necessary, for it too has no chance against the "forces of hatred" (ibid.).

What follows is Bonhoeffer's call for an ecumenical council of peace, a call that was echoed worldwide fifty years later in the 1980s peace movement in the churches. Only a great council where Christ's church comes together from every corner of the world could speak the word of peace with a voice "that the world, grinding its teeth, cannot but hear; and the peoples will rejoice because this church of Christ takes weapons out of the hands of its sons, forbids their use in the name of Christ, and proclaims the peace of Christ over the furious world" (ibid.). Bonhoeffer was well aware that only the ecumenical body of churches "can make this radical call to peace" take effect and that the peoples of the world—"East and West"—are in fact awaiting this (ibid.)! And he adds the provocative question, perhaps with Gandhi in mind, "Must we let ourselves be put to shame by the non-Christians of the East?" (ibid.).

Half a year later, in January 1935, Bonhoeffer reported, in his "Memorandum to the Ecumenical Youth Commission" in Geneva, news about his concrete work activities since the conference in Fanø. Initial progress, however small, had certainly been made in Germany: "There appears to be a willingness, most likely due primarily to the pressure of the growing military atmosphere, to take the Christian Gospel of peace seriously" (DBW 13, 505). Thought had been given to founding a Christian community that would attempt to live strictly in the spirit of the Sermon on the Mount: Christianity today can convince others only through "a clear and uncompromising stance" (ibid.). The ongoing conflicts between the churches in Germany appeared to be moving more and more in the direction of a conservative form of Christianity "that would be very congenial to the conservative mentality now spreading in all directions through the military circles of the Reich and the industrially minded regime" (ibid.), observed Bonhoeffer in this letter. He voted to convene an international youth conference where the question of conscientious objection would be discussed. He also proposed a topic for discussion there: "The use of force, its rightfulness and its limitations" (ibid., 506). Bonhoeffer concluded by declaring that "The theoretical basis of pacifism will remain very weak until an answer is found to this fundamental question" (ibid.). How true! The fact that he recognized this deficit indicates that Bonhoeffer was also aware of both the complexity and the potential for conflict inherent in an ethics of peace.

It is characteristic of Bonhoeffer's pacifism that in spite of his every "No" uttered in principle as a response to the question of war, he rejected any rigorously unreflective pacifism that categorically refused *a priori* to consider the question of force. Another characteristic is that his pacifism was theologically rather than politically motivated, without disregarding concrete political and social dimensions. Quite the contrary! Also characteristic of Bonhoeffer is that he dared to say "No!" to war, beginning with his own person.

When universal military duty was definitively reintroduced in May 1935, Bonhoeffer indicated to his students in the newly founded Preaching Seminary of the Confessing Church in Zingst that he did not preclude for himself the possibility of refusing to serve, should it come to that. For us today, it is hard to understand that at that time such a step was almost inconceivable, especially for a German Evangelical theologian: "In the First World War (and later in the Second) there was no recorded instance of a Lutheran pastor refusing to bear arms."[7]

A few years later, beginning in 1940, Bonhoeffer set foot on a different path of refusal: that of conspiracy. The official charges against him as an alleged negotiator for the Resistance included among other things "sedition against the military." He had accepted the risk of illegality as a negotiator in the interest of peace, a peace he hoped to achieve through an overthrow in Germany.

Before the outbreak of war in March 1939, Bonhoeffer wrote in a very personal letter to Bishop Bell, with whom he had been on friendly terms since his pastorate in London, about his sense of isolation, his doubts, and his feeling of helplessness before the coming induction of those born in 1906. He feared compromising the Confessing Church, which had no choice but to act with respect to the issue of military service, as it was in fact doing under the circumstances, through a refusal on his part to serve. "I would do immense harm to my brothers should I resist in this respect, since the current regime would view this as typical of the animosity of our churches against the State," he wrote (DBW 15, 625). Moreover, it was impossible for him to swear the mandatory oath of loyalty to Adolf Hitler. What he did not say explicitly in this letter, but is nevertheless self-evident, is that such open refusal would have direct, unforeseeable implications for him, possibly including the death penalty. Bonhoeffer emphasized at that time that he did not know how he would behave under other circumstances: "But as things stand now, I would do violence to my convictions as a Christian if I were to take weapons in my hand in the 'here and now' " (ibid.).

With his pacifism, Bonhoeffer liberated the Christian view of peace from the backwaters and resignation of pure interiority and other-worldliness in which it had threatened to atrophy. He wanted to make the word "peace" resound anew and restore to it its early Christian impact for the sake of God and the world. Backward as his understanding of the State sometimes appears to us today, he was just as far ahead of his contemporaries, particularly his Christian contemporaries, in the area of pacifism.

To us, it may seem to be a shortcoming "that neither then nor later did Bonhoeffer devote the theological attention to democracy as a life form, which later times view it as deserving."[8] But this makes his advance into new territory all the more astonishing and encouraging. At a time when nationalism and Christian faith, along with confessionalism and Christian faith, had entered into an ingenuous and apparently long-lived alliance, he made it clear that Christianity at odds with itself is a contradiction in terms.

Bonhoeffer dealt with the question of peace by beginning with the question of the credibility of a united Christianity; in so doing, he put his finger on the ecumenical wound. By their very nature, protestation for peace and personal commitment to ecumenical unity were—and continue to be—inextricably related to one another. Only the one church of Christ can be a church for the world, and it can be so only in this way.

16

The Search for the Lost Church

We, like God, expect the church
to produce truly free men and women,
highly effective free men and women,
since freedom for them is not only a right
but also a sending.

Georges Bernanos

For Bonhoeffer, the church of Jesus Christ was a house of life, a place of community, a sign of God's presence in the world and a witness to it—he longed for it to be all these things. In contrast to many of those in theology and the church, it was not something he spoke about only critically while keeping his distance, or something he accepted only with clenched teeth and mockingly. "Church" had been one of the basic themes of his theology and his life since his university studies. It was his interface with the world, the place where God's will was concretized and His proclamation voiced. Bonhoeffer believed and hoped that the Christian church would truly be the church *of Jesus Christ,* and he devoted his abilities and his whole person to this end. Experiencing the church and hoping to experience it were for him not marginal issues but issues central to Christian existence.

Bonhoeffer's first, almost sensual experience of "church" occurred in his encounter with living Catholicism during an extensive stay as a student in Rome. A few years later, while studying on a scholarship in New York, he was a regular guest in black church communities in Harlem, where he came into contact with an immediacy, a spontaneity, and a mutual support among church members in their services and communities that was unknown to him up to that time: "This was the second time that Bonhoeffer experienced what 'Church' can be."[1] The experience was formative with respect to two dimensions of his later personal and professional life and theology, namely, his life within the (nearly) worldwide ecumenical movement, and his life within the Confessing Church in Germany. In actual fact, however, the two di-

mensions were inseparable from one another during the further course
of his life and thought.

Before turning to these two concrete dimensions of church in
Bonhoeffer's thought, however, it is necessary to recall briefly once again
the preeminent meaning of "church" for him in general.[2] This is already
evident in the titles of many of his works, in particular his dissertation
Sanctorum Communio, the university lectures he presented in the summer of 1932 at the University of Berlin on "The Nature of the Church,"
his essay entitled "What Is Church?" written in January 1933, and
finally his "Draft for a Paper," which was drawn up in prison in 1944. It
is also evident not only in his other works but—from beginning to
end—in his wholly actualized existence and work as a theologian.

For Bonhoeffer, the individual and the church enter into what Luther called a "joyful interplay." The responsibility of the individual
man or woman of faith for the church and in turn its responsibility
for that person has been expressed classically once and for all in the basic
Evangelical affirmation of the universal priesthood of the faithful. Bonhoeffer takes this up, for example, in his dissertation (DBW 1, 162) and
modifies it in his own fashion, writing that ". . . every Evangelical Christian is a dogmatist" (ibid., 172). When leaving Berlin shortly thereafter, in
order to begin his vicariate in Barcelona, nothing saddened Bonhoeffer
more than the knowledge that he was leaving behind his church services
for children. He relates in his diary how moved he was when the pastor
of the church community included him in the community's prayers in
the presence of the children at the last divine service he attended there;
"Wherever there is church there is never loneliness," he notes in retrospect (DBW 10, 21).

The notes that have come down to us from his lectures on "The Nature of the Church" indicate the liveliness and originality Bonhoeffer injected into his development of the topic of the church, the encyclopedic
span of his knowledge, and how much he demanded of himself. He
defines "church" as "God's dwelling place in the world," but warns immediately against rootlessness, arbitrariness, and pandering to the world
(DBW 11, 244). A church that aims to be omnipresent ends up being
nowhere. Rather, it is much more important that the church be the
"critical center of the world" (ibid., 248), whether in Galilee or in
Wittenberg with Luther. In the further course of his lectures Bonhoeffer concerns himself with the relationship between theology and
the church and between Christ and the church; that is, with the character of the church as a whole. Finally, in the last part he discusses the relationship between the church as "worldly" and as Christian, arriving at
the conclusion that ". . . worldliness is to be taken seriously because the

church's godliness is to be taken seriously: that is what is Christian about the church" (ibid., 301).

Bonhoeffer again attempted to define the church's place in the world in a speech entitled "Theological Foundations of the World Council's Work," delivered in that same summer of 1932 at the International Youth Conference in Ciernohorské Kúpele. The word of the church to the world is fully authoritative only if it stems "from deepest knowledge of the world; it must address the world in all of its current reality" (DBW 11, 332); otherwise it is merely a word of weakness. This (ibid.) is where Bonhoeffer makes the statement—already quoted—that is so important for understanding his thought: "Therefore the Church may not proclaim immutably true principles, but only mandates that are valid today. For that which is 'forever' true is precisely 'today' untrue: God is 'forever' *God* for us precisely *'today.'*"[3]

To illustrate this idea, Bonhoeffer uses the examples of war and personal property, where a "Yes, but . . . ," or better a "No, but . . ." is impermissible. For example, it is an abomination that a church which condemns war both generally and in principle should justify a specific war by arguing that *this* particular war ("Yes, but . . .") is, after all, necessary. Speaking of the gap between luxury and poverty, he also declares that it is an abomination that the church should forbid the concrete redistribution of property using the argument that the inviolability of property is, after all, God's will. He demands categorically that the church, if it has truly received its mandate from God, "must proclaim this in the most concrete form possible, acting from deepest insight into the matter, and must issue a call to obedience" (ibid., 333).

Bonhoeffer wanted to see this decisiveness regarding basic ethical problems both in himself and in the church. When it comes to issues involving the world, a church can be neither credible nor in tune with the Jesus-event if it states its positions without factual knowledge and in complete abstraction, or if it promptly relativizes, or even suspends, its response in concrete instances. The church cannot exist in an ivory tower but must stand with both feet on the ground. In this speech, Bonhoeffer addresses in ever-new variations the tension-laden, dramatic relationship between the church and the world. The church must exist—in the words of John—"in the world," but it does not draw its existence "from the world." It must live in a dialectic between the poles of being "in this world" and "not of this world." For it to live in this world always means with responsibility for this world rather than in a state of inner absence. It must confront the conflicts of this world and speak the language of this world. But it must also be mindful of the fact that its roots and the guarantee of its existence are not "of this world."

This dialectic between church and world leads Bonhoeffer to the insight and position that the church is church only as the church *for* this world! "It is—to put it in exaggerated terms—'church for the world' inasmuch as it dares in the obedience of faith to be uncompromisingly a church *against* the world."[4]

This line of thought leads from dialectic to the clear-sighted critique of the church that Bonhoeffer formulated in Tegel Prison. His understanding of "church" took on a sharper, more consistent focus during this time; and in view of the customary understanding of the church that prevailed up to that time, it is no exaggeration to say that in this regard his was a lone voice in the wilderness. "He saw through the thesis of the church's apolitical character, and saw that it sprang from an interest in self-preservation. He also saw through the entanglement between the church's civil character and the vested interests of those who wished to maintain the status quo."[5] Until Bonhoeffer took up the subject, the understanding of "church" in his day remained largely unquestioned; but he saw that its wellspring was a specific view of the church and a desire to present it as an organization which is its own end, one which logically enough does (almost) anything necessary in order to secure its own existence.

It took years and decades after the end of the Second World War for the realization to take hold among Evangelical persons—and here we are speaking only of them—that church is the church *only* when it is the church for others, and it strays from its own self when it identifies with the need to maintain its own existence. The church loses its soul when it revolves around itself. Such self-rotation prevents it from fulfilling itself. It can be the church only when it is *not* the church for itself. Accordingly, Bonhoeffer expressed the following in the baptismal text he wrote for his godchild in May 1944: "Our church, which has fought only to preserve itself in these years, as if it were its own end, is incapable of bearing within itself the word of reconciliation and salvation for mankind and the world" (DBW 8, 435). And a few weeks later he noted in his "Draft for a Paper": "Crucial: Church in self-defense, risking nothing for others" (ibid., 558). During the course of further reflections on suffering caused by the church in the past, and hope for its future, he goes to the heart of the matter in a statement that sounds easy, but is difficult to put into practice: "Conclusion: the church is the church only when it is for others" (ibid., 560). This is one of the most frequently quoted statements made by Bonhoeffer—in this book as well—and one the church must ever call to mind anew in its practical activities.

Bonhoeffer's views of church and worldly Christian existence, combined with his ecumenical impetus, helped ignite movements such as political service within the church, liberation theology, and the anti-racism programs and actions initiated by the World Council of Churches. One of the peculiarities of Bonhoeffer's view of the world and the church was that this ecumenical impetus was not a result but a precondition for his thoughts about the church. He was one of the first to look beyond nationalistic Christian interests; ecumenism for him was not simply one conclusion reached in a doctrine of the church, but was instead a prerequisite for his ecclesiology, part of the essence of the church. In his dissertation *Sanctorum Communio,* he drew a picture of this ecumenical foundation of the church as extending to the entire inhabited globe, using "Geneva and Stockholm" to represent ecumenical centers and/or conferences: ". . . the body of Christ is Rome and Corinth, Wittenberg, Geneva, and Stockholm, and the members of each and every church community together constitute the one whole community of the church, the *sanctorum communio*" (DBW 1, 152–53). Even at that early time (ibid., 191), "church" for Bonhoeffer was the *una sancta,* the *one* holy church; this and nothing else is what he said later in his *Ethics:* ". . . the church of Christ is one, embracing all races of mankind" (DBW 6, 85).

Even if the ecumenical movement at that time was not, in practice, one that included the Roman Catholic Church, and thus *all* churches—a sore spot in the understanding of ecumenism to the present day—it is nevertheless a fact that Bonhoeffer always thought of Rome when ecumenism was at issue, beginning with his stay in Rome as a young student. The diary he kept of his time in Italy in 1924 (DBW 9, 81ff.) and many statements in his letters from prison written exactly twenty years later, when his friend Eberhard Bethge was in Italy, document this affection; and when Bonhoeffer stayed at the Ettal cloister in the early 1940s, he carried on intensive discussions with Catholics not only about issues of dialogue among the churches but also about illegal political activities.[6] At the peak of his own ecumenical work, however, from the beginning to the middle of the 1930s, "ecumenism" for Bonhoeffer meant that the non-Catholic churches should approach one another and cooperate across national boundaries. He saw clearly that it would be unrealistic to attempt more than this.

This form of ecumenism was regarded as offensive enough during that period of secular and church history. For outsiders, those in the ecumenical movement were regarded as bumpkins without national ties; above all, they were suspect in the nationalistic Protestant circles of Germany. In circles such as these, their meetings in those years must have appeared strange and offensive as, for example, the meetings between

North American clergymen and representatives of the Russian clergy during the time of the Cold War.

Bonhoeffer, who ignored the possibility of losing prestige at home and had no fear of contacts abroad, had carried this vision of the ecumenical church since his year of study in New York from 1930 to 1931. Up to the middle of the 1930s, he was full of ideas and enthusiasm, and he injected numerous new impulses into the work of the ecumenical movement. But concrete, continued work in and for ecumenism came to a halt with the rigid bans on travel abroad imposed in 1937 upon representatives of the churches in Germany. Even before that, however, there had been disagreements between Bonhoeffer and the "top level" of the World Council. These conflicts came about due to internal church disputes: the decision-making bodies in Geneva repeatedly arbitrated against representatives of the Confessing Church. This ultimately led Bonhoeffer to break with Geneva, and it was only his work for the Resistance group within the military from 1940 on, and his consequent travels as a conspirator, that prompted him to renew his contact with church officials in Geneva. But he also experienced a different sort of ecumenism in a fully unexpected manner: in the conspiracy movement; and at the end, in prison, he came in contact with persons of every worldview and in particular of every confessional provenience far beyond the limits of institutionalized ecumenism.

This "ecumenism of resistance" refused to be degraded into an "ecumenism of powerless victims." As Bonhoeffer wrote to George Bell, the English Bishop of Chichester, with whom he felt a bond of special trust, following a meeting held at the beginning of June 1942, "This spirit of community and Christian brotherhood will bear me up through the darkest hours. . . ." (DBW 16, 773). After Bonhoeffer was isolated on April 8, 1945, in order to go before a drumhead court, he asked his fellow prisoner, the Englishman Payne Best, to tell Bishop Bell the following: "I believe with him that the foundation stone is our universal Christian brotherhood, which supersedes all national feelings of hatred" (DBW 16, 468).[7]

In spite of his intense hope for ecumenical unity, Bonhoeffer was neither uncritical nor naive in this regard. From the very beginning he demanded a theology of ecumenism. As early as 1932, he was already analyzing the implications of this missing theology, namely, the lack of appeal ecumenical thought and action had in Germany, and the resulting susceptibility to nationalistic sound and fury: "Because the ecumenical movement has no theology of its own, the ecumenical idea today, in Germany for example, has been rendered insipid and meaningless by the political wave of nationalism among young people" (DBW 11,

328f.). The theology of ecumenism: is it a black hole in Christian dog-matics and proclamation of that day, and still to be desired in our own?

Bonhoeffer saw the lack of solid theological foundations for ecume-nism in another area as well, when noting the lack of unyielding support from many representatives of the ecumenical movement for the belea-guered church in Germany. On the one hand, he underscored in 1935 the sympathy and solidarity of ecumenical centers with the Confessing Church: "Differences of opinion within the church have made the Evangelical ecumenical movement more visible in the last two years than ever before" (DBW 14, 378–79). On the other hand, for example, in a communiqué he wrote to General Secretary Henriod in 1934, he openly castigated the "dilatoriness of ecumenical action" (DBW 13, 120) and the indecisiveness and indifference with which developments in Germany were being observed. If those representing ecumenism could not comprehend that and for what they must decide, then they were no longer the church but "a club whose shiftless members merely gave nice speeches" (ibid.).

Whereas Bonhoeffer's call was loud and clear, the reaction of those within the ecumenical movement to the internecine struggles of the churches—German Christians here, Confessing Church there—was not always so. There were exceptions, however: Bishop Bell, for ex-ample, unflaggingly supported the latter; in an open letter to the *Times* in 1936 he summed up his position briefly and clearly: a blow against the Confessing Movement would be a blow against Christianity.[8]

German Christianity and ecumenism were a contradiction in terms; this was clear to Bonhoeffer from the very beginning. His personal ecu-menical commitment had its roots in his understanding of Christ and his confession of Christ. From beginning to end, the impact of ecumenical Christian existence was intrinsic to his profession of being a Christian. In an essay he wrote in the summer of 1935, entitled "The Confessing Church and the Ecumenical Movement," he described the theoretical and theological foundations for the indissoluble relationship between Christian profession and ecumenism: "Evangelical ecumenical unity," he wrote, can become reality only through discipleship of the New Testa-ment event (not simply the New Testament glad tidings!), a discipleship in which "the church of Christ does not stop short at national and racial borders but reaches beyond them" (DBW 14, 379). In the succinct com-ments following this passage, Bonhoeffer perhaps developed the theology of ecumenism he found so painfully lacking: he links the current issue of Christian profession with the mission and reality of those united ecumen-ically; and he elevates the entire complex of thought to a higher level by discussing the dialectic of unity and truth.

It would be well worthwhile to study this essay from the perspective of today's ecumenical movement. In light of Bonhoeffer's own specific situation, the essay emphatically illustrates his personal view of the church: "One of the characteristics of his understanding of the church is precisely his dialectic between the profession of faith and the achievement of ecumenical unity. . . . His theory of the church is a theory of the Confessing Church and as such a theory of ecumenical unity; each is the key to understanding the other."[9]

The fact that he was more or less alone with this characteristically individual thesis is hardly surprising in view of German Christianity's distaste for trailblazing ideas at that time. German ideology of the day, with its vision of the "nation as one family," tended on the contrary to draw lines and raise fences of division, and large circles of Christianity in Germany went along unquestioningly, at least as far as their faith was concerned. Even within the Confessing Church, it was not a matter of course to view the profession of Christian existence as inextricable from the ecumenical movement. Apart from Bonhoeffer's later decision to participate in political conspiracy, it was also his enthusiasm for ecumenical unity that made him an outsider within the ranks; there is no doubt that he had the status of a minority voice in his chosen church, the Confessing Church: "Bonhoeffer's nearly unique position in the church's struggle stems from the fact that personal ecumenical commitment and struggle within the church, disparate tasks though they appear to be, were for him both biographically and theologically parts of the same whole."[10] His years of work in the ecumenical movement and the Confessing Church overlap one another just as ecumenical unity and the Confessing Church overlap in his theological thought.

But what was really behind the issue of the Confessing Church and the German Christians? In other words, what was the so-called "church struggle," and Bonhoeffer's attitude and position regarding it? This question can only be answered against the backdrop of the National Socialist system. To put it theologically, the basic issue was that of the First Commandment: who is God? National Socialism's totalitarian claim consisted in demanding full and complete possession of the *whole* person at *all* stations and in *all* aspects of his or her life. Its claim to absolute authority consisted in understanding itself as the *one* valid and rigorously required worldview, with moral consequences designed to render all other existing standards and values ineffective. These claims to total and absolute authority manifested themselves ultimately in the *apotheosis* of the "Leader"; unconditional glorification of Hitler and unconditional subjection of the individual went hand in glove with the glorification of the "German race." This in turn implied the denigration of all non-Arians, and found its only possible conse-quence in the systematic persecution and extermination of those who thought differently or were themselves "different."

The National Socialists' church policies, implemented with utmost skill, aimed from the start to render the churches powerless and in-distinguishable from one another. In response to its organizational compactness and centrally established hierarchy, the Roman Catholic Church was brought to heel, so to speak, from the top down: in the sum-mer of 1933 Hitler signed the Concordat with the Holy See. Regarding the "Evangelical Church," as one historian put it, "Developments were more complicated and dramatic than in any other institutional area. The reasons for this were both organizational and ideological and concerned the structural problems of German Protestantism."[11] Here there could be no question of proceeding in accordance with the Concordat. The re-gime was constrained to take a different route in order to eliminate the Evangelical Church as a hypothetical opponent. From the start, there-fore, systematic use was made of a policy aimed at rendering the church innocuous. In spite of much turbulence, this was very successful in the long run.

The susceptibility of large circles of the Protestant population for National Socialist ideology and their admiration for the new govern-ment, at least during the initial years, were most prominent in the Ger-man Christian Movement, which was instrumental in rendering the Evangelical Church powerless to resist the magnetism and dominance of National Socialism until inner church conflict finally broke out openly.

Although this Faith Movement of German Christians was not primarily an offshoot of National Socialism, it nevertheless served the government as a most welcome instrument for its church politics. In its earliest form it had existed as a diffuse, religious-national mélange since the end of the German Empire. Like a schoolchild trying to get a star next to his or her name, in June of 1932 it issued its (in)famous Guidelines, a basic program containing National Socialist ideology in its pure form.

In his opening words at the International Youth Conference in Cier-nohorské Kúpele, Czechoslovakia, at the end of July 1932, Bonhoeffer spoke of "the grave issue of Christian responsibility for the political de-velopment in Germany" (DBW 11, 348–49). Hitler's party, he said, was abusing the opportunities offered by democracy and striving to set up a dictatorship; it was even extending its influence into the church. Bon-hoeffer's demand on that occasion was a program in direct contrast to the Guidelines of the German Christians (ibid., 349): "Christians must unite to fight the forces that are seducing nations to a false nationalism, promoting militarism, and threatening the world with an unrest that could lead to war."

The history of the German Christian Movement is one of a speedy rise to influence within the Evangelical Church, followed by a rapid downfall. Its relationship to the top National Socialist leadership was that of a close liaison which soon led it to compromise itself. Its over-zealous effort to be more nationally socialistic than National Socialism itself was rewarded with little thanks from the latter. It acted as a lackey during the brainwashing of the Evangelical churches by the new system of oppression. Church elections in the year 1933 ensured the German Christians of a relatively strong influence in numerous ecclesiastical decision-making bodies.

On July 23, 1933, the same Sunday as these church elections, Bonhoeffer preached a sermon on the topic of the church. He preached, for those "of you who have lost your church, . . . let us go together in search of the eternal church" (DBW 12, 466). He was preaching about the "church of the little flock, the church out there in silence, the church in the face of death" (ibid., 467). He referred to the slogan "church must remain church" of the group campaigning against the German Christians under the name of Gospel and church, encouraging them by saying: "We say to the church not just, 'Remain church,' but rather 'Profess, profess, profess . . . that Christ alone is the Lord, and that only from His grace do you have life as you are. . . .' The Confessing Church is the eternal church, for Christ protects it. That it is eternal is not visible in this world. It is not endangered by the world, . . . and it often seems to be altogether hidden and lost. But to it belongs the victory, because Christ, its Lord, is with it and has overcome the world of death" (ibid., 470).

For the time being, however, the German Christians carried the day. They had successfully done their bit for the Fatherland and for Mother Church; from that time on, few national churches remained ostensibly intact, since they had in fact been largely dismantled by the German Christians. As an irony of fate, only a few months later, in November 1933, the German Christians were abandoned by the government after a spectacular rally in Berlin's Palace of Sport; thereafter it regarded them as only laughable at best. In retrospect, however, it may be said that it would not have been possible for an opposition movement to arise so quickly within the church, nor would a return to the texts of the New Testament have taken place so quickly, without the somewhat successful efforts of the German Christians to infiltrate the church with a Christianity in National Socialist colors.

The occasion for forming such opposition to the German Christians within the church came in the autumn of 1933. It took the form of an instruction issued by the German Christian-dominated leadership of the church to apply the Arian Paragraphs to church members.[12] In protest, two theologians in Berlin, namely, the pastor Martin Niemöller and the Assistant Professor Dietrich Bonhoeffer, wrote a letter to church leaders in which they proclaimed the *status confessionis*, the status of the confession of faith. Not long afterwards, as one of the consequences of this "Note of Protest," a declaration was sent to the Evangelical pastors and distributed by them with the signatures of twenty other signatories, and this in turn was signed nearly immediately by two thousand pastors. At the initiative of Niemöller, an emergency alliance of pastors was formed in September of 1933, and from this sprang the Confessing Church.[13]

This church took on its decisive profile at the Synod of Barmen in 1934; the Theological Declaration and its six theses formulated there, with Karl Barth as the guiding spirit, is rightfully regarded as the most significant document of the Confessing Church. Bonhoeffer, who at that time was already serving as a pastor in London, was in constant contact with it and was appointed director of one of its first Preaching Seminaries in the town of Zingst on the Baltic Sea in 1935. These were the happy days of the Confessing Church, the time of the Councils of Brothers, of lived profession in church communities, of newly established training institutions.

But in April 1934, Bonhoeffer had already given Erwin Sutz an evaluation of the situation which, when read in retrospect, is stunning in its clarity of vision. He sent it to him in Switzerland: "And even though I am working with all my strength in the opposition movement within the church, I see quite clearly that *this* opposition is only a very preliminary station on the way to quite another opposition, and that almost none of the men involved in this first, preliminary skirmish will be involved in that second battle. And I think that all Christianity must pray with us that it may come to a 'fight to the death' and that people will be found who are willing to suffer this" (DBW 13, 128). Only then, and then only perhaps, will God again acknowledge his church. At the end of this letter he included a resigned and longing confession: "I do not know how long I will remain a pastor, or even a member of this church. Perhaps not much longer. I want to go to India this winter" (ibid., 129). Here again, his—never fulfilled—desire to visit Mahatma Gandhi and learn from him and from India!

Bonhoeffer's ambivalence toward the Confessing Church—because its words and actions were too indecisive for him—is also expressed in a letter he wrote to the Danish Bishop Ammundsen in August 1934. In preparation for the Conference of Fanø[14] he confessed that he "is more apprehensive about many of our own people than about the German Christians when thinking about Fanø" (DBW 13, 179) and that he is oppressed by the constant need to take care not to appear unpatriotic under any circumstances. Bonhoeffer called for unreserved openness regarding obedience to the State "for the sake of Jesus Christ and ecumenical unity," and voiced that the "decision is at the door: National Socialist *or* Christian" (ibid.). What he by no means wanted was "continued meretricious vegetation"; the only help now lies in "*whole truth* and *truthfulness*" (ibid.).

The dilemma of the Confessing Church was, among other things, that it was unwillingly shackled from the beginning in two ways: it originated in opposition to the German Christians, but for this very reason found itself, from year to year and from one situation to the next, more and more openly in opposition to the National Socialist State. On the other hand, it was by nature incapable of fundamentally doubting the validity of those in "authority." Its main activity consisted in permeating the national Evangelical churches—in a sometimes quasi-subversive manner—with Christian faith and Christian ethics. It attempted to bear witness within the National Socialist State and, if necessary, against it, to the Christian credo by opening the eyes of those in church institutions and church communities to the need of confessing faith and action. What is especially impressive in retrospect is that the Confessing Church had broad-based support from the individual church communities. One critical contemporary, a church historian, called these Confessing Church groups the "miracle of the Confessing Church."[15] On the whole, however, its history was one of courage commingled with timidity, protest, and accommodation to the situation. It was not concerned with opposing the State, but at least tried to accept the consequences of its profession of faith. Strictly speaking, however, it did not itself engage in battle within the church.

In any case, the concept of struggle within the church was and still is variously interpreted. It may be helpful to approach it from different points of view. It reflected not only a struggle within the Evangelical Church but also a campaign by the National Socialist State against the church(es) and the resistance of individual Christians—but not the institutional church—to the National Socialist State. It began immediately after the establishment of the National Socialist system of oppression and took place on various levels. Regarding the relationship between the State and the church, the State made a highly successful attempt to keep the church on a tight leash; where this did not succeed, the churches were simply eliminated from participation in public life by the National Socialists. In extreme cases, it led to imprisonment and the execution of Christians of all confessions. Within Protestantism, the struggle within the church took the form of an attempt by the Confessing Church to make the church Christ-like—in opposition to the German Christians and in spite of intervention by the State. Finally, within the Confessing Church it took the form of an attempt—eventually abandoned—to overcome various watered-down interpretations of "protesting" Protestantism for the sake of an effective confession of Christ in word and deed, both within and in opposition to a National Socialist State.

The "struggle of the church" did not raise much of an echo in German public life, and it was gradually forgotten during the war years. In addition, the activities and significance of the Confessing Church, already diminishing after 1937–1938, were much reduced as many of its ordained ministers, particularly younger ones, were called to military service. The end of the war meant the end of the Confessing Church as well, and as the directing body of the institutional Church gradually resumed authority, it naturally supplanted the Confessing Church's Council of Brethren as an effective element. Nevertheless, it remains a fact that Protestantism in Germany in the second half of the twentieth century has perhaps learned more from the errors and failures of the Confessing Church than from the short list of its successes.

How can Bonhoeffer's position regarding the Confessing Church best be summarized? He was both a driving force in it and a provocateur, one of its leading thinkers but also an outsider, an advocate and a critic. He belonged to a minority within the Confessing Church and at the same time worked loyally for it. As much as it pained him that it did not go further, he nevertheless felt close ties to it. *He* regarded it as being too tame, and *it* regarded him as being too radical. Even in the autumn of 1933, that is, before it actually began, he reflected with his friend Franz Hildebrandt whether it would not be more to the point to enter the unaffiliated Free Church, in light of their own church's silence regarding the Arian Laws.[16] A year later, he wrote to Erwin Sutz the lines quoted earlier: "It is high time to stop this theologically justified reticence regarding the actions of the State—which is after all nothing but cowardice. 'Open your mouth for those who cannot speak!' Who in the church still remembers this dictum, and that it is the minimum requirement of the Bible in such times? And then the questions of military weaponry and war, etc., etc." (DBW 13, 204–5).

In spite of many reservations with respect to the Confessing Church and in spite of many disappointments with regard to it, Bonhoeffer identified with it. It was "his" church, and he defended it with all his might against outside attacks. In a long essay entitled "On the Question of Community in the Church," which he wrote in 1936, he discussed at length the complicated inner relationship between the profession of faith, orthodoxy, and the communion of those within the church as viewed in the light of (church) history, theology, and the history of the contemporary world. Then, in the final section, he took up the implications of the highly moot thesis that "Whoever knowingly separates himself from the Confessing Church in Germany separates himself from salvation" (DBW 14, 676). Bonhoeffer makes it clear that, for him, the emphasis here is on the words "knowingly" and "factually," which is to be interpolated here. The intention of this sentence was not to claim perfection for the Confessing Church, but to assert the need for a church that *professed* itself as belonging to Christ alone, and thus clearly distinguished itself from an apolitical church, one against Christ. A church that feels itself obliged to National Socialist ideology is, for him, per se no longer church. Helmut Gollwitzer delivered the most pointed commentary on all the polemics against this dictum of Bonhoeffer's in a reply that appeared some months later in the same journal as Bonhoeffer's essay: "The criticism of some of Bonhoeffer's statements demonstrates how rare it is to read correctly and understand at one and the same time" (ibid., 681).

How much Bonhoeffer clung to the Confessing Church in spite of all reasons to the contrary is reflected in his diary and the letters he wrote during his second stay in the United States. They bear eloquent witness to the loneliness he felt, his trust in God, his doubt, and his inner liberation. In the early summer of 1939, when he had the opportunity to emigrate in light of the certainty of approaching war, he decided after periods of exhausting uncertainty to return home. Friends and colleagues wanted to make it possible for him to live and work in the United States. But "I feel irresistibly drawn back to the Confessing Church," he wrote to Erwin Sutz, a day before embarking (DBW 15, 215). He wrote to Reinhold Niebuhr: "My brothers in the Confessing Synod wanted me to go to the United States. Perhaps they were right in pressing me; but it was wrong of me to go" (ibid., 644). In a long letter to his friend Paul Lehmann, one of the primary organizers of his stay in the United States, he explains in detail his reasons for returning home: "I feel drawn to my brothers in their battle. . . . The political situation is terrible, and I have to be with my brothers when things come to a head" (ibid., 209).

It is possible that for Bonhoeffer the church was never so near to him as when he was physically farthest away from it. But he again became a lonely traveler at his own risk not long after his return.

17

And the Jews?

The day the synagogues were stormed, the church,
their sister, should have stood by them. That that
was not the case says everything. But where was I?

Reinhold Schneider

The following lines are taken from one of the reports written by Bonhoeffer and Friedrich Justus Perels, who was also executed shortly before the end of the war, in Berlin during October 1941: "Without any warning, the Berlin police or Gestapo appeared in apartments in the night of October 16 . . . and took the designated persons to the police station; from there they were transported in groups to the synagogue in Levetzow Street. . . . Destinations mentioned in rumors, if at all, were all somewhere to the East. . . . That these actions will continue is indicated by the fact that new eviction notices and lists reached the families on the evening of the 17th and the morning of the 18th of October. Since these additional families now know the implications of these missives, their despair is unparalleled" (DBW 16, 215ff.).

By documenting this state-ordered, systematic, and perfectly executed campaign of terror against Jews, Bonhoeffer and Perels, who was a legal advisor for the Confessing Church until 1940, hoped to prompt persons in influential positions to intervene; these were the "first reports about the beginning of mass deportation written by members of the inner-German opposition."[1] Copies of these reports also went to Bonhoeffer's brother-in-law Hans von Dohnanyi, and thus to the Resistance group within the military and the offices of ecumenical institutions in Geneva.

Like an arrow on a signpost, the phrase ". . . their despair is unparalleled" found within the remarkably noncommittal, factual language of the reports, points to the suffering that lay behind and before these human beings who as Jews were discriminated against, stigmatized, herded together, and finally destroyed. The intention was to reveal their suffering to those who were moving toward, or actually already in opposition to, this movement within their own countries and to the Christianity of the ecumenical world, that is, in the most familiar sense of the word itself, to the entire world.

Here, the arrow sets the direction for inquiry into the question of "Dietrich Bonhoeffer and the Jews."[2] What was the nature of his relationship and behavior toward the Jews in theory and practice? How did he feel about them, this man of extremes, this unique member of the Confessing Church, this man of two worlds; this conspirator whose journey into the Resistance ended in death? As is the case with other issues relative to Bonhoeffer's theological and ethical existence, for many persons of his own time he went too far, and for many of our day not far enough.

Within the context of this book, an outline of this issue can of necessity only be compressed; it cannot provide a response that is "short and to the point" or black-and-white. Bonhoeffer's theological conceptualization (that is, Bonhoeffer and the Jews in the sense of Judaism), and Bonhoeffer *in abstracto*, will be touched upon here only briefly.[3] Instead, we will discuss Bonhoeffer *in concreto*, in the sense of his attitude toward the Jews of his own time and his own place.

But first a few statements about Bonhoeffer and Judaism are in order. There are indications that his inner connection with the people of the Old Covenant and with Old Testament faith and thought grew increasingly intense during the course of his life, as well as more and more distant from the customary public understanding of the connection between Judaism and Christianity, between the Old and New Testaments. For instance, as early as 1933, when he wrote an introduction for the published version of his course "Creation and Fall," he concluded with the pointed claim "that God is One God in all of Holy Scripture; the church and the science of theology stand and fall with this belief" (DBW 3, 23). And 10 years later, in Berlin's Tegel Prison he repeats this claim nearly word for word: "It is after all one and the same God" (DBW 8, 277). For Bonhoeffer, "the Bible" was never the New Testament alone. Indeed, it is striking how frequently he refers to Old Testament texts in his sermons and explanations of biblical passages.[4] Especially during his time in Finkenwalde, the themes articulated in Judaism and Christianity were more or less constantly present for him. His last printed work, which appeared in 1940, was the brochure *The Biblical Book of Prayer: An Introduction to the Psalms.*

Bonhoeffer's closeness to the Old Testament became clearest to him during the time he spent in Tegel Prison. According to his own report, he read it two-and-a-half times during his first seven months there "and learned much" (DBW 8, 188). On the Second Sunday of Advent in

1943, Bonhoeffer wrote to Bethge that "I notice more and more, by the way, how much I think and feel in terms of the Old Testament; in fact, I have read the Old Testament much more than the New Testament in the past months" (ibid., 226). It also became fully clear to him during this time that his partiality for this world and his pious openness for life in this world—pious because it was anchored in God—had great affinity with the Old Testament: "This world may not be given up too soon. It is the link between the OT and the NT." A letter he wrote on June 27, 1944, also concludes with this conviction (ibid., 501). In the context of the often-quoted statement "God is in the midst of our life beyond it" found in the often-quoted letter dated April 30, Bonhoeffer writes: "The church is not found at the point where human powers fail—in borderline situations—but in the town marketplace. That's what the Old Testament tells us, and we read the New Testament much too little in light of the Old" (ibid., 408).

A study of Bonhoeffer's explicit relationship with the Jews can only be carried out while keeping in mind the warning issued by Pinchas Lapides, the great (to be emphasized here, Jewish!) religious philosopher who emphasized more than a quarter-century ago: "Whoever wishes today to analyze Bonhoeffer's position regarding the Jews and Judaism must above all avoid the hubris of retrospect."[5]

Bonhoeffer had the good fortune to grow up in a family that had a capacity for tolerance and an inclination to show respect and friendliness toward others, and he felt his family's protectiveness toward himself, especially later, in times of personal danger. It is impossible to point out too often the eminent meaning of this family for him. In his biography of Bonhoeffer's life, Bethge highlighted his immunity even in younger years to nationalistic and extreme positions of conservative thought.[6] Without going more deeply into Bonhoeffer's political consciousness, it can safely be said here that anti-Semitic tendencies were inevitably foreign to him from the very beginning: inevitably because persons of Jewish origin belonged to his family's circle of friends, and questions of discrimination simply never arose. For example, Bonhoeffer's twin sister married Gerhard Leibholz, whose non-Arian extraction, as it was termed at the time, later compelled them to emigrate to London. And his friend Franz Hildebrandt, a fellow theologian like himself who was likewise both active in, and in doubt about, the Confessing Church, was of Jewish extraction. He too eventually fled to England. So much for Bonhoeffer's personal credentials.

The year 1933 marked a turning point in German attitudes toward Jewish persons, and this of course not only for Bonhoeffer. He undertook several activities that year in response to what was at that time customarily

called the "Jewish question": he lectured and produced essays, memoranda, postulates, and leaflets. After the National Socialists came to power
in the spring of 1933, the latent anti-Semitism of the day, which was
rooted in a virulent strain of anti-Judaism, became the well-documented
State-legalized animosity and suppression of everything Jewish. In a mixture of the systemic and the arbitrary, the segregation of so-called non-
Arians and their persecution as a logical consequence was initiated.
"Spontaneous" boycotts of Jewish businesses were paralleled by passage of
the law entitled Law for Reestablishment of the System of Professional
Civil Servants, which contained the so-called Arian Paragraphs.

Within the Evangelical Church in particular, the question arose as
to whether or not this law and all its consequences applied to Evangelical Christians of Jewish origin who were also civil servants. More specifically, the question concerned baptized persons of Jewish extraction.
The German Christians, as already described, had already taken up their
positions; the Confessing Church was still in its birth pangs and actually
did not yet exist as such. Bonhoeffer, who was at that time an Assistant
Professor at the University of Berlin, saw the application of this law as a
"sign of complete division within the church,"[7] and in a letter he wrote
to his friend and colleague Erwin Sutz in Switzerland, he remarked that
the Jewish Question was causing a great deal of trouble for the church:
"those here who are usually the most sane have completely lost their
heads and their Bibles" (DBW 12, 58). He was busy preparing a lecture
in that month for a critical circle of pastors; the lecture appeared in the
summer of 1933 in two church journals, bearing the title "The Church
and the Jewish Question."

This text is one of the best examples of the way individual sentences
in Bonhoeffer's writings have been torn from their context and their
meaning distorted. Although his line of argumentation cannot be followed step by step here, we can present the main ideas.[8] But we must
remember that this text was written by a theologian of Lutheran provenience who had just reached the age of twenty-seven years. Although
he had been taught by Karl Barth, the reformed "patriarch" who viewed
the politics of the State with a critical eye, Bonhoeffer still thought to
some extent in very conventional theological terms. In spite of many
passages that seem problematic from our perspective today, Bonhoeffer's
observations regarding the so-called Jewish Question at that time are
marked "by their fundamentally theological character, their surprising
perspectives, and their clear decisiveness."[9]

It was, by the way and to anticipate somewhat, none other than the
eighty-eight-year-old Karl Barth who wrote to Bethge in 1967, after
the latter's biography of Bonhoeffer was published, that "Above all, it

was new to me that in 1933 and thereafter, Bonhoeffer was the first, and, in fact almost the only, one who tackled and dealt with the Jewish Question so squarely and energetically. I have long blamed myself for the fact that—at least during the struggle within the church—I did not also publicly declare it to be a decisive issue (for instance, in the two Barmer Declarations I wrote in 1934)"![10]

What then are the views Bonhoeffer expresses in the initial statements of his position made during the year 1933? He begins by identifying the one element that is new in the purely racist discrimination of the State against Jews: "The fact that a Jew is subjected by the State to special laws on the basis of his race alone, independently of his religious affiliation, is unique in history and poses for the theologian two new problems that must be treated separately" (DBW 12, 350). These problems are that it must now be asked (1) how does the church judge this action on the part of the State and what must its own response be? and (2) what position is the church to take toward baptized Jews in the individual churches? Both questions can only be clarified by examining the concept of "church." Bonhoeffer then goes on to describe in systematic and nuanced form the relationship between the church and the actions of the State. It becomes typical during the course of this description that he is reformulating basic theological pronouncements previously considered matter-of-course, only to relativize them promptly or even negate them through a "but" or an "on the one hand."

The first conclusion he draws is that it is the task of the church always to ask the State "whether it can take responsibility for its actions as being *legitimate for a State,* that is, as actions that bring about law and order rather than lawlessness and disorder" (DBW 12, 351). He then applies this question pointedly and concretely to the signs of the times (ibid., 352), namely, the signs evident in the spring of 1933: the church must put this question in all directness to the State *today* regarding the Jewish Question.

Viewed generally, the church has a number of alternatives in choosing its behavior toward the State. The first is to ask the question already mentioned, regarding the responsibility of the State. Here Bonhoeffer presents a sort of "three-stage plan" that bears a peculiar resemblance to his own biography. Stage 1: question the humanity and legitimacy of the State's actions (the key idea here is the church's mission as a watchman of society). Stage 2: help the victims of State despotism (the key idea here is political diaconate). And Stage 3: as *ultima ratio,* exercise direct political intervention (the key idea is active resistance).

Bonhoeffer elaborates Stage 2 only briefly (DBW 12, 353): "The church has an *unconditional* obligation to the victims of *each and every*

social order, even when they are *not* part of the Christian community";
he then quotes Gal 6:10: "Do good to *everyman*" (italics by the author).
This is followed by Bonhoeffer's unusually vivid—and later, rightfully
famous—statement that forms the culminating point of this entire text:
Stage 3 consists "not only of binding up the wounds of those who have
been run over by the wheel but of thrusting oneself between the spokes
of the wheel" (ibid.) in order to bring it to a halt.

Posthumously, "thrusting oneself between the spokes of the wheel"
almost became Bonhoeffer's insignia. In passing, it is interesting to note
that he may have used this image to reverse a statement made by the anti-
Semitic theologian Adolf Stoecker. And in his famous lecture "Politics
as Profession,"[11] Max Weber also used the image in the same sense as
Bonhoeffer. This formulation, which is apparently quite common, is
also found, for example, in Søren Kierkegaard's diary.[12]

Bonhoeffer emphasizes that the necessity of Stage 3—that is, of
thrusting oneself between the spokes of the wheel—is "to be decided
in each case by an 'Evangelical Council'"; but with respect to the Jewish Question, the conditions for Stages 1 and 2 are already fulfilled
"today" (DBW 12, 354). These conditions are met—at the latest—the
moment the State dictates to the churches, for example, that they are
to expel baptized Jewish persons from their ranks. Bonhoeffer makes it
unmistakably clear that the church in this case is *in statu confessionis,*
that is, in a situation demanding an ultimate profession of faith. Thus
he comes to the following conclusion: "Such expulsion remains . . . impossible for the church" (ibid., 357). Or, as he says even more emphatically during the further course of his reflections: "This is where the
church shows whether it is still the church or not" (ibid., 358).

Bonhoeffer speaks bluntly in his remarks that address "The Church
and the Jewish Question," especially with regard to the consequences for
a church that calls itself Christian. However, there is no doubt that par-
allel to these remarks—or even better, written between the lines—there
are also theological reflections that are difficult for modern Evangelical
theology, which views itself as a "theology after Auschwitz," to understand. It is all the more astonishing, on the other hand, that they contain
a statement that in those days approximated a critique of ideology: to
call the Jews "the Jewish race" is to establish a "biologically questionable
category" (DBW 12, 356).

Bonhoeffer's other initiatives with respect to the church and the Jews
in 1933 include a memorandum he wrote in English entitled "The Jewish-
Christian Question as *status confessionis,*" which he directed toward ecumenical decision-making bodies abroad; it contains the quintessence of
The Church and the Jewish Question. In that summer he also composed a

series of theses entitled "The Arian Paragraphs in the Church," where he dealt sharply with the church politics of the German Christians and concluded that endorsing implementation of the Arian Paragraphs was a "heresy" that destroyed the substance of the Church. As a consequence, truth could "only be served in one way, namely, by leaving the church" (DBW 12, 412).

During these months, Bonhoeffer was also working with others on the *Bethel Declaration*. This was a comprehensive profession of faith—a defense of faith within the church, as it were—occasioned by the differences in opinion that were emerging more and more bitterly within the Evangelical Church, between it and the so-called Faith Movement, that is, the German Christians. This text went through numerous revisions and peer reviews, until it finally emerged in highly watered-down form, in other words, without the original chapter on "The Church and the Jews." In protest, Bonhoeffer removed his name as co-author.

In the autumn of 1933, together with his friend Franz Hildebrandt, Bonhoeffer lodged a concrete protest against the pro-regime attitude of the official church body, heavily colored as it was by the German Christians. This took the form of a leaflet passed out at a National Synod in Luther's city of Wittenberg. The effort proved to be futile. But one result of his "bull-headed" insistence, just prior to that time, was the establishment of the Emergency Council of Pastors, from which the Confessing Church arose in the following year.[13] Bonhoeffer himself left Berlin and Germany in October in order to assume his first truly pastoral position at one of the German churches in London.

In the British metropolis, Bonhoeffer came in contact with the so-called Jewish Question on a completely different level: it was no longer a question of inner church politics, risks, and intrigues, or one of theological rights and impossibilities; instead, the issue became quite concrete and personal. London was already becoming a refuge for displaced persons from Germany, and the German communities, including Bonhoeffer, had more than enough opportunities to experience the meaning of "binding the wounds of whose who fall under the wheels." In 1935 he returned to Germany in order to take over the direction of one of the first Preaching Seminaries of the Confessing Church. Bonhoeffer's thought in the years that followed led more and more in the direction of a theologically-based conviction that the time had now come literally to ward off disaster by instigating the above-mentioned Stage 3, that is, by "thrusting oneself between the spokes of the wheel." He also became convinced that baptized Jews had long ceased to be the central issue.

A dictum of Bonhoeffer, the protesting Protestant "troublemaker," later became famous, for it expresses his attitude regarding the Jewish

Question *as well as* what might be called the Christian Question: "Only he who raises his voice for the Jews should be allowed to sing Gregorian as well."[14] For a better understanding of the *Sitz im Leben* of this saying, which is now almost a household word, we should note that, without a doubt, he uttered it with the curates of the Confessing Church's "illegal" Preaching Seminary in mind. In the middle of the 1930s they were practicing, perhaps with more gusto than skill, the melodies of Gregorian chant. He may also have been thinking of the members of the Berneuchen Movement, who believed that their own salvation and that of the church lay in a renaissance and intensification of the liturgical life of the church. And he was certainly thinking in principle of a *conditio sine qua non* for Christians of all times, that is, as an absolutely essential condition for the spiritual life that can only be legitimated by simultaneous "Pro-Test," that is, by giving oneself for others. Concretely in Bonhoeffer's day: for the Jews. And today?

This saying of Bonhoeffer's—"Only he who raises his voice for the Jews should be allowed to sing Gregorian as well"—is highly relevant today in two respects. Even in a time of new interior life and spirituality, Christian faith must always and *also* consist in "raising one's voice for the Jews," although in later decades this has become more a formality than it was in Bonhoeffer's time. Yet even today, it is not *merely* a formality, as recent events have taught us: Paul Spiegel, the Chairman of the Central Committee of Jews in Germany, reports that after the Düsseldorf synagogue was set on fire in the autumn of 2000, he was asked by Jews whether it was not time to leave Germany.

Bonhoeffer's statement, "Only he who raises his voice for the Jews should be allowed to sing Gregorian as well," reflects his "weakness" for a passage in the Old Testament that he often quoted: "Open your mouth for those who cannot speak!" ("and for all who are abandoned," as Luther's translation continues the passage in Prov 31:8). For Bonhoeffer, public advocacy for those who are compelled to maintain silence was one of the basic duties of Christian life and the life of the church. Christianity's silence during his time was for him the heart of its failure to act as church. It was also one of the reasons he finally embarked in 1940 on the narrow path of conspiracy, consciously accepting isolation even within his own church. It was while living in this inner and outer isolation that he continued to write his *Ethics,* up to the time of his imprisonment.

The manuscripts of the years 1940–1941 contain a confession of the church's guilt. "Almost no other text is to be recommended as highly for meditation on the German catastrophe and its consequences as this one," wrote the theologian Ernst Lange twenty-five years later.[15]

Bonhoeffer wrote: "The church . . . remained silent when its duty was to cry out, because the blood of the innocent was crying out to heaven. It did not find the right words in the right way at the right time. . . . The church confesses that it saw the arbitrary use of brutal force, the outer and inner suffering of countless innocent human beings, oppression, hatred, and murder without finding a way to hurry to their aid. It has incurred guilt for the life of the Weakest and Most Defenseless of the Brethren of Jesus Christ" (DBW 6, 129–30). The unusual capitalization here is explained by the fact that the final sentence was added subsequently by Bonhoeffer. In particular, Bethge has demonstrated more than once that Bonhoeffer was using the phrase "Brethren of Jesus Christ" at that time to refer to Jews. In another passage in his *Ethics*, for example, Bonhoeffer wrote pointedly in this sense: "To cast the Jews out of Western society is of necessity to cast out Christ; for Jesus Christ was a Jew" (ibid., 95).

By this time—we need only remember the deportation reports from the autumn of 1941—Bonhoeffer had irrevocably crossed the threshold into a double existence of subversion. A thorough study of his attitude toward the Jews shows that "it was the escalation of discrimination against the Jews that prompted Bonhoeffer to escalate his own opposition toward the NS-State into active resistance."[16] It was at this time that he deliberately assisted others, such as Charlotte Friedenthal, in fleeing, thus participating in the activity that has gone into the history books as Operation Seven.[17]

What lies behind this? Charlotte Friedenthal, an Evangelical Christian of Jewish extraction, was one of the most active and persistent members of the Confessing Church in Berlin. She was the driving force behind many initiatives that were of a social, charitable, and also theological nature; as a very close colleague of the Spandau Superintendent Martin Albertz, a man of integrity and thoroughness, she acted more or less as the "business manager" for the directors of the Confessing Church. In the autumn of 1941 there was reason to fear that she too would be deported. At the intervention of Bonhoeffer, among others, however, it proved possible through Swiss "church channels," especially at the request of Karl Barth, to provide her with a visa for travel abroad. In the meantime, however, a law was enacted that forbade Jewish persons to leave Germany for any reason whatever, so her permission to reside in Switzerland became useless. From the beginning of 1942, she was compelled to live in a Jew House, and to expect deportation as inevitable. At Bonhoeffer's request, Charlotte Friedenthal was placed under military protection by Hans von Dohnanyi, and it was only this that made it possible to strike her name more than once from the "orderly list" of those to be deported. The conspirators then hit upon a new, somewhat grotesque, and risky idea: Charlotte Friedenthal should leave Germany as part of Operation Seven.

The idea was "grotesque" inasmuch as the whole of Operation Seven was grotesque in nature. Hans von Dohnanyi, with the knowledge and support of Admiral Canaris, the head of military intelligence, set in motion a hazardous plan to make it possible for a group consisting initially of seven persons of Jewish extraction to flee the confines of the Sovereign State. The number doubled as planning continued. Officially, these persons were designated as agents of the military intelligence service who were to travel "legally" via Switzerland to South America for corresponding activities there. Preparations and planning for this dangerous undertaking required a high degree of care and deception, in order to cover completely all bureaucratic tracks, while avoiding any breath of suspicion on the part of the Gestapo and the Schutzstaffel (SS), and to ensure financial security for the "travelers abroad" once they were in Switzerland.

Their detailed reports on what they experienced in those months in 1942 reveal moments of deepest dismay and unrest, maximum tension and humiliation, but also moments when they encountered liberating, compassionate, and reliable responses they had hardly dared to hope for. The Star of David, for example, was mentioned time and again: did the law requiring Jews to wear it apply to them as well, or was it necessary for them by all means to avoid doing so as "V-agents" of military intelligence? Then, after crossing the border, how should one respond to the friendly but firm request in Switzerland to take it off once and for all? There was the abrupt refusal of one of the group members the first time he was confronted concretely with the idea that he must go in disguise and who, failing to understand that it was no more than that, asserted he could never work as a representative of this government office, not even for the sake of being able to leave.

In short, Charlotte Friedenthal, officially an agent of Operation Seven, boarded the night train from Berlin to Basel on September 4, 1942, and the main group followed on the night of September 29. A final straggler followed in mid-December 1942, thus bringing the refugee project Operation Seven to a successful conclusion. In all, fourteen persons were rescued from the jaws of death by genocide, and Bonhoeffer's intermediation was of decisive importance for one of them—namely, Charlotte Friedenthal.

Both Hans von Dohnanyi and Dietrich Bonhoeffer were arrested the following year, on April 5, 1943. Both were executed on April 9, 1945—von Dohnanyi in the concentration camp in Sachsenhausen, Bonhoeffer in the concentration camp in Flossenbürg. The inquest into

Operation Seven played an important role in the interrogation of both men, as did, by the way, their attempts to help a relative of Friedrich Justus Perels, the above-mentioned co-author of the deportation reports. His uncle, who was also of Jewish descent, was imprisoned at the time in a so-called internment camp in Gurs in Southern France, near the Pyrenees. Although unsuccessful at first, Bonhoeffer was eventually able to gain information about Gurs from the Ecumenical Fugitive Office in Geneva; he then turned for help to von Dohnanyi, who managed to have money, papers, medicine, and clothing smuggled into the camp. Emil Perels survived the genocide of the war.

How best to sum up Dietrich Bonhoeffer's stance regarding the Jews? In view of the initial wave of discrimination against them, followed by the application of open persecution, a distinction must be made. What is certain is that Bonhoeffer's attention was first caught by the situation of Jews within the church, and that in spite of all the new theological directions he ventured into, he was a man faithful to the traditions of the church, especially Lutheran thought, and was unable to rise above this as quickly and as thoroughly as we perhaps might wish in retrospect. But what is also certain is that it was precisely Bonhoeffer who suffered most from the fact that the church during those years thought only of saving its own neck. Writing in Tegel Prison at the beginning of August 1944, he noted the following in his "Draft for a Paper": "Very much burdened and weighed down by thoughts about tradition. The stumbling block: the church thinks only of self-defense. Risks nothing for others" (DBW 8, 558). He had witnessed that the Christian church proves itself to be the church of Christ by intervening with no thought for itself on behalf of others. In the draft just mentioned he came to the following conclusion (ibid., 560): "church is the church only when it is for others."[18]

In terms of promptness, clarity, and decisiveness, Bonhoeffer's reaction to the so-called Jewish Question was almost seismographic—far more so than the response made by most of his Protestant contemporaries. For him, it was a question of the profession of Christianity, and by the spring of 1933 he had already begun to focus the church's attention on this. Years later, at the beginning of the 1940s, when working on the *Ethics,* he wrote: "It is the Jew who keeps the question of Christ open" (DBW 6, 95). Bonhoeffer made this sentiment clear to others through his concrete work in the Confessing Church, through the "illegal" training of young theologians in that church, and as a trailblazer of ecumenical unity. As a consequence of his now fully independent theological thought and as an unarmed combatant, so to speak, in the resistance, he made full use of the extensive connections he formed during his earlier ecumenical work, in order to pass on information to the rest of the world and initiate individual actions for providing assistance.

It is possible that, from today's point of view, Bonhoeffer did little, perhaps too little, for the Jews of his time. For Charlotte Friedenthal, it was a great deal. In any case, it must be said of Bonhoeffer that "He was one of the few who wormed their way out of complicity with those promoting the 'final solution.' That makes him one of the irreplaceable links to the victims, the survivors, and the inheritors of the Holocaust."[19]

18

Conspiracy, Not Collaboration

Without the feeling of oneness with those in danger
I would be a hopeless fugitive from reality.

Jean Amery

It is not only the "hubris of retrospect" Pinchas Lapide warned
against[1] that must be avoided in attempting to sketch Bonhoeffer's
thought; it is equally dangerous to equate today's view of reality with
that of his day. We who look back tend to project involuntarily points of
view and interpretations onto events of the past, even reconstructing
whole scenes and scenarios which were not (yet) elements of the time.

For example, we have come to speak matter-of-factly about Dietrich
Bonhoeffer's determined entrance into the Resistance. That is how it
appears to us in retrospect. But Emmi Bonhoeffer, the widow of his
brother Klaus, reports that she first heard the term "Resistance Movement" in 1947 in Switzerland: "My brother-in-law in Zurich said to me,
'Hopefully, things will be a little easier for you now, inasmuch as your
husband died in the Resistance.' 'In what?' I asked. 'In the Resistance.
That's what it is called here.' I swallowed hard and said, 'Yes, you could
put it that way.' Why was the term new to me? Because none of us had
heard of it."[2] Nevertheless it was a fact, even if not perceived or designated as such. In the consciousness of those involved, however, it
was certainly perceived in another way. The picture of the Resistance
Movement in National Socialism usually conveyed to us is one of lonely,
heroic resolves formed on firmly identifiable dates, which then led irresistibly into the Underground. In reality, the Resistance Movement
was different, which by no means lessens the deep respect we have for it
today, even though we may have arranged our lives with resigned com-
fortableness in a situation of incomparably greater political freedom.

The outlines of Dietrich Bonhoeffer's concrete life and thought already sketched here make it clear that what impelled him to political action and the path of resistance was not something of a political nature,
but something theological. This too does not lessen his standing in our

eyes; quite the contrary! It is precisely here that we find the element that later had such a liberating effect on the ongoing work of the church and theology: resistance was—and still is—possible in a State founded on injustice, inhumanity, and force, not only *in spite of* Christian faith but also *as a consequence of* Christian faith.

With regard to Bonhoeffer, it may be more appropriate to say that he refused allegiance to a system of terror in his time, rather than unreflectively applying to him the resounding title of "resistance fighter." The latter implies a heroic decision and a militant attitude, and both were foreign to Bonhoeffer. Rather, his decision began with involuntary collaboration in the form of intense, open exchanges of opinion in the home of his birth family. Above all, he became at least partially informed about the existence, intentions, and methods of a resistance group within the military intelligence service through discussions with his brother-in-law, Hans von Dohnanyi (a study of the role of the women in this "dynasty" is sorely needed!). In order to arrive at a proper understanding of the situation, it is important to understand that "the small reserves of mutual trust that are indispensable for discussion and decision-making in a resistance movement were most likely to exist within the circles of the family, and among old school and university friends";[3] it was—above all—the (extended) middle-class family, in the wider sense, that proved its value "as a unit of interaction and loyalty."[4] It is therefore no coincidence that Ernst Kaltenbrunner, the SS jurist and later director of the Head Office for Security in the Reich, referred in his report of October 1944 to the "oppositional attitude of the entire clan."[5]

It is of course more in connection with Dietrich Bonhoeffer than with the other members of his family that questions arise concerning the justification for and necessity of open resistance on the part of Christians against the National Socialist State, including possible motives and goals, and the shape it actually took. These are among the most hotly disputed questions that pertain to the relationship between church and State (not only in that day). The basic complex of associated problems justified by and justifiable for Christian reasons cannot, of course, be taken up here. Suffice it to say that the churches' attention, including that of the Confessing Church, tended to be fixed on issues of self-preservation. Above all others they were unworthy servants not only when confronted with the genocide of European Jews, but also when faced with the persecution and annihilation of many other groups of human beings, programs of euthanasia, the conduct of war, etc.

The Christian churches never issued a call for direct resistance against a State that was trampling under foot the image of mankind.

They were, like many other institutions in German society, involuntary helpmates of the National Socialist system of oppression, unable or unwilling to cast doubt on the wheelings and dealings of official power. In particular, those who followed the Protestant Lutheran tradition found it wearisome and fateful—if not impossible—to stand up against the State.

Nevertheless there were Christians within the churches of both confessions who rendered passive or even active resistance against National Socialism, with full awareness of the fact that this was life-endangering. Rare as the passive enduring of situations involving persecution had become in the history of Christianity since the time of the catacombs, how much more seldom had the churches experienced the necessity for passive or active resistance against the State! Thus it also came about in the Third Reich that Christians only rarely opposed the State of their own accord; the usual pattern was to travel a roundabout way from the unavoidable need for self-defense to intercession for others who were persecuted, and in this way finally to arrive at opposition against the State. Thus their resistance was not primarily political in character but was motivated by their faith, and only thereafter allied with political resistance. Many remained nameless. One who did not was Dietrich Bonhoeffer.

We will not delve into the question of how and where Bonhoeffer should be integrated into the spectrum of the Resistance in Germany here, for a great deal of historical-critical research already exists on the subject, along with much infighting among historians concerning the best way to describe it. Since the 1980s, scholars who study resistance movements have come to use the term "national-conservative resistance"[6] for civilian resistance, especially resistance against the military use of force; the idea is to use this approximate term as a lowest common denominator, so to speak, for forms that are widely disparate in character.[7]

The resistance group that took shape within the Office of Foreign Affairs and Intelligence in the High Command of the Wehrmacht, directed by Admiral Wilhelm Canaris, experienced similar difficulties with nomenclature. The group included Ludwig Beck, Hans Oster, Hans von Dohnanyi and, beginning in the autumn of 1940, Dietrich Bonhoeffer as well. Bonhoeffer scholars have suggested this group be called the Republican-Protestant Group,[8] assuming that labels such as "republican" or "liberal-conservative" are at all necessary.[9]

Regardless of the way this question is resolved, it is important to note that the basic political and social attitudes of the resistance group Bonhoeffer joined did not necessarily correspond to later views of parliamentary government or direct democracy: they were elitist and aristocratic in nature. Nor did the group's motivation correspond to democratic standards of our own day. For us to *acknowledge* this is justifiable; to turn it into an *accusation* is not. Its members themselves made no political claims. During one of Hans von Dohnanyi's last visits with his wife Christine in prison, he said to her, "Dietrich and I were certainly not acting as politicians. It was simply the inevitable response any honorable human being would make."[10]

It is uncontested that the middle-class origins of most of the members quite naturally gave the group its basically conservative character. But in spite of all the conservative patterns of thought, in the case of the "Bonhoeffer-Dohnanyi Circle"—the name bestowed on the group that arose among the members and friends of the Bonhoeffer family in Marienburger Allee in Berlin—a civil-liberal strain predominated. This was the seedbed for the group's opposition to the National Socialist State—as well as its readiness to venture into the danger of opposition! From the inner circle of the family alone, Dietrich Bonhoeffer, his brother Klaus, his brother-in-law Rüdiger Schleicher, and Hans von Dohnanyi, all lost their lives because of their participation in the Resistance. In Dietrich Bonhoeffer's case in particular, albeit not for him alone, the actual political consequences far exceeded the bounds of his originally conservative political thought.[11]

In any case, appellations such as "civil" resistance are not particularly helpful here, now that they have become watered down into more or less negative clichés: "The problem of 'entente' between the National Socialist Movement and the established power elite, together with national-conservative elements, has been strongly emphasized by . . . scholars who study the Resistance; however, the problem requires . . . very careful differentiation and should in no case prompt generalized conclusions about 'civil' resistance."[12] The important fact is that one such as Dietrich Bonhoeffer distanced himself from complicity and collaboration with those in power, that he refused to be a part of it, that he was thus against it, and that he knew full well that he was thus risking his life.

His actual role in the Resistance group within military intelligence circles can be sketched only briefly here. He was assigned to the Munich representative of the intelligence as a "V-man" (German: "Vertrauensmann," undercover agent) but remained in close contact with the "Berliners." In what sort of activities did this opponent of the regime engage? His was a type of practical resistance "in which attempts to prevent crime and help persecuted individuals were carried out with the same energy and willingness to take risks as preparations for the coup or the 'post-Hitler' era."[13]

The first direct contact between Bonhoeffer and the Resistance, apart from his constant contact with Hans von Dohnanyi, had already taken place in 1938. Beginning in the autumn of 1940, he functioned officially as one of its informants; to this end he was exempted from military service and, in the disguise of a courier, was able to perform "courier" services of a quite different sort. His trips to Switzerland, Scandinavia, and Italy served to establish and/or maintain contact with Resistance groups abroad and to carry out various types of assistance.

It will suffice to mention here only a few examples of Bonhoeffer's activity during that time. Bonhoeffer made a statement in the autumn of 1941 that emphasizes his realistic evaluation of the situation and his own point of view with regard to it: "Only the military itself is capable of removing the present regime from power: every workers' rebellion is bloodily quelled by the SS" (DBW 16, 537). Another statement often quoted is the response Bonhoeffer made to Willem Visser't Hooft from Holland, later the General Secretary of the Ecumenical Council of Churches, who asked him what he prayed for under the current circumstances. According to his biographer, Bonhoeffer responded, "If you really want to know, I am praying for the defeat of my country: I believe that is the only way to pay for all the suffering my country has caused in the world."[14]

In retrospect, one of the most moving examples of the kind of conspiracy Bonhoeffer engaged in was his last meeting with Bishop Bell in the summer of 1942, in the Swedish town of Sigtuna. During the meeting Bonhoeffer informed the English bishop in detail of the group's plan for a coup, along with names, projects, goals of the group, and its vision of a German State after the putsch and the war; he then asked the bishop to pass on this information to his government. An extensive historical and political study of "Sigtuna and its implications" could easily be carried out, quite apart from the dramatic, detailed reconstruction of the events themselves![15]

The motivation, stages, and stations that led Bonhoeffer into the Resistance, as well as his role in that group, have been published in detail in the third and last part of Bethge's biography, and in various other works by Bethge.[16] In addition, broad-based monographies exist,[17] along with explanatory documentation collected for the fiftieth anniversary of Bonhoeffer's death.[18] A wealth of source material covering the years 1940 to 1945 is also available in the sixteenth volume of *Dietrich Bonhoeffer: Works.*

Given the goal of the present work, only a few of his own statements will be given as a way of facilitating insight into the way he himself perceived the road he traveled. His reasons for embarking on this road can be left aside; instead, the accent here is on the experiences and conflicts that resulted from this choice, since everything mentioned up to this point makes it clear that Bonhoeffer's faith in God, in the discipleship of Christ, and his hope in the reign of the reality of the Holy Spirit, made it impossible for him to collaborate with inhumanity. He was able to speak out of love for the world, for mankind, and for life in this world, as an advocate not of war but of peace. Thus, faced with the persecution of the brothers and sisters of the Nazarene, he went underground and lived a double existence that eventually cost him his life.

One problem, however, hampers the attempt to track his understanding of himself as a "resister" and his understanding of the practice of resistance (keeping well in mind that this practice involves subversive action!): direct utterances from Bonhoeffer's own pen are almost nonexistent. We do have, however, one essay entitled "The Last 10 Years," written at the turn of the year 1942. And scattered utterances spoken by Bonhoeffer in the years previous foreshadow his later affinity for opposition and resistance, at least when interpreted in retrospect. (The previous chapters have already dealt with the topic of this later affinity in his political ethics.)

Matters in Germany had already reached a critical point in the restless early summer of 1932, when Bonhoeffer preached a sermon in the Kaiser-Wilhelm Memorial Church in Berlin. Referring to the admonition in Colossians to "seek that which is above, not that which is below" it is as if he were turning the text inside out and interpreting it to emphasize that Christians may indeed look for that "which is on earth"—precisely because they are Christians! Playing off of Nietzsche's critique of Christianity and Marx's dictum about religion as the opiate of the masses, he asks "whether we Christians have the strength to witness to the world that we are not daydreamers with castles in the clouds; that we do not simply accept things as they are; that our faith is indeed not an opiate that leaves us satisfied in the midst of an unjust world. Instead, we protest all the more persistently and single-mindedly on this earth, precisely because we look for that which is above. We protest in word and deed . . ."! (DBW 11, 446).

Many passages in this sermon, by the way, relativize and reverse the superficial image of Bonhoeffer as a conservative—if not reactionary—thinker (see above). This sermon also reflects his lucid awareness of the coming, inevitable clash with those seeking power in Germany: "Must it be the case that Christianity, which was once so tremendously revolutionary in character, now remains conservative for all time? That every new movement must blaze its own trail without help from the church, and that it always dawns upon the church twenty years later for the first time what has actually happened? If so, then we need not be surprised if a time again comes for our church when the blood of martyrs is required" (DBW 11, 446). The exhortation to seek what is above can mislead us to a "betrayal of the earth," to a spurious sense of being in God's hands, so that we erroneously come to rest "in the midst of the most flagrant injustices in the world" (ibid., 448).

For Bonhoeffer, there was no question of trying to withdraw, either through escape into an inner world or through flight into the outer world. In a letter he wrote to Reinhold Niebuhr, explaining his reasons for returning to Germany in the summer of 1939, he emphasized: "I must be present to live through this difficult epoch of our national history with the Christians of Germany. I will have no right to work for the restoration of Christian life in Germany after the war, unless I share the trials of these times with my people" (DBW 15, 644).

As a motif, the fatality of withdrawing into a private world surfaces again in the section of Bonhoeffer's *Ethics* entitled "Ethics as Creation," where he describes various forms of contempt for other human beings. We succumb, he says, to the temptation to be contemptuous of other human beings when we see through the mechanisms of the world and consequently "withdraw out of disgust for others, leaving them to their own devices, preferring to tend our own gardens rather than be part of a community in public life" (DBW 6, 73). This is also true, he remarks as an aside, when we tend toward tyrannical contempt for others. Such contempt for others, he writes, is "perhaps more high-class and more honest, but it is also less fruitful, less active. It can no more survive God's Incarnation than the tyrannical form of contempt for others. He who is contemptuous of others despises what God has loved; indeed, he despises the very figure of the God who has become man" (ibid.).

This is probably the key point that moved Bonhoeffer to join the political opposition. The only alternative left to him personally, given his background and the actual situation, was collaboration with what later came to be called the National-Conservative Resistance. This movement united individuals with very different points of view: "In many respects these were outsiders . . . who, in spite of unspeakably difficult conditions and in full awareness of the apparent hopelessness of the task, had decided to try to bring down the government as a way of crying 'halt!' to the tyranny of absolute inhumanity that was embodied by Hitler, while the vast majority of the nation and its elite groups remained silent."[19] It should be noted that other actual and potential resistance groups had been neutralized at an early date, or were doomed to failure from the beginning.

Bonhoeffer did not find it easy to make the decision to engage in conspiracy as a means of opposing the tyranny of contempt for others. What is notable about this decision from today's point of view is rather *how much* difficulty he had in making it: he acted in full awareness of wrongdoing and guilt, not at all self-righteously or complacently, or as if what he intended to do were matter-of-course. Collaboration—even at a distance and indirectly—in putsch plans that necessitated the deliberate use of force in order to succeed was equivalent, for him, to disobedience of God's commandments.

The dilemma Bonhoeffer faced was that he would incur guilt not only if he stood idly by as a spectator of violence *but also* if he participated even indirectly in putsch plans, violence, and concrete actions designed to take human life while in the guise of an agent of military intelligence. Even though his decision arose out of ultimate necessity, and was as such the *ultima ratio,* in his eyes it was and remained disobedience. Such disobedience, however, remained the only way for him to obey God!

His ethics of responsibility as a guideline for living made him willing to accept responsibility for this deliberate incurrence of guilt, without desiring to turn it into a new principle of action. He could not deny that an "exceptional, borderline situation was coming into being that required the application of violence [as] *ultima ratio*" (DBW 6, 274). However, this borderline situation and its guilt remained for him a unique exception, precisely as his own decision to collaborate in conspiracy, and the guilt it involved, was and remained for him likewise a borderline case, a unique exception.

This grappling with *complicité,* with entrapment in the meshes of guilt and a conscious willingness to accept guilt, is expressed in many different contexts in his *Ethics.*[20] Bonhoeffer wrestled with these ideas, sometimes without explicitly mentioning them, in distinguishing between an ethics of attitude and responsibility, or between an ethics of principles and situations, or when dealing with matters of conscience, with the limitations of ethical action and its correspondence with reality, and with the very real questions of truth, truthfulness, and a life lived according to basic patterns of responsibility *and* freedom. He wrestled with striking intensity, and found his answers in the person and glad tidings of Jesus Christ.

Only *one* example of how these glad tidings gave him direction as he faced the undeniable guilt incurred by man is the following passage from his manuscript "The Structure of Responsible Life": "The wellspring of my conscience and its guiding light is not any law, but the living God and living human beings as I encounter them in Jesus Christ. Jesus became a Law-breaker for the sake of God and man. . . . Thus

Jesus Christ liberates conscience for the service of God and neighbor; He liberates conscience precisely at the point where man enters the community of human guilt. . . . Unlike a conscience that is bound to the Law, the liberated conscience is not fearful; rather, it is wide open for the neighbor in real need. Thus in Christ, it can be at peace with the responsibility of bearing guilt for the sake of a neighbor" (DBW 6, 279).

These difficulties are also discussed in the one extant fragment we have from his essay entitled "What Does It Mean to Tell the Truth?" (DBW 16, 619ff.). He wrote this essay during his first autumn in prison, when he was in a situation that forced him constantly to tell lies "for the sake of his neighbor," that is, for his fellow conspirators already in prison (including for a time his sister Christine von Dohnanyi), for those still at large, and in order to save his own life. We who look back often find it difficult to realize how much Bonhoeffer suffered for his involvement with the Resistance, and how this constantly led him to reflect on the complex problems associated with guilt.

This soul-searching is mirrored in his famous essay entitled "The Last 10 Years," which he wrote at the turn of the year 1942–1943 for his fellow travelers—Bethge, von Dohnanyi, and Oster—in order to take stock, as it were, of the previous ten years; the same essay was later used as a preface for his notes and letters from prison. The essay contains reflections of a personal, political, social, and theological nature that are at times almost prophetic in their impact, as well as intellectually astute and frighteningly up-to-date. What is unusual about this text (more precisely, this series of individual vignettes) is the plethora of thought-provoking statements it contains, quite apart from the concrete intention and situation in which it was written.

The text contains numerous statements Bonhoeffer made that are striking in their relevance, not only for his own time *but for ours as well.* For example, he describes with crystal clarity the potential danger of the "good old" German virtues: "The man of duty will end up doing his duty to the devil as well," he warns (DBW 8, 22). Under the heading "Civil Courage," he concludes: "It was only a question of time before it became clear that Germans are missing one all-important basic insight: the need for free, responsible action, even at the cost of one's career and assignments" (ibid., 24). Life, he says, plays itself out not only in the area of personal responsibility but also in generational interplay: Bonhoeffer demands that the last question asked by a human being who has a sense of responsibility should not be "how I can get out of this heroically, but rather [how] future generations are to survive" (ibid., 25). This can be heard against a different background but with no less validity in our own day. The section Bonhoeffer entitled "On Stupefaction" could not be more relevant for our own time of multi- and mass media (self-) brain-washing. It is a realistic commentary on conditions that existed in his own time, as well as ours today.

This is also true of what is probably the focal passage of the entire essay: "Standing idly by and observing lethargically are not Christian attitudes. The Christian is called first and foremost to take action and to suffer, not by his own personal sufferings but by those of his brethren, for whom Christ suffered" (DBW 8, 34). The response to the self-critical question Bonhoeffer posed to himself, to his friends at that time, and to us today remains unchanged: "We have witnessed evil and remain silent, . . . our experience has led us to mistrust others, so that we often withhold the truth and the open words we owe them. Unbearable conflicts wear us down or perhaps even make us cynical—are we still of any use?" (ibid., 38). These lines express the conflict of conscience and identity constantly suffered by those involved in the conspiracy.

In particular, those who opposed the regime from within the German Central Intelligence Agency were compelled by circumstances "not only to willingly assume a high degree of personal risk but also to do violence in public to their own convictions"; and this "to a far greater degree than was required of those who in any case inwardly oppose dictatorship."[21] The identity crises that are a normal part of secret service activity were aggravated in their case by their plans for a putsch.

Also undeniable is the fact that this text, "The Last 10 Years," contains statements by Bonhoeffer that are almost bound to rub us the wrong way at first glance—and perhaps at the second as well. Passages from the section entitled "A Feeling for Quality" come to mind, where he describes "mob" tendencies and "rabble-rousing," finally arriving at the following conclusion: "In other eras it was perhaps right for Christianity to bear witness to the equality of all human beings; but today Christianity must passionately defend respect for the private sphere and human quality" (DBW 8, 32). Still, this is the same Bonhoeffer who concluded in another text, entitled "The View from Below," which was also probably written at the end of 1942 and later tacked onto the essay discussed here: "It remains an experience of incomparable value that we have learned at some point to see the great events of world history from below—that is, from the perspective of those disowned, mistrusted, badly treated, deprived of power, oppressed and derided; in brief, those who suffer" (ibid., 38).

The feelings and insights underlying these lines took on fullest meaning for him in a previously unknown and—in the end—irrevocable manner, with his arrest on April 5, 1943.

19

Fascination of a Fragment:
Resistance and Surrender

Who knows
what God can make of the shards of our lives
if we give them entirely over to Him.

Blaise Pascal

Caesuras in the life of a human being are always perceived and interpreted in all their poignancy and implications only by that person.
Naturally, there are caesuras whose significance is indeed recognized by
others; but even in that case, their deeper dimensions are comprehended
only to a very limited degree. Bonhoeffer's arrest on April 5, 1943 was
such a caesura.

It is not possible here even approximately to do justice to the
psychological aspects of this last phase of his life. Bethge's biography
contains appropriately reserved but nevertheless highly instructive details. Moreover, a study published in the 1980s undertook with empathy
and competence the task of bridging the gap between psychological and
theological commentary—an approach again taken up in the background material of the newly revised edition of *Resistance and Surrender*
within *Dietrich Bonhoeffer: Works.*[1]

The inner and outer stresses Bonhoeffer was exposed to are indicated here only briefly but must always be understood as if written in invisible ink between the lines of his letters, texts, and other notes from
prison. He was abruptly catapulted out of all the existing relationships of
his life, out of his work and career, his love and friendships, his parents'
home and his family, his church and the Resistance as well. What lay
before him was the unknown: court trial, interrogation, sentencing—
ending in what? Fear of torture. Fear of giving in. Fear of betraying
accomplices in the conspiracy or of exposing friends and family to
persecution and arrest. Fear for himself. For his own existence in the
present and future. Fear of losing himself. Fear of despairing. Hope of

contact with the outer world. Of contact with fellow prisoners from the circle of conspirators. Hope of success in the assassination and putsch attempts, which had been futile up to that time. Hope for an "afterwards"—after removal of the National Socialist regime from power, after release from prison, after the end of the war.

During the first two weeks Bonhoeffer was subjected to extreme prison conditions that were specifically designed to break him down; his *Incarceration Report after One Year in Tegel Prison* (DBW 8, 380ff.) is a dispassionate record of his experiences during this period of solitary confinement, which made a joke of any human dignity. His living conditions improved thereafter: Paul von Hase, the town commandant with responsibility for the German army's Tegel Detention and Interrogation Prison, who was later involved in the assassination attempt on July 20, 1944 and executed as a consequence, was Bonhoeffer's uncle. He was able to bring about some easement of Bonhoeffer's prison conditions. Nevertheless Bonhoeffer remained under great duress. "Prison shock" and "prison trauma" are the scientific terms used for such experiences. A violent interruption of one's previous existence in the form of outward changes can gravely endanger one's inner existence, that is, one's identity. The perception of oneself as living and moving in a halfway reliable continuum of time and space begins to break down. The pillars of one's own world no longer provide support.

Some of Bonhoeffer's notes written in May 1943 speak for themselves: "Separation from others, from work, from the past, from the future, from honor, from God" (DBW 8, 60–61). And "continuity broken off with the past and the future . . . suicide, not from feelings of guilt but because basically I am already dead; bottom line; that's it" (ibid., 64). Eberhard Bethge stresses the importance of viewing this mention of suicide with some reservation—at least partially—in view of the possibility of torture. To view suicide as a way of directly avoiding any possible betrayal of information under the pressure of interrogation and torture is part of the *condition humaine,* a condition of the subversive life of a conspirator. Bonhoeffer appears never to have spoken or written of suicide thereafter.

His life was dominated in the following months by intense correspondence, at first with his parents and some of his relatives, and with his fiancée. Maria von Wedemeyer had written to him from the moment of his arrest, and he was allowed to answer her letters beginning at the end of July. In November 1943, he also began to correspond with Eberhard Bethge. The history of these letters from and to Tegel Prison is a dramatic history in itself. It would be a worthwhile study to pursue how and in what way much of the correspondence between Bonhoeffer and Bethge was smuggled past the censors. Or to study the fact that these letters survived the chaos of war, and especially the war's end, and how this came about. Or to study the way they were first published at the beginning of the 1950s, not to mention the story of the correspondence between Maria von Wedemeyer and Dietrich Bonhoeffer! Their letters reveal a love that had to put its hopes in the future because it had no past, but it was at the same time vulnerable to the uncertainty of that future. These letters will not be studied in detail here, because they belong completely to the realm of Bonhoeffer's personal life.

Likewise many remarks Bonhoeffer made in the collected letters and texts compiled as *Resistance and Surrender* belong to this immediately personal, emotional sphere and will not be mentioned individually here precisely for that reason. Their proper place is among the letters and personal notes. (They are most likely one of the reasons that fascination with *Resistance and Surrender* continues to this day.) They include remarks on his deepest personal feelings and interpretation of life, comments about his relationships with those who were closest to him, and statements about his inner well-being, whether in actual fact or exaggerated out of consideration for his parents. Also not mentioned here, but always to be borne in mind, is the fact that many of his statements are deliberately encoded, so to speak, in view of his past and continued subversive activities. Our attention here will be focused on his theological reflections.

Before doing so, however, a word must be said about the way the texts from Tegel Prison came into being. It would appear that in occupying himself primarily with belletristic texts (novel, drama, narration) (DBW 7) during his first year in prison, Bonhoeffer was trying to find his way "back to the roots" of his own inner and outer existence. He also composed prayers for other prisoners, as well as reports—for instance—on experiences during an air raid and his arrest, and essays where he attempted to come to terms with his current inner conflicts and near-despair. "What Does It Mean to Tell the Truth?" (DBW 16, 619ff.), for example, is one of these, along with another—no longer extant—study he wrote on the "Sense of Time." Then, beginning in the spring of 1944, his letters take on the pronounced theological character that led Bonhoeffer himself to call them the "theological letters" (DBW 8, 513). Their impact is in fact that of theological essays, although they bear all the more authenticity and urgency precisely because they are letters containing questions and unfinished trains of thought, rather than essays cloaked in letter form.

In May he wrote the *Baptismal Day Thoughts* and in the following months, from early summer 1944 until autumn, he wrote poems. Concerning the poems Bonhoeffer observed on June 21, 1944, "These un-born children of mine leave me pretty much at a loss as to what to think about them or how to judge them" (DBW 8, 491). His letters and poems are mutually explanatory, and decades later the latter in particular would bring countless people who knew nothing about his letters or earlier books into contact with him. The openly theological correspondence between Bonhoeffer and Bethge continued until September; on October 28, 1944, two days before his own arrest, Bethge destroyed the last letters received from Bonhoeffer, so that the "classical" theological letters and the already-mentioned "Draft for a Paper" belong to the period from the end of April to the end of August 1944. The government's efforts to destroy all opposition and resistance groups were redoubled following the miscarriage of the assassination attempt on July 20, 1944, and in September following the discovery of the Zossen Files. These were previously undetected ledgers kept primarily by Oster, Beck, and Hans von Dohnanyi, which laid bare their identities as conspirators. This meant the end for the already imprisoned members of the Resistance group within military intelligence. Any hope for a "trial" that was even partially legal became illusory from that time forward. On October 8, Bonhoeffer was transferred from Tegel Prison, which had been heavily bombed and mostly destroyed by the allies by that time, to the so-called Gestapo basement of the Office of Security in the Reich in Berlin's Prinz-Albrecht-Straße. Still extant from the time thereafter are the letter he wrote to Maria von Wedemeyer on December 19, 1944 (*Love Letters from Cell 92*, 208ff.); the poem *By Goodly Powers;* the letter he wrote to his mother on her birthday, December 28, 1944 (DBW 8, 609); and the letter he wrote to his parents on January 17, 1945, which was apparently the last letter he ever wrote (ibid., 610–11).

The idea of collecting the letters that record what later became known as the Tegel Prison theology and making them available to others is mentioned briefly in the letters themselves. Bonhoeffer wrote on July 8, 1944 (DBW 8, 513), "By the way, I would very much appreciate it if you would not throw away my theological letters. . . . I might want to read through them later for my work." In the same letter (ibid., 512) he responds to Bethge's request to send excerpts from them to their closest friends from the days in Finkenwalde, friends such as Albrecht Schönherr and others. Bonhoeffer replies that Bethge may of course do so, but "*I* myself wouldn't do so, because I venture to express myself so off-the-cuff only to you, hoping that this will clarify them for me as well. But just as you like."

Bethge kept the letters and not only made them available to friends of the House of Brethren, but also published parts of them six years after the end of the war as *Resistance and Surrender: Letters and Notes from Prison* in a first, short edition. This choice of—what would become—a legendary title was taken from a letter Bonhoeffer wrote on February 21, 1944, where he expresses his disappointment that preparations for his trial are going nowhere and his hope of being released from prison has once again evaporated: "I have often asked myself here where the need to resist 'fate' comes to an end and the equally important need for surrender begins" (DBW 8, 333). One must resist fate with the same determination as one submits to it when the time has come. His conclusion: "There is, therefore, no principle for determining where the line lies between resistance and surrender; but both must be put into practice, and both must be exercised determinedly. Faith demands this nimble, vital action" (ibid., 334).

The reaction of ecclesiastical and theological circles to Bonhoeffer's *Ethics,* which appeared in 1949, was for the most part cool; thus the resonance subsequently evoked by the Tegel Prison texts was totally unexpected. More complete editions and translations into seventeen languages (to date) followed, along with fully revised editions of these texts. For theological texts, the number of reprintings is unusual, extending to Volume 8 of *Dietrich Bonhoeffer: Works,* based on a review and new deciphering of difficult passages in the original writings and containing the complete *Correspondence,* including the extant letters from his relatives and friend. It is undeniable that *Resistance and Surrender* probably reached more people "among the Christians and non-Christians of the world than any other book by a German theologian."[2] These texts, written in prison in Berlin during the final two years of what has been called the Thousand-Year Reich, were instrumental in bringing about Bonhoeffer's reknown as "the best-known and most often-quoted theologian of his century, among Christians and non-Christians in both the East and the West."[3]

This stands in stark, startling contrast to the diffidence Bonhoeffer himself openly confessed, often with greatest self-doubt: "All this is still only the very beginning, and I am guided here, as usual, more by my instinct for upcoming questions than by any clarity about the answers," he remarked on June 8, 1944 (DBW 8, 476). "I'm currently working my way gradually into a non-religious interpretation of biblical concepts. The task itself is clearer to me than the way I am to go about performing it," he stated at the beginning of the theological part of his letter dated July 16, 1944 (ibid., 529). Two days later he wrote, "I apologize for the fact that all this is still expressed so clumsily and inadequately; I feel this very keenly" (ibid., 537). And his "Draft for a Paper" ends with the passage: "All this is very rough and abbreviated. But I just want to make an attempt at simple, clear expression of a few things we usually like to sweep under the rug. Whether this succeeds, especially without the help of discussion, is another question. My hope is to do a service for the future of the church" (ibid., 561).

Was his hope fulfilled? A judgment on Bonhoeffer's historical impact—an impact on theory *and* practice within the church—is not at issue here. What is certain, however, is that almost none of his other works raised as intense, enduring, and fruitful an echo as his Tegel Prison theology did. The secondary literature on its many key passages and topics is as countless as the sand on the seashores, and one might think there is nothing more to say about them. Often, however, these texts have the disadvantage of being very difficult for the so-called interested layperson to understand. They have been endlessly repeated, misunderstood, quoted out of context, truncated, and sugar-coated. They have also been interpreted with insight, with perception, with feeling, and doubtlessly with theological accuracy. They contain a theology whose implications and consequences have been—and still are—discussed very heatedly today; the battles occasioned by it have been numerous and fierce. For many persons and groups, *Resistance and Surrender* served as a "booster charge" both for their theology and their faith, a first mover toward personal commitment to the church and the public arena. It has, as Bonhoeffer hoped, *already* "done the church a service" (see above), and one hopes that there is still much it will be able to do "for the *future* of the church."

Bonhoeffer's theological reflections in *Resistance and Surrender* are "prison theology." They came into being in a situation that put both Bonhoeffer and his time to the extreme test (which does not at all lessen their value and impact—quite the contrary!). We can never ignore the *Sitz im Leben* of any text if we wish to do justice to it and the person who wrote it at all. This fact is especially important for understanding *Resistance and Surrender.*

For example, Bonhoeffer's notes and letters from prison indicate that he experienced more glaringly and directly than on the "outside" the complete absence of religion among his fellow prisoners. Even where this was most expected, in the nightly torment of air raids when they were powerless to take cover, the religious questions and feelings that manifested themselves were at best rudimentary. When Bonhoeffer attests to the fact that human beings of today are simply no longer capable of being religious, and asks why "this war, in contrast to all those before it, does not engender a 'religious' reaction" (DBW 8, 403), he is echoing his concrete experience of this religious vacuum: "The truth of these statements reflects the truth of Bonhoeffer's concrete experience within the context of prison: he was observing and registering the break-down of religion as a self-evident factor."[4] Many of the insights he formulated in Tegel Prison reflect his daily situation. These were not, however, a mere record of facts. They express—at times tentatively and hesitantly, at other times more focused and pointedly than ever before—thoughts and personal experiences that had long been present in Bonhoeffer's life. Moreover, new lines of thought, triggered by his living conditions in prison, also began to take shape.

The fragility of his situation, the experience of failure and resistance, the fact that his future was completely up in the air, the abrupt uprooting from "normal" ways of thinking and living, led Bonhoeffer to theological insights and faith that would otherwise be unthinkable today, although he himself would never see this happen. The power of the questions, doubts, and insights he formulated in *Resistance and Surrender* is also due precisely—but not only—to their immediate context of experience. This gives them credibility, and as a consequence "many individuals, especially those in situations of oppression, at least have an inkling precisely here that Christian faith comes to meet them in the most pertinent possible manner . . . these theological reflections pointing to the future arose from Bonhoeffer's reflections on his experiences in the Resistance."[5]

Bonhoeffer's prison theology had a liberating impact. It opened up new theological horizons and introduced a new understanding of theology as a ferment for uniting theory and practice in faith. It encouraged new directions, a concrete public diaconate, and new perspectives in theology, such as liberation theology. In Germany, liberation theology was inseparable from the name of Johann Baptist Metz, a Catholic theologian, or the specific theology of Dorothee Sölle, a Protestant theologian whose work extended from *Vicariousness* to *Mysticism and Resistance,* although she criticizes Bonhoeffer in the first book and hardly mentions him at all in the second. *The Crucified God* of the Protestant theologian Jürgen Moltmann would likewise have been nearly unthinkable without Bonhoeffer's Tegel Prison theology, which opened up the possibility of a Christ-like faith and liberated life with and before God, in a world without God. The Protestant theologian Eberhard Jüngel sums up Bonhoeffer's impact: "With this christological approach to understanding the godlessness of the world, thus making it fruitful for understanding God, Bonhoeffer brought to light a situation that is fundamental for Christian faith in God."[6] Bonhoeffer also moved countless lesser-known human beings to turn their steps—sometimes once again—toward the Christian faith.

Bonhoeffer's relationship to God, with Jesus Christ as its central focus, withstood the test of imprisonment; it was, however, far different from what is traditionally understood as "religion." With this as a foundation, he began to draft his views of what he called "a world come of age," "religion-less Christianity," and "the church for others." In spite of much initial discrimination and animosity within ecclesiastical circles, the publication of these notes and letters, under the title *Resistance and Surrender*, ushered in a new epoch of Bonhoeffer's presence in a world where there is an excess of surrender to the world as we know it, and a paucity of resistance to the world as we know it: does the world we live in resemble the world come of age that Bonhoeffer described and envisioned?

·Bonhoeffer's Tegel Prison theology remained of necessity only fragmentary, although these fragments were to have an astonishing future. They were, however, also fragments with a past. The basic thoughts Bonhoeffer set down on paper in his prison cell had already been forged in outline form by the theology and practice of his previous life; now they appeared with new impact under different conditions of life and thought. The old and new contours of his theology and its political consequences had a mutual effect on one another. Both statements are true: Bonhoeffer's political thought moved more and more in the direction of political resistance as a consequence of his theology; and his "older" theology took on new contours as a consequence of his political thought.

20

Christianity Beyond Religion

This my work
is more about seeking than finding;
of that which was found
only a little bit is truly certain;
the rest, however, is marked as "problem
still to be solved."

Augustine

Loss of the religious *a priori*, religion-less Christianity, the non-religious interpretation of biblical concepts, the world come of age, the suffering God, the church for others: these are the great themes of the Tegel Prison letters, written in the spring and summer of 1944. But these themes had also appeared in earlier writings, one example being the theme "religion-less Christianity."

We treat this theme in detail here, as being representative of other lines of Bonhoeffer's thought expressed in *Resistance and Surrender*. It is all the more representative inasmuch as it was not at all something substantially new within his thought, but represented the continuation of a line of thought that previously existed in outline form. In prison, however, it took on new clarity and a new impact. Thus it serves as a paradigm both for Bonhoeffer's Tegel Prison theology and the constructive ambivalence of openness and identity that characterizes his thought.

Here again we inevitably come across a response to the often-discussed question—mentioned more than once in this book—concerning continuity and discontinuity in Bonhoeffer's thought.[1] The expression "continuity of thought" as it is used here does not mean a system of thought that is so self-contained it excludes new impulses; instead, the term is used here in the sense of a coherent, consistent body of thought still in process; a body of thought that throws open new doors without falling into the pitfall of arbitrariness; a body of thought that moves forward without losing or denying its own identity. All answers to the question of continuity must remain in any case (re-)constructions, indeed if not a result of projection or at least interpretation. Still, such attempts are indispensable for those of us who have no choice but to try to understand the thought and work of another human being after the fact and from the outside. We must, however, at least be aware of this.

Numerous monographs have dealt with the interpretation and meaning of Bonhoeffer's term "religion-less Christianity," often enough with a glance toward its current relevance for our time.[2] Ernst Feil above all wrestled vehemently and repeatedly for decades with the question of religion-less Christianity under various aspects.[3] There have been instances when discussion of the (ir)relevance of Bonhoeffer's religion-less Christianity for our times led to downright theological and ideological feuds. However, that is a subject which does not concern us here, since our goal in this context is to trace the development of this theme while concentrating wholly on Bonhoeffer himself.

Religion-less Christianity surfaces as a thematic concept in Bonhoeffer's writings for the first time in his letters from prison, although it is formulated only twice in this particular way. It is, however, the foundation for many other reflections expressed in *Resistance and Surrender,* and it bears special implications for theology in two senses: "according to" Bonhoeffer and "after Bonhoeffer." Furthermore, it has its roots in all of his previous thinking. The same is true of another of his thematic concepts which, while not identical with religion-less Christianity, is closely related to it: the "non-religious," or the "worldly," interpretation of biblical concepts. Our emphasis here will be on religion-less Christianity.

This viewpoint first began to play an explicit role in the Tegel Prison texts, where Bonhoeffer carried to a logical conclusion what he had earlier described and laid down as a principle in other works and in other words: overcoming the forces that separate the world from God, religion from reality, faith from life, the church from daily routine. The traces—or even better, the paths—leading to his view of a religion-less Christianity extend far back, although he did not designate it as such earlier. However, they are clearly evident in retrospect. Although they are to be found in various terrains of his theology, in different facets and with differing degrees of emphasis, they are nevertheless impossible to overlook. An especially clear example is found in the talk "On Jesus Christ and On the Essence of Christianity," which Bonhoeffer gave in 1928 while a curate in Barcelona. In it he paints an ironic picture of religion in the house of modern man, that is, as a "best room" that has nothing to do with work, everyday life, and normality. He polemicizes against this form of "religion in the salon," a sugar-coated faith for Sunday services that turns the Nazarene into a bowdlerized figure: "He did not go to the cross in order to ornament and decorate our lives" (DBW 10, 302). He speaks out sharply against a type of good-humored religious disembowelment of the Christian glad tidings: "The religion of Jesus Christ is not the dessert that comes after the meal but is rather the bread itself, nothing else" (ibid., 303). The fact is that Christ has become reserved as an affair of the church alone, not an affair of life, and in this way He has been banned completely from the house of life and confined to the temple and the church.

Bonhoeffer then speaks about the Jesus of Nazareth who lived and worked quite un-religiously, quite contrary to the customary human views of religion. He contradicted these views—and liberated us from them. In this talk, Bonhoeffer says that "The solution, or better the paradox, lies in Jesus' unheard-of new vision of God" (DBW 10, 314). God comes to man in His own way, independently of the religious images man makes of Him, and independently of the religious requirements man imposes upon Him (and himself). Man cannot attain God, nor need he even wish to do so. God comes to man precisely when man's illusion is that of a distant God. Here Bonhoeffer uses the unusual term "un-religion": "When man is merely a hearer, a recipient, in other words, when he appears furthest away from God in his un-religion, his un-morality: that is when God is closest to him. . . . We think we have discovered in ourselves something like God, something divine that lifts us to the plain of God and authorizes us to make demands. Thus religion and morality become the worst enemy of God's coming to man, that is, of the Christian glad tidings; and thus the Christian glad tidings are at their root a-moral and a-religious, paradoxical as that may seem" (ibid., 315).

For Bonhoeffer, it was clear that at the center of the Christian glad tidings we find neither the proclamation of a new religion nor signposts pointing to a new, but in the final analysis merely another, path of man to God. Rather, we find a surprise: God's path to man is a highly a-religious path. At the center of the Christian glad tidings stand love and death. The human Jesus is the personified love of God for man, and His death documents the fact that this love does not end, even before the most ridiculous, brutal death of mankind. God's solidarity with man becomes evident in God's pure abandonment of Jesus; the cross becomes, according to Bonhoeffer, "the center and the paradoxical symbol of the Christian glad tidings" (DBW 10, 320). With this cross standing, so to speak, in the background, he contrasts the Christian glad tidings with religion and religions, not as a know-it-all who plays off the diverse paths of man to God one against the other, but rather in the sense of being a liberating manifesto of God's love for man: "Christ does not bring a new religion;

rather, He brings God" (ibid., 321). As Bonhoeffer wrote in his Tegel Prison cell on July 18, 1944, "Jesus does not call us to a new religion but to life" (DBW 8, 537).

In another talk he gave in 1932, while a lecturer in Berlin and Potsdam, we find his views and hopes for a religion-less and worldly Christianity and what he requires of it, even though he does not use precisely these terms. He begins this talk,[4] entitled "Thy Kingdom Come: The Prayer of the Church for God's Kingdom on Earth," by asserting that "We are off the beaten path or even secularists; what that means is that we no longer believe in God's kingdom" (DBW 12, 264). One situation ("off the beaten path" is a term found in Nietzsche) leads man "off the beaten path and into religious flight from the world," and is a denial of God's kingdom *on earth* (DBW 12, 265). The other situation (by "secularists" he means Christians who accommodate) leads to love of the world for its own sake, and is a denial of God's kingdom on earth. As a result, Bonhoeffer comes to the following conclusion: "But after all, being off the beaten path and secularism are only two sides of the same coin—*namely, disbelief in God's kingdom*" (ibid., 267).

Christians exist with both God *and* the world, with God *in* the world. And that means: worldly Christianity, a religion-less Christianity. In Bonhoeffer's eyes, for man to be Christian and for the church to be Christian they must be fellow travelers with the world; God's kingdom "comes whenever the church remains in firm solidarity with the world while awaiting the kingdom from God alone" (DBW 12, 270).

It is important not to skip over the final words of this sentence in seeking to understand the concept of religion-less-worldly Christianity; for it is precisely in this sense that Bonhoeffer understands religionless—that is, worldly—Christian existence: "God wants to be revered by us here on earth, in our brother, nowhere else. . . . If we open our eyes and are realists, then we see that we belong to Him here" (ibid., 276).

In his letters from the early 1930s, Bonhoeffer also expresses—in very personal diction that is often not at all hopeful, but on the contrary rather despairing—his conviction that Christianity in its present form has no future as a religion. What is necessary in this world is to speak about God quite differently, to bear witness to Christ in a quite different way than what has borne the signature of "religion"—at least in the West—up to now. Perhaps salvation will come once again out of the East; this time, perhaps from India?

Many years previous to this time, Bonhoeffer had developed a half-formed plan, as already mentioned, to visit Gandhi in India. There, he hoped to acquire radically new impulses for himself and his church. In October 1931, likewise during his time as an instructor in Berlin, he wrote to his friend Helmut Rößler: "There is one great country I still hope to see, with the question whether perhaps the great solution will come from there: India; for otherwise it would seem to be over; it would seem that Christianity has begun to die the death. Is our time up? Is the Gospel to be given to another people, to be preached perhaps with *completely* different words and deeds? What is your own view of the 'foreverness' of Christianity in light of the world's situation and our own lifestyle?" (DBW 11, 33). As if continuing this passage, Bonhoeffer wrote to his brother Karl-Friedrich from London in February 1934: "Every day I become more and more convinced that Christianity in the West is coming to an end—at least in the form it has had up to now, and as it has been interpreted up to now. Therefore, before I return to Germany I would like to go to the East" (DBW 13, 75). Gandhi confirmed to Bonhoeffer that he would be cordially welcome in Ashram, provided that he—Gandhi—were not residing in prison at the time, but Bonhoeffer's plan never materialized.[5] As things turned out, his path was to take him from London directly to Zingst, and from there to Finkenwalde: to "life together" in the house of "brethren."

For Bonhoeffer, the shape and interpretation of Christianity as practiced in the West up to his own day had already come to the end of the road. Could a fully different shape and interpretation be possible, namely, that of a "religion-less Christianity?" as he put it ten years later in Tegel Prison, and a "non-religious interpretation of biblical concepts"?

The Tegel Prison theme of religion-less Christianity is also found in *Discipleship*. In the Foreword to that book, he poses the question as to what the meaning of discipleship can be for people today—"the worker, the businessman, the farmer, the soldier"—and whether it is not the case that "Christians and those working in the world are experiencing an unbearable sense of being torn apart from one another" (DBW 4, 23). For Bonhoeffer, God Himself mended this sundering of religion from life by living in Christ a human life in a human body. And thus life lived in the discipleship of Christ is a full, undivided life as a full human being. Here again life in Christ is different from religion (which is not to be taken as "victory" over religion).

In a later chapter in *Discipleship*, Bonhoeffer writes that "A truth, a doctrine, a religion needs no specific locale. It is bodiless. It is heard, learned, comprehended. That's all. But God's Son become man needs not only ears or hearts, but also bodily human beings who follow in His footsteps" (DBW 4, 241). In the final chapter he again draws a line between the Gospel and discipleship of Christ on the one hand and religion on the other, when he asks how man can (again) become the image of God. Bonhoeffer's response: "God sends His Son; and only in that can there be help. No new idea, no 'better' religion can reach the goal. A human being comes to mankind" (ibid., 299).

Such forerunners of individual elements that later developed into the Tegel Prison theology are common. For example, in the diary he kept of his journey to America in the summer of 1939, Bonhoeffer used drastic words to express his resentment of "religious idolatry" (DBW 15, 225). Even at that time he was already tending to have no regrets about the creeping breakdown of even the tiniest particle of religiosity as a matter-of-course part of life—man's "religious *a priori*," as he was to call it in Tegel Prison. Following a religious service he found intolerable—"The whole affair was nothing but a well-mannered, opulent, self-satisfied celebration of religion"—he asked himself, "Are people really unaware that they can do quite well and be better off without 'religion'?" (ibid.). But then he adds, "But where would we be without God Himself and His Word?" In an essay he wrote on North American Protestantism after his return to Germany, under the title "Protestantism Without the Reformation," he summed up his experience in America as follows: "Taken as a whole, theology and the church in America have never been able to understand the full meaning of God's word in the sense of 'critique.' They fail to comprehend in the final analysis that God's 'critique' also extends to religion, to the Christian mentality of the churches, and to the sanctification of Christians—and that God has founded His church beyond all religion and ethics" (ibid., 459).

As Bonhoeffer became more involved in conspiracy, he observed that he was distancing himself more and more from religion and religiosity. Emboldened by his "current activities in the worldly sector," as he wrote in a circumlocutory manner to Eberhard Bethge in June 1942, he sensed how a "resistance to everything called 'religious'" was growing within, "often even to the point of instinctive revulsion, and that is certainly not good" (DBW 16, 325). He was by nature not religious, but he continues on, "I must constantly think about God and about Christ; and I find myself very much drawn to all that is genuine—to life, freedom, and mercifulness. But religious trappings go very much against my grain" (ibid.). He was aware that the sentiments and thoughts he was voicing were not new, but his feeling was that, for him, in this respect something "simply has to give" (ibid.).

It is clear in retrospect that theologically something inside him did indeed "give," to stay with his image, in Tegel Prison for the first time; however, even before that time it was already in the process of "giving" more and more. Bonhoeffer was at work at that time on his *Ethics*, which contain the most pronounced premonitions of the theological conclusions he would draw two years later in the incomparably more extreme situation of imprisonment. Bonhoeffer had learned his lesson about critiquing religion and understood that Christ-centered faith is only an illusion as long as it serves merely "to religiously round out a profane world view" (DBW 6, 32). God is either 100 percent real in the world or not at all—*tertium non datur,* there is no third possibility. God's reality cannot be divided into religion on the one hand and reality on the other. It is not higher than the world, but is rather congruent with it. It is precisely at this point that one of Bonhoeffer's most important statements comes in: "What is important, therefore, is *to be part of God's and the world's reality in Jesus Christ today,* in such a way that it is impossible for me to experience the reality of God without the reality of the world, or the reality of the world without the reality of God" (DBW 6, 40–41).

This is the epicenter from which Bonhoeffer develops the whole of his *Ethics.* What is of Christ is within our reach only through what is of the world. There is no "island of the blessed," no place of refuge, no quiet little religious room where we are alone, "no place where the Christian can withdraw from the world either outwardly or within the inner sphere," pleasant as this might be (DBW 6, 47). "Wholly Christ's, he simultaneously stands wholly in the world," he writes (ibid., 48)—because Christ was wholly the world's, we might add. Worldly existence and Christian existence are not simply two sides of a coin but are at one and the same time the *whole* coin. That is true of the life of the individual Christian—and of the life of the church as *sanctorum communio.*

We are dealing here with more than merely an anticipatory element of the Tegel Prison motifs of religion-less Christianity and church for others. Rather, these statements are the motifs themselves, even if not yet couched in exactly these terms: "The church can defend its own sphere . . . only by battling, not for that sphere but for the salvation of the world. Otherwise the church degenerates into a 'religious society,' fighting for its own existence, and thus automatically no longer God's church in the world" (DBW 6, 49–50). Here we already find indirectly in his *Ethics* the concept of his "Draft for a Paper," which he sketched out in August of 1944 in his Tegel Prison cell, and in which he developed the motif of the church for others.[6] Elsewhere in his *Ethics,* he indirectly describes the meaning of the expression religion-less Christianity in the letters from Tegel Prison: the church does not deal "first and foremost in essence at all with man's so-called religious functions but rather with man himself as a whole, as existing in the world, and with everything that implies. The church is not about religion but about the figure of Christ and how it takes shape among the masses of mankind" (DBW 6, 84). This statement makes clear once and for all: against the background of Bonhoeffer's religion-less Christianity, it is only a short step from the *Ethics* to *Resistance and Surrender*.

At more than one point, the Tegel Prison letters are a personal manifesto of his resentment toward everything religious. Bonhoeffer worked out for himself specific rituals of piety in his prison cell, without returning to the fleshpots of religion. In a personal vein, he wrote to his friend Eberhard Bethge on November 21, 1943 that he had taken over the custom of Martin Luther, among others, of blessing himself during morning and evening prayers with the sign of the cross, assuring himself in the same breath: "Don't worry! I will certainly not leave this place as a *homo religiosus!* Quite the contrary, my distrust and fear of 'religiosity' have become greater here than ever before" (DBW 8, 197). Something within him balked at religious prattle. He wanted no part of "religious blackmail," like that exerted on his fellow prisoners by panic and fear during bombing attacks (DBW 8, 301).

His final step into the lines of thought later subsumed under the title "Prison Theology" was taken in the letter he wrote to Bethge on April 30, 1944, where we come upon Bonhoeffer's religion-less Christianity, which triggers one question after another in him. As if desiring to calm his friend and comfort him in advance, he emphasizes at the beginning that Bethge truly need not worry about him personally: "The only thing that might surprise you or even cause you worry would be my theological thoughts and their consequences. . . . What I can't stop thinking about is the question, what is Christianity? or even, who is Christ for us today?" (DBW 8, 402).

Starting from this overall question about the identity of Christ in a religion-less age, Bonhoeffer's reflections focus on the conceptual image of a religion-less Christianity. His premise: we may no longer take any kind of religious *a priori* in man for granted, as if it were self-evident that he has a sort of religious antenna. Bonhoeffer's plea and hope is for a religion-less-worldly Christianity and a non-religious interpretation of biblical terms. His postulate: precisely because it is the church of Jesus Christ, the church must understand itself as the church for others—as the church for the world, independent of religiosity and religion. He takes it for granted that the future of religion-lessness has already begun: "We are headed in the direction of a completely religion-less time; because human beings are the way they are, we simply cannot be religious any longer" (ibid., 403). The rug is being pulled out from under the feet of Christianity, which arranged things so comfortably for itself in the past; "Only a few last, intellectually dishonest 'heroes' remain, at whose doorstep we are allowed to land 'religiously' " (ibid.)! Bonhoeffer asks—rhetorically—whether, in view of their doubtful probity, it is really a good idea for us to swarm to this group of people, full of zeal, or pique, or indignation ". . . and try to sell them our wares? Is it right for us to pounce upon a few poor souls in their moment of weakness and violate them, so to speak, religiously?" (ibid., 403–4).

It is of course clear to him that this is precisely what we do *not* want. But if the Western form of Christianity is, after all, nothing other than the "final stage on the way to complete religion-lessness" (DBW 8, 404), then what will be the situation of the church? For Bonhoeffer, one question after another follows: "How can Christ also become the Lord of those who are religion-less? Can there be such a thing as 'religion-less Christians'? If religion is merely the cloak of Christianity—and this cloak has looked very different in different eras—then what is 'religion-less Christianity'?" (ibid.).

This is the first time that the great theme of religion-less Christianity has been specifically mentioned. That it in any case does *not* imply a renunciation of every type of cult is made clear by the questions that follow like an unleashed avalanche—questions about the meaning and practices of the church, about communities of faith, about preaching, about liturgy. In short: about Christian life in a religion-less world.

Bonhoeffer goes on to ask how we can speak of God—"in an age without religion, an age when conditions are no longer amenable to it, an age without metaphysics and interiority" (DBW 8, 405)—and immediately raises the objection that perhaps we can no longer speak of Him at all as in the past. And he asks, "How do we speak . . . in a 'worldly' way of 'God,' how can we be 'religion-less-worldly' Christians, how can we see ourselves as . . . called to leave everything behind when we cannot see ourselves as religiously advantaged but rather as belonging completely to the world? Christ is then no longer an object of religion but rather something fully different: truly Lord of the world. But what does *that* mean? What is the meaning of cult and prayer in religion-lessness?" (ibid.).

And at the end of this long letter he again returns to the theme of religion-less Christianity: "I think these days a great deal about the shape of this religion-less Christianity, and what it looks like" (DBW 8, 408).

Bonhoeffer does not therefore identify religion-less Christianity with the elimination of cult and prayer, but rather asks about their proper place in a future, more specifically, in a religion-less Christianity. The time of religious preserves—namely, metaphysics and interiority—has come to an end; the matter-of-course areas reserved on a planning grid for things like God have become irrelevant for people of today. For Bonhoeffer, metaphysics means here the habit of seeing God *behind* things, as something *not of* this world (meta-physical!). And interiority means here the issue of "rest for the soul," of the need of individual conscience, and of longing for deliverance. The key words "metaphysics" and "interiority" as he understands them are essential to a type of religious thinking that reserves for God the "outside," the world, or the "inside" of man but never the whole world or the whole of man.

Given that these preserves of God are also now disappearing due to growing religion-lessness, two alternatives remain for the Christian faith of the future: either it will itself be swallowed up by religion-lessness, as religious views that were self-evident in the past gradually disappear, or it will detach itself from the religious condition and find a new path of its own. This religion-less path might even lead the man and woman of faith in a fully new way, fully in the sense of earliest Christianity, to where he and she rightfully belong: into the world for which God did *not* consider Himself as being too good. And God would then no longer be banished to religious exile, whether it be that of metaphysics or that of interiority, but would rather be proclaimed and realized—in a religion-less-worldly manner—in the midst of the world.

However, Bonhoeffer also asks himself precisely *how* it is possible to speak of God in a religion-less and worldly manner and interpret the contents of biblical proclamation in a non-religious manner. He does not exclude the possibility that it might even be necessary to fall silent about God (do we see the basic idea of a negative theology shining through here?). Bonhoeffer speaks directly about the lines of thought familiar to him from contemporary theology of his time. For him, Rudolf Bultmann's concept of demythologization, as he remarks in a letter dated May 5, 1944, "did not go 'too far' as most have felt, but rather not far enough" (DBW, 8, 414). Karl Barth, for whom Bonhoeffer's profound respect cannot be doubted, was in his view the first to step into the breach and fight for a theological critique of religion; thereafter, however, his theology of revelation stranded on the shoal of "positivistic revelation" (ibid., 415). (Much as he himself was rooted in dialectic theology with his own verdict on religion, he nevertheless distances himself from Barth with this verdict on the positivism of revelation.)[7]

In this context it again becomes clear that Bonhoeffer's basic understanding of Christian proclamation is that it constantly interprets anew the Gospel of John (1:14), as translated by Luther: the Word became flesh and dwelt amongst us. The issue is the Incarnation, that is, God's insertion of Himself into this world by "becoming a body" and being in this world; the issue is the fact and meaning of Jesus Christ's life, death, and resurrection; at issue are the consequences of this Incarnation. The proper place for proclaiming this Incarnation is neither the abstract world of metaphysics nor behind the walls of religious interiority. It is not to be achieved with an individualistic doctrine of salvation. Thus he wrote on May 5, 1944, "The issue is not some other world beyond this one, but rather this world precisely as created, preserved, subjected to laws, reconciled, and renewed. That which is beyond this world is in the Gospel and wishes to be *for* this world" (DBW 8, 415).

But how do we speak of this Incarnation, and how do we act in accordance with it? How do we interpret it in a non-religious way, and how do we practice a non-religious Christian existence? Bonhoeffer was unable to outline a program that would respond to these questions. But he does indeed give us an idea of what he had in mind in a vision that even today has hardly been realized. As he wrote at the end of his *Baptismal Day Thoughts*, penned for his godchild Dietrich Bethge in May 1944, "It is not our business to predict the day; but that day will come when human beings will once more be called to utter God's word in such a way that the world responds by changing and renewing itself. It will be a new manner of speech, perhaps fully un-religious, but also liberating and redeeming, like the speech of Jesus" (DBW 8, 436).

For Bonhoeffer, the Incarnation of God in Jesus Christ is the most important reason for doing away with the customary—religious—interpretation and the customary—religious—practice of Christian proclamation. He does not mourn the disappearance of the religious as an *a priori*; rather, his hope is precisely that it will evaporate; that there will be a "reformation" of the Christian glad tidings, so that they permeate the whole of human life and not merely the religious dimensions of man's existence. The intention of Christianity is not to search for, and find, man first and foremost in his gray zones or his shadows, but rather to affect man as a whole and not—at best—only at the religious outer limits of his existence; God's will is namely, writes Bonhoeffer on May 29, 1944, "that we know Him in life and *not finally* when we die; in health and strength, and *not finally* when we suffer; in our actions and *not finally* when we sin" (DBW 8, 455; italics by the author, S.D.). God's will is that we comprehend Him "not in the unsolved problems of life, but rather in those situations where indeed answers have been found . . ." (ibid.)!

Up to that time, the "claims" had been clearly staked out: here *ratio*, there *religio*, such that the latter labored under a loss of face and territory, and is resorted to more and more only when people do not know where else to turn. Only the uncharted areas of human knowledge are acknowledged as its domain, although these are constantly shrinking before what is referred to—not merely by coincidence—as the "triumphal advance" of the sciences. What is true on the level of knowledge of the (natural) sciences is also true, according to Bonhoeffer, for the existential level of man as an individual. God does not want a dual system. God's intention is not to be for us only when our powers of understanding, or our strength to perform, or our lives come to an end: not merely in the existential, social cauldrons of life. In the same letter he writes, "Here too, God is not simply a stopgap measure; God must be recognized in the midst of life, not merely at the limits of our possibilities. . . . The reason for this is found in God's revelation through Jesus Christ. He is the center of life and has by no means come to provide answers for unsolved problems" (DBW 8, 455).

Bonhoeffer was aware that his paradoxical view of a religion-less Christianity was eliciting more questions than answers, and that this was nothing more than a gradual approach to a complex set of problems for which there were no model solutions at hand. In practical terms, what does he mean when he writes, as he did on June 8, 1944, that the concepts in the Bible "must be interpreted from now on in a way that does not take religion as a precondition . . . for faith" (DBW 8, 482)? The comparison he makes in this context may be helpful: just as the New Testament rescinded the law of circumcision as an essential precondition for Christians, so also in our time it might be possible to rescind the law that religion is a prerequisite for Christian proclamation and existence—in the form of a religion-less Christianity. Only in this way might it be possible to win a place for God—again?—in the world and not in the alleyways, not merely somewhere behind the world (metaphysics), not merely in the private religious sphere (interiority). "Squeezing God out of the world, out of the marketplace of public human existence," Bonhoeffer concludes a month later, "resulted in the attempt at least to keep hold of Him in the 'personal,' the 'interior,' the 'private' sphere" (ibid., 509). The question arises whether today just the opposite may not be true, that is, whether countercurrents of religiosity within and without the Christian churches are not—once again—fixated on precisely this area? And are they not once again, to use Bonhoeffer's words, "squeezing God out of the world, out of the marketplace of human existence"?

The expression "religion-less Christianity" appears in Bonhoeffer's writings for the first time in the Tegel Prison letters, more precisely in the first of his "theological letters," written at the end of April 1944, and the questions concerning the possibility, or impossibility, of a religion-less Christianity remained a central focus of his thought through the weeks immediately following. Nevertheless the vision of a religion-less Christianity—and this is the point to be made here—was present in his thinking long before that time, even though he did not call it by that name. It remained present in the letters he wrote later, in the summer of 1944, when it became connected to other basic motifs in his thought, and it remains a question—as well as a challenge—to the present day.

21

A World Without God

> As the power of man's inner gaze and insight
> grows, distance also grows—the space, as it
> were, around him: his world gains in depth,
> his purview takes in ever-new stars,
> ever-new puzzles and images.
>
> *Friedrich Nietzsche*

Tightly interwoven with Bonhoeffer's view of religion-less Christianity is that of a world come of age. Together, these two themes form the warp and woof of mutual interrelationships in which one conditions the other. Both of these key ideas—today perhaps even more than in Bonhoeffer's time—describe a question more than a fact. It can be said with certainty that, for Bonhoeffer, neither one was negative in character—quite the contrary! He did not view religion-less Christianity as a stopgap solution, but as a utopia. That this is not *yet* the case in our day is self-evident, but—we may hope—it can still become reality. What Bonhoeffer saw in a world come of age was not a lamentable state of enmity toward God but a systematic process of intellectual and spiritual liberation of the Christian world in the West from forces that traditionally have prevented it from thinking for itself and governing itself. For Bonhoeffer, both ideas contained hopeful perspectives for the present and the future. Rather than fearing that they might already represent reality or might take on shape in the future, he took this reality for granted.

Bonhoeffer's conception of a world come of age appears for the first time in a letter he wrote on June 8, 1944. In it we notice immediately that he clearly distinguishes between God and "God": "There are those who try to persuade a world come of age that it cannot live without a 'God' who refuses to let it think for itself" (DBW 8, 477). But the world can indeed do so—and not badly at that. The conditions and possibility for faith in a world that has become a-religious are already at our disposition. "God" has been eliminated, or at least become a matter of indifference to mankind. In the face of such a godless style of living and thinking, Christian faith is thrown back onto the core of the Christian glad tidings and the permanent mission and opportunity offered by its proclamation: How can Christ be proclaimed in this world? How can He become real and effective in it? Bonhoeffer states it even more pointedly when he writes, "The issue is: Christ and the world come of age" (ibid., 479).

In his Tegel Prison letters, Bonhoeffer uses the expression "world come of age" in a way very similar to what the sociology of religions and the philosophy of history call "secularization"; society is becoming ever more worldly. We hear echoes here of Immanuel Kant, who spoke of "man's awakening from his self-imposed immaturity," and Max Weber, who spoke of the "demystification of the world." Bonhoeffer hit upon this line of thought as a consequence of his detailed study of Wilhelm Dilthey's work during his first year in prison, especially *World View and Analysis of Man Since the Renaissance and Reformation* in the early summer of 1944.[1] Dilthey, a student of cultures, a hermeneutist, and one of the pillars of Life Affirmation philosophy, was highly esteemed as a representative *and* interpreter of the liberal arts in Europe.[2] With regard to the practice and theory of secularization, his influence on Bonhoeffer was far stronger than that of Kant or Weber, and it was from Dilthey that he adopted the notion of a world come of age.[3]

In general, this idea refers to the notion that the course of Western history is dominated by a tendency toward autonomy, which appears to reach its culmination in the twentieth century. Society and modern occidental sciences are in an irresistible process in which now one, now the other is dominant. Through this process they are liberating themselves more and more from their traditional *religio*, that is, their ties— meaning here, to Christian religion—and are taking on independent stature. One of the conditions *and* implications of this emancipation of man is the autarchy of his thought, such that it is a waste of time to try to trace the fine line between cause and effect.

This complex process of enlightenment and coming of age on the part of Western man, as well as the results of religion-lessness can also be interpreted as the almost-logical implication of certain elements of biblical faith. The mental and physical subjection of the world was legitimized by the mission given at the creation of the world in Genesis: "subdue the earth; and have dominion over it." (But this is an issue in itself with regard to interpreting the process of secularization.) A world that has been conceived and made subject as a terrain for scientific and technical intervention no longer needs "God" as a pillar of being, as an omnipresent beacon of enlightenment or an iron-clad formula that explains the world. He becomes obsolete, and human beings have recourse to Him only in times of utmost need: He has become superfluous as far as "real" life is concerned. They no longer need the directing forces of clergy and church, for they are able to take the world and their existence into their own hands.

Bonhoeffer's reflections on the world come of age, reflections he jotted down in preliminary form in correspondence with others and that, in the end, remained unfinished, belong to the realm of the dramatic—that is, very heated—debates over secularization theory, which are still widespread today in philosophy and history, in sociology and theology. It is interesting to note that in his *Ethics*, Bonhoeffer used the term "secularization process" to refer to secularization (DBW 6, 103), a viewpoint that differs from that of the world come of age, as he called it, which he spoke about during his later imprisonment. The section of his *Ethics* entitled "Heritage and Decline" contains passages, as the title implies, in which his assessment of this process is less approving than that associated with the Tegel Prison theme of the world come of age. But the *Ethics* contains forerunners of the "world come of age" and religionless Christianity.

In another passage, Bonhoeffer takes up Lessing's remark about intellectual integrity: "Intellectual honesty in all things, including questions of faith, is the highest good of liberated reason and has been one of the moral requirements of Western man" (DBW 6, 106). The same motif is also found in Friedrich Nietzsche's nihilism, for example, and Max Weber's demystification analysis in the form of high expectations of oneself, and Bonhoeffer used it in a letter he wrote in Tegel Prison on July 16, 1944 (DBW 8, 533), in connection with the problem and possibility of knowing God in a world come of age.[4]

It was not Bonhoeffer's intention to suggest that Western godlessness should simply be equated with the end of faith and the growth of antagonism toward the church. In another passage found in "Heritage and Decline," Bonhoeffer states, "Rather, side by side with the religious-Christian coloration of godlessness we have called 'hopeless godlessness,' there is also a highly promising godlessness whose speech is anti-religious and anti-church" (DBW 6, 115). This is the protest against those forms of "pious godlessness" with which one meets in the churches. When making this distinction, Bonhoeffer calls to mind Luther's remark that the godless man's curse can be more pleasing to God than the "hallelujah!" of the pious, which he was so fond of quoting. This was the passage from Luther[5] that left such a deep impression on Karl Barth when he and Bonhoeffer met for the first time.

Now, thirteen years later, while in Tegel Prison during the spring of 1944, Bonhoeffer writes to his friend Bethge of his attempts to identify the extent to which people still believe in the "transcendent" (DBW 8, 355), and he asks him about his experiences in this regard. Earlier, at Christmas in 1943 (ibid., 259), he had asked Bethge to make a list of what the people he dealt with really believed in. Bonhoeffer's intention during those months was to draw as accurately as possible a picture of the religiosity of human beings in everyday life. Is God a presence in their concrete lives? Does He play any role at all? And if so, what role?

Accordingly, Bonhoeffer concludes the same letter that speaks about the world come of age for the first time, the letter he wrote on July 8, 1944 (see earlier), as follows: "The movement in the direction of human autonomy that began around the thirteenth century—I do not want to enter the fray over the precise moment— . . . has come in our time to a certain completion. Man has learned to stand on his own two feet in all of the important areas of life without using the 'working hypothesis of God' as a crutch" (DBW 8, 476). The expression "working hypothesis of God" also has an interesting history; it was used by Carl Friedrich von Weizsäcker in his book *On the World View of Physics*, which Bonhoeffer had read.[6] He goes on to develop his analysis of the current situation of the church and theology in view of the modern world which both is religion-less *and* has come of age. After becoming superfluous first in the areas of science and art and then in ethics, this working hypothesis of God has also become unnecessary with respect to questions of religion during the last hundred years. It has become clear, Bonhoeffer writes, "that everything gets along even without 'God,' and in fact just as well as before. So also in the area of science, God is being pushed further and further into the background of everyday human life; He is losing ground" (ibid., 477).

Even today, some Christians still regret the fact that God—that is, the God of the working hypothesis, the God of the stopgap—gradually lost ground and prestige. What is striking is Bonhoeffer's emphasis even at that time that this development had been interpreted with rare unanimity by both Catholics and Protestants as "the great falling away from God and from Christ" (DBW 8, 477); the further this movement proceeds, the more it becomes in fact anti-Christian. He observed that "The world that awakened to itself and to the laws governing its life is self-assured to a degree that seems uncanny" (ibid.). In a way that is critical of himself and the church, he describes—sometimes with an ironic or even sarcastic undertone—the weary reactions and efforts, which he regards as questionable, to halt the process of

God's shrinkage. According to Bonhoeffer, Christian apologetics are again immediately called for here.

One method would be for faith to pounce upon the "last questions" (in every sense of the expression) of man, that is, questions such as guilt and death, and to "exploit" them, to put it crassly, as justification for its own existence. Bonhoeffer's caveat is "We live so to speak from these so-called 'last questions of man.' But what will happen should they be answered one day?" and he points to the already influential "secularized offshoots of Christian theology, namely existential philosophers and psychotherapists" (DBW 8, 478). In his eyes they have done slipshod work in taking over a tradition of Christian Methodism by first convincing people that the human situation is hopeless and then using this bleak prospect to paint their own promises of salvation in even rosier colors.

Bonhoeffer expresses here—and not only here—his reservations about existential philosophy and psychotherapy. In December 1943, for example, he wrote to a friend about his ever-deepening "disgust for everything involving psychology" and his "aversion to 'soul analysis' " (DBW 8, 235). His aversion to psychotherapy as a consequence and game played by psychoanalysis is, from his viewpoint, certainly explicable as being, among other things, part and parcel of the "social genes" he inherited from his father. Karl Bonhoeffer was a psychiatrist through and through, in an era that found it difficult to reconcile psychiatry with the techniques of psychoanalysis and/or depth psychology, which was a circumstance that often led to implicit resentments.[7]

Dietrich Bonhoeffer's critical evaluation of existential philosophy, which appears in undisguised fashion for the first time in a letter he wrote to Bethge on June 8, 1944, is not directed so much against existential philosophy as a current of contemporary philosophy, for he regarded this philosophy with great respect in spite of having substantial differences with it. Bonhoeffer had delved into existential philosophy, in particular that developed by Martin Heidegger, during his academic activities. In his professorial dissertation *Act and Being* he expressly used categories taken from Heidegger and worked "at length with his ontology."[8] Then, in the inaugural lecture he entitled "Man in Contemporary Philosophy and Theology" presented in Berlin in 1930 (DBW 10, 363ff.), he again devoted himself to it in depth, giving it its proper due—indeed with critical distance, but also factually and without polemic.

However, in the context of the world come of age and in light of attempts to give the world a bad taste for those who live in it, as it were, and even to denigrate its denizens, Bonhoeffer repeatedly attacked existentialist philosophy and psychotherapy. In a letter he wrote on June 30, 1944, he accuses these disciplines of using "cunning methods to this end" (DBW 8, 503–4). Later, in a letter he wrote on July 8, 1944, he clearly states his intentions: "My goal is to ensure that no one succeeds in smuggling God into a final, secret hiding place; but instead to ensure simple recognition of the fact that man and the world have come of age, to ensure that man is not 'harassed' in his worldliness but is confronted by God precisely where man is strongest" (ibid., 511). He then argues for a renunciation "of any kind of 'tricks of the black robes' " (ibid.). In the same breath, he again mentions existential philosophy and psychotherapy. His line of argumentation is always the same: he rejects them to the extent that they are perfect examples of frequent, sly tactics of manipulation, just one more attempt to expose human weaknesses and exploit life's lowest points, in order to be celebrated all the more as bringers of salvation.[9]

There is no need to ask here whether and to what extent Bonhoeffer's negative critique was justified. More to the point for church and theology are the strategies those he prefers to employ, in order to prevent a "world come of age" (the English translation of Bonhoeffer's "mündig gewordene Welt"). We return to the letter he wrote on June 8, 1944, where he speaks tersely about this situation: "The attacks of Christian apologetics against the world's coming of age is in my opinion (first) senseless, (second) bad manners, and (third) un-Christian" (DBW 8, 478). They are senseless because they resemble "an attempt to make an adult revert to puberty" (ibid.). They are bad manners because they simply abuse and burden human beings with their own shortcomings; they are un-Christian because they mistake Christ "for a specific stage of religiosity" (ibid., 479).

Bonhoeffer goes on to subject the diverse reactions he perceives in Protestant theology and the church to a scathing critical analysis; this includes, among other things, liberal theology, old and new Lutheranism, as well as liturgical and social trends. Here again, with a glance toward Barth's theology of revelation, we meet with the positivism of revelation, but less disparagingly here than in the earlier context. His sharpest criticism is reserved for the Confessing Church, which, on the whole, has forgotten what is forever indispensable: Barth's fundamental approach. The church has made itself comfortable in the positivism of revelation and, moreover, become "caught up in conservative restoration" (DBW 8, 481).

Bonhoeffer counters this development with the firm and hopeful conclusion that "The world's coming of age is now no longer an occasion for polemics and apologetics; instead, the world is now truly understood better than it understands itself, namely on the basis of the Gospel and Christ" (DBW 8, 482). In his opinion, it is in a world that is no longer religious that the world and its inhabitants can become aware of themselves; and Christ's reality can have a greater impact on a world come of age than a world wearing disguises of religion.

The lines of his theology from Tegel Prison come together like the spokes of a wheel with a common center. The focus of his reflections on loss of the religious *a priori*, on the renunciation of God as a working hypothesis, on religion-less Christianity, and on a world that has gotten rid of "God," is simply that "Jesus Christ takes possession of the world come of age" (DBW 8, 504).

Bonhoeffer's thought during that time might be best characterized as a "theology of coming of age." But must it be viewed as "merely" a borderline theology or even a theology of exile? Was it the product of a unique situation that made it impossible to see "reality"—at least any longer? By no means! To marginalize his theology in Tegel Prison is just as unwarranted as to glorify it blindly as a verbalized and inspired theology of modern times. To dismiss it as the product of extreme stress would be dishonest, but to canonize it without thinking would also be senseless.

On the other hand, can we speak of a "theology" of the Tegel Prison letters at all without ignoring the fact that Bonhoeffer himself expressly wanted them to be viewed as inquiries, preliminary reflections, and ideas in outline? And today, do we really live in the "world come of age" that Bonhoeffer envisioned and identified? Did Bonhoeffer himself live even at that time in such a world? Is it not instead a fact that many indications in his own time, and ours as well, contradict such an interpretation? The *full* extent of the mass destruction of human beings—even though it will never be fully comprehensible—was not even known until after 1945. What Adorno called the "breakdown of civilization" ushered in by the Second World War and the Holocaust is a memory still far too clear for us to view our present-day world as a "world come of age." And whether the status quo of this world in the new century that has now begun meets the definition of a world come of age is no less doubtful.

In spite of all these questions about Bonhoeffer and ourselves, his theology of a godless world is a solid theological response, in contrast to all the cries of lamentation that accompanied secularization. As a theological analysis and response, it is sober, offensive, and full of hope, without a trace of Schadenfreude or a sense of Götterdämmerung. In contrast to religious laments or any other sort of dirge regularly intoned even today as an accompaniment to supposedly irreversible processes of autonomy, Bonhoeffer's interpretations of the world, his insights, and his call to arms provide us with a sound basis of thought. He was the first theologian to consistently welcome secularization instead of complaining about it. He accurately diagnosed the world's break with "God." Nevertheless he never feared that in this world, with all its apparent godlessness, God Himself might have broken with the world.

This was, however, a different God from "God the Super-Power," engendered by and corresponding to man's fantasies of omnipotence and dwelling far beyond all worlds. This God was also different from the God who was degraded to an explanation for the workings of the world, a mere premise and last end. This was the God who suffers with and in the world.

22

God in the World

Once more we gaze upon the Jew Jeschua
Ben-Joseph from Nazareth,
who hangs derided and abandoned on the cross
. . .

His voice is heard through the centuries:
"Whatever you did for the least of my brothers you
did for me."

Schalom Ben-Chorin

Bonhoeffer's reflections on the non-religious proclamation of the
Christian glad tidings in a world come of age take on a different,
more intense tone in subsequent letters and notes, in particular those
written during the crucial month of July 1944 and—above all—the long
letter he wrote on July 16, 1944.

Returning once more to his earlier reflections, Bonhoeffer embarks
on a sweeping journey through history. Beginning with the modern era
and its salient points in the history of thought and the natural sciences,
he focuses on the "*one* great development, the growing autonomy of the
world" (DBW 8, 530). His method singles out highlights from theology
and ethics, politics and jurisprudence, philosophy and physics, while
also referring back to their foundations in classical antiquity and the
Middle Ages. Everything revolves around the declaration that we live
in the world and must indeed do so *etsi deus non daretur:* "as if there
were no God." Bonhoeffer quotes this, but then translates it as "even if
there were no God" (ibid.). He came across this phrase, expressed by the
seventeenth-century Dutch civil rights champion Hugo Grotius, along
with its translation, in the writings of Dilthey.[1]

Bonhoeffer bestows special importance on this *etsi deus non daretur*
as a principle of thought. Since he consistently assumes that man now
lives in a world come of age, he also consistently assumes that man no
longer needs the one who functioned as "God" during the stages of
man's adolescence, whom man now actually gets along without. God has

become as superfluous as a working hypothesis not only in ethics, politics, the natural sciences, and philosophy but also—and he refers here to
Feuerbach—in religion, and it is simply a matter of intellectual honesty
to admit this.[2]

"Where then is there still a place for God?" asks Bonhoeffer, as he
rejects all avenues of escape, all "emergency exits from the suddenly narrow confines of such a place," including the *salto mortale*, the "desperate
leap" back into the Middle Ages: "The basic principle of the Middle
Ages . . . is heteronomy in the form of clericalism. A return to it can only
be an act of despair, paid for with the sacrifice of intellectual honesty"
(DBW 8, 533). This longing for a return to the past is futile; it is "a day-
dream set to the melody of the German song: 'Oh, to know the way
back, the long road to childhood's land.' But there is no such way," he
says (ibid.). In order to be honest we must live in the world—*etsi deus
non daretur*—as if there were no God. But—and here is where Bonhoeffer's altogether ir-religious worldview receives its final, most provoca-
tively contradictory focus—"We acknowledge this in the very presence
of God! It is God Himself who compels us toward this realization. . . . It
is God Himself who gives us the understanding that we must live as
men and women who can get along in life without God. The God who
is 'with us' is the God who abandons us," he writes (ibid.). He then turns
to Mark 15:34, to the cry of Jesus of Nazareth in the face of inexorable
and terrible death: "My God, my God, why have You abandoned me?"

In this passage from his letters we encounter Bonhoeffer's understanding of God and Christ, of man, and of himself in its most concise
and deliberately paradoxical form. The point where God and the world
intersect is precisely the nadir of human existence. Jesus of Nazareth, in
the wasteland of the loneliness of death, is both abandoned man *and*
abandoned God. This is what "incarnation" means. God does not en-
throne himself over the world, but dies the death in this world. It is in
the very sacrifice of His omnipotence that He becomes—omnipotent. It
is His powerlessness that bears us through life and death. In Bonhoeffer's words, "God allows Himself to be crowded out of the world
and onto the cross; God is power-less and weak in the world; it is precisely in this way and only in this way that He is 'with us' and helps us"
(ibid., 534).

This is the immanent scandal of the Christian faith; it is the protest
of the cross simultaneously counterpoised against all sublimely religious
visions of divinity and their fantasies of grandeur. It is here that the
fundamental difference between Bonhoeffer's view and all the other—
religious—views of God, habitually formed by man in both the past and
present, becomes glaringly evident. "Here lies the all-important point of

difference from all religions. Man's 'religiosity' makes him turn in times of need to God's power in the world," Bonhoeffer goes on to write (DBW 8, 534), and he calls to mind the great, magical God, the *deus ex machina*, the God lowered to the stage in classical Greek and Roman drama by a crane. This is the so-called "God" to whom man invariably appeals in moments of need and whom he views, according to the exigencies of the moment, as an anchor in the storm, a good luck charm, a religious stage prop, or a rabbit from the hat.

But the God of the New Testament is neither a cosmic "Terminator" nor a God of glory and happy endings. This travesty of a human being abandoned to despair on the cross is at odds with all religious images; but God is present in Him. The biblical route Bonhoeffer travels has nothing religious about it: "The Bible causes man's eyes to turn to God's powerlessness and suffering; only the suffering God can help him" (DBW 8, 534). And that means: religion-less Christianity. Only as the world comes of age, and precisely in doing so, does it bid farewell to images of God that have little or nothing in common with the biblical God. The world then opens its eyes, Bonhoeffer says, "to the God of the Bible, who establishes His power and His place in the world through His powerlessness" (ibid., 535). And it is here that the non-religious, worldly interpretation of the biblical proclamation must begin.

This interpretation consists of a peculiar turning away from the "God principle"; it also consists of an exchange of roles, thus further subverting the rules of the religious game and—what is more—reversing them once and for all. Bonhoeffer traces a line from Golgotha back to Gethsemane. In a letter dated July 18, 1944, he writes that Jesus' question to his disciples in Gethsemane, whether they could not keep watch with Him for even one hour, is the "opposite of everything that the religious person expects from God" (DBW 8, 535). Man's response to the suffering God can be either a renewal of disdain or a readiness for "compassion," for suffering with Him. "Man is called to suffer together with God, a suffering occasioned by the godless world," writes Bonhoeffer, and it is precisely here that the chance for man's liberation from all religious preconceptions and distortions lies (ibid.). By allowing himself to be taken up into God's passion, a passion in the world and occasioned by it, man discovers the world—and his own life—anew. He can then live a worldly life. He becomes completely human, without religious schizophrenia. Bonhoeffer describes this process as follows: "Christian existence does not mean being religious in any specific manner; . . . rather it means being a true human being, not a specific type of human being. No, Christ creates the human in us. It is not a religious act that makes a Christian, but participation in God's suffering in the midst of our life in this world" (ibid.).

For Bonhoeffer, the Bible, especially the New Testament, richly documents this participation in God's suffering in the midst of our life in this world. This participation is invariably acted out in the whole of life, and is never merely partial. To walk in the footsteps of Jesus of Nazareth does not mean to live religiously, but—simply to live. Thus Bonhoeffer can say in this context, "Jesus does not call us to a new religion, but to life" (ibid., 537). It is a life that embraces man's participation in God's powerlessness; life in a world that has the courage to systematically dismantle the stage scenery of religion and truly come of age. It is a world open to a God who is fully different from what we have called "God," different from the traditional, the religious God. Bonhoeffer's hope is that "the world come of age is more God-less and thus perhaps just for that reason nearer to God than the world that has not yet come of age" (ibid.).

The poem "Christians and Heathens," written in that very summer of 1944, contains the quintessence of Bonhoeffer's unique theology of the cross. It sets out a "third way," in a world that is fully different from that of religious images of God or anti-religious rejection of God. In briefest form and with a minimum of tools, with very few and very simple words, Bonhoeffer traces in this poem the path of man's search and God's quest. It is a search and a quest that shatters past stencils of religious thought and faith and depicts a reality that aims to be the salvation of the world, the whole world.[3]

Religion-less-worldly Christian existence for Bonhoeffer is a concrete consequence of God's Incarnation into this world. The "this-worldliness" of Christianity—as he terms it and lived it—is a result of God's having become man in Jesus of Nazareth. It is because God *was* man that a Christian can *be* man in the daily-ness of human existence in this world, with all its high points and moments of exultation, its imponderabilities and blind alleys. Thus he wrote on July 21, 1944, the day after the attempt to kill Hitler had failed: "In these last years I have come to know and understand the profound 'this-worldliness' of Christianity more and more; the Christian is not a *homo religiosus* but a human being through and through, just as Jesus was, and probably in contrast to John the Baptist" (DBW 8, 541).

Bonhoeffer knew that the perspectives he developed in prison, and in life as a whole, drastically changed for the worse as a result of the failure to kill Hitler. Gethsemane can be everywhere. It reveals God's distance from us, and also His nearness; it marks our world as God's venue, as both the curse and the refuge of man. In this world of being "we fall completely into the arms of God and no longer take our own suffering seriously, but rather that of God in the world; we then keep watch with Christ in Gethsemane," he noted elsewhere in the same letter (ibid., 542).

The glad tidings that constitute the core of Christianity are tidings of God's existence in the man Jesus of Nazareth and of man's co-existence with this Jesus in the Gethsemanes of the world. Bonhoeffer planned to draw up a "balance sheet" of this Christianity in a work he was drafting during those weeks, under the title *An Inventory of Christianity*. Thereafter he wanted to take up the question, "What is Christian Faith?" and then, in a third step, to draw the "Conclusions" (DBW 8, 556). Here we find for the last time some of his thoughts on a religion-less-worldly Christianity in a world come of age, on God's being in this world and our participation in this being of God. "Our relationship to God," says Bonhoeffer, "is not a 'religious' relationship to the highest, mightiest, best being we can conceive of—all that is not true transcendence—but rather our relationship to God is that of a new life in 'being for others,' in participation in the being of Jesus" (ibid., 558). Bonhoeffer uses three examples to demonstrate that this core of the Christian glad tidings— "God as man!" (ibid.)—is not compatible with any of the similar but illusionary contents of other religious systems; nor with oriental religions or Greek mythology; nor with the thought structures of postclassical times.

By rights, this core of the Christian glad tidings should make itself felt through the agency of the Christian church; but Bonhoeffer dryly attests that the existing churches and their diverse theological constructs bypass this in both their faith and their lives. Pietism, for example, is for him the "last attempt to preserve Evangelical Christianity as a religion"; Lutheran orthodoxy is "the attempt to preserve the church as the Institute of Salvation" (DBW 8, 557). Finally, Bonhoeffer's verdict on the Roman Catholic Church and the Confessing Church is that they are closed societies whose purpose is the preservation of vested rights. In short, "church is church only when it is for others," and he names the concrete consequences already mentioned:

> In order to make a fresh start, it must give all its possessions to those in need. Pastors must live exclusively from the free gifts of their church communities and must, if need be, practice a worldly profession. They must take part in the worldly tasks of life in human society without lording it over others, but as helpers and servers. They must tell those of all professions what life with Christ means and what it means "to be for others" (ibid., 560).

Is Bonhoeffer's understanding of "religion-less Christianity" in such a "church for others" realistic? Has the future of such a church already begun? How solid is his "theology of powerlessness in a world come of age?"[4] How convincing is his interpretation of the Christ-event as the presence of the suffering God?

This is not the proper place for a discussion of these questions. Nor is this the proper place for a comprehensive portrayal of Bonhoeffer's Tegel Prison theology. (*Resistance and Surrender* contains many other thought-provoking statements, especially those of a very personal nature. These reflections can only be fully understood in any case by each reader for himself.)

However, three points of view call for special attention now that the main lines of Bonhoeffer's general theological thought in *Resistance and Surrender* have been presented. First, Bonhoeffer follows a path also marked out by the historian and philosopher Karl Löwith, in Löwith's book *From Hegel to Nietzsche*. Even though Bonhoeffer rarely refers to this book explicitly, his reflections on religion-less Christianity and the world come of age make it clear that he himself had traveled the road to what has been called in modern times "the death of God, from Hegel to Nietzsche," only to go beyond Nietzsche. It is also clear, even though this is merely suggested in his final letters, that he had done his homework regarding the critique of religion. (Bethge once remarked on this subject that the questions Ludwig Feuerbach put to theology—and, according to Bonhoeffer, never answered—occupied Bonhoeffer throughout his life; above all, the question as to whether or not the conclusions derived from theology are true, and to what extent they correspond to life in the real world.[5]) This was not the first time Bonhoeffer had responded to these questions, but the theology he developed in Tegel Prison offers his most direct response to Feuerbach's critique of religion. "Feuer" in German means "fire," and "Bach" is a flowing stream; like Karl Barth before him, Bonhoeffer had indeed passed through this "river of fire." In response to the central point made in Feuerbach's critique of religion—namely, that religion is simply a product of human projections—Bonhoeffer presented an interpretation of the Christian proclamation without coming *expressis verbis* to a clinch with it. The congruence between the suffering God and suffering man in the Christ-event does not correspond in reality to religious images of God and man.

Second, nearly a year before his arrest in May 1942, Bonhoeffer wrote in a letter to the family of his twin sister Sabine Leibholz that "suffering and God are not a contradiction in terms, but these two are intrinsically inseparable; the idea that God Himself suffers has always been one of the most convincing teachings of Christianity for me"

(DBW 16, 759). This idea of the Suffering God has been in the middle of theological and depth-psychological crossfire in recent years, and certainly with justification. However, the truth and validity of this idea cannot be established by means of theories and/or abstractions. It belongs less to the dimension of insight than to that of actual experience in human life, and it can prove itself only existentially—or not at all.

Third, "The—'grown-up' and mystical—understanding of suffering,"[6] which Dorothee Sölle claims is unique to Bonhoeffer, bears striking resemblance to the understanding of suffering and God held by other persons of faith at that time. Although coming out of different traditions of faith and thought, they sometimes found themselves in similar life situations. We mention here, for example, Leo Baeck, Abraham Heschel, Kazoh Kitamori, and Ronald Gregor Smith.

Pinchas Lapide impressively pointed out parallels between Bonhoeffer's theology of the cross and the Jewish theology of God's suffering; and between particular ideas Bonhoeffer expressed in Tegel Prison and those expressed by Rabbi Leo Baeck in his concentration camp: "I am not sure whether Bonhoeffer knew that such questions and thoughts are part of the bedrock of Judaism," he remarked.[7] He then mentions in this context letters written by persecuted Chassidic rabbis from Poland and Russia, whose striking echoes he had found in Bonhoeffer's letters.[8] He also mentions Rabbi Abraham Heschel's theology of God's suffering. Years ago, Jürgen Moltmann was one writer who studied these thoughts on *God's Pathos*,[9] which Heschel developed in the mid-1930s. In connection with Bonhoeffer, he also mentions the Japanese Lutheran theologian Kazoh Kitamori and his book *The Theology of God's Pain*, written in 1946.[10] Clements emphatically called attention to the striking parallels between Bonhoeffer's thought developed in Tegel Prison and those formulated by his contemporary, the Scottish Evangelical theologian Ronald Gregor Smith.[11]

However, above all, we must mention here Simone Weil, whose writings reveal an extreme fascination with the suffering, defenseless God. This French mystic never identified herself with her Jewish origins nor did she ever convert to Catholicism, in spite of all her inner affinity for it. But at the beginning of the 1940s—not long before Bonhoeffer wrote "Before God and with God we live without God" (DBW 8, 534)—she noted that the absence of God is the mode of divine presence. And she said it another way as well: "The seeming absence of God in this world is God's presence."[12]

Can it be that these are traces of a like-mindedness that has nothing to do with religion and confessions, whose dimensions and significance for our faith we have yet to recognize?

23

Death and God in Counterpoint: A Fugue

Crucified time and again
Christ
in wood and stone
copper and iron
glass and plaster
But the resurrection
Rainer Kunze

In light of classical, systematic, purely theological, and philosophical analysis, it is surprising that Bonhoeffer rarely addressed the two most difficult questions posed by theodicy, that is, the defense of God's dispensation in view of evil and unspeakable suffering, and death: "Where are we in death?"

Bonhoeffer did not explicitly process these issues as theoretical disputes about the way we arrive at truth or as they apply to pastoral counseling of the bereaved. His sermons of course touched on them directly or indirectly, but even there rather infrequently. Nevertheless, both had long been present at least latently, and at times manifestly, in his thoughts—theodicy less, death more.

We come upon the reason for this largely marginal role of theodicy in Bonhoeffer's writings in a letter he wrote to his brother-in-law Hans von Dohnanyi, exactly one month after both men had been arrested, and there is nothing to add to his clear, firm declaration. There is in him "not one atom of reproach or bitterness," when he speaks about what happened, for "such things come from God and from Him alone, and I know . . . that before Him there can be only submission, waiting, patience—and gratitude. Thus any question about the 'why' of things falls silent, because it has already learned the answer" (DBW 8, 59).

For Bonhoeffer, questions about the meaning and justification of suffering in this world were neither abstract nor comprehensible apart

from the suffering made manifest in Christ. He heard it in the cry of despair on the cross, and from there he heard the response as well. The response did not come in the form of a "solution to a riddle" but as an echo
of his own—despairing—question and as a promise of God's reality,
which does not go to pieces even in suffering. In Tegel Prison—as we
saw in the preceding chapter—Bonhoeffer arrived indirectly at answers
to questions of theodicy he had not asked in quite *this* form. Nevertheless his answers provide possible responses to the question of theodicy,
or at least learning to live with faith in the presence of this question.
Questions about the meaning of one's own *passio*, one's own suffering,
are subsumed in God's suffering with us: "Man goes to God in his
need," Bonhoeffer writes, and ". . . only the suffering God can help him"
(DBW 8, 515 and 534).

It is God who then casts light on the question of death, which
Bonhoeffer thought about his whole life—though perhaps less as a question than as the actual fact of death. Death was the backdrop, the background motif, for life as he lived it; and it was the yeast of his faith.
Bonhoeffer's first direct confrontation with death came in the spring of
1918,[1] when one of his brothers died on a battlefield in the First World
War. As children attempting to cope with the fear and fascination of
death, his twin sister recounted her fantasies about death and eternal life.[2]

A literary sketch written by Bonhoeffer reveals his deep dismay at
his incurable fear of death, along with his efforts to master it. The sketch
was probably written in 1932, when he was in his mid-twenties, and, although written from the perspective of the third person singular and
thus kept "at arm's length," it is unmistakably autobiographical in character, interpreting retrospectively his perception of death and dying during childhood and adolescence. He describes the magnetic attraction he
felt for death and his—hypothetical—hope of meeting it calmly and
sovereignly; but he also recounts how the thought that one day he would
actually, truly die, and must do so, caused him to become paralyzed by
fear and panic, feeling like one possessed. This realization overpowered
him like an incurable disease, one that renders physicians helpless: "The
disease was that he saw reality as it is, and the disease was incurable"
(DBW 11, 374). From that point on, he buried something deep within
himself, which he neither spoke nor thought about for a long time. The
text concludes: "His favorite topic of discussion and imagination had
suddenly acquired a bitter taste. From then on he fell silent about
welcoming pious death, and erased it from his memory" (ibid.).

Sometime later, during his stay in London, Bonhoeffer again took up
the issues of death and dying. He chose as a text for his sermon on All
Souls Sunday in the year 1933 a line from the apocryphal Old Testament

book of Wisdom ("But they are at peace," Wis 3:3) to discuss questions that assail *all* human beings: "Where are our dead? Where will we be after our own death?" (DBW 13, 325). Here he attempts to express the flood of emotions that threaten to overwhelm us at the death of someone near to us; feelings of irrevocability, of the nothingness of one's own life, of infinite and unbridgeable separation. These are followed by a resignation, a coming to terms ". . . with the fact that it is over for them, that they have retreated into the nothingness from which they once came" (ibid., 326). But over against our fears for the dead—and for ourselves—and over against the suffering of those who are dying, God Himself raises His voice and assures us that His presence does not end even in death.

Bonhoeffer takes up this theme repeatedly in his sermon, declaring that "where we see nothing but hopelessness and nothingness, God says, 'But they are at peace'" (DBW 13, 329). This "But" from God runs counter to our patterns of inquiry; it is absolutely incomprehensible, something altogether new and final. We can have complete confidence in this "But" from God. Bonhoeffer is certain "that life really begins when it ends here, and all this is only the introductory scene before the stage curtain opens" (ibid., 329–30). Such were his thoughts when he was in London in 1933, at the age of twenty-seven years.

A week before the Second World War broke out, Bonhoeffer chose "Death in the Christian Proclamation" as the title for a guest lecture he was invited to give at the University of Edinburgh. In choosing this title, "he thus returned during a time of impending evil to a theme that had occupied him during his growing years,"[3] a theme that remained with him from that time on. Immediately after the outbreak of war in September 1939, he wrote a group letter addressed to the members of the (officially illegal) collective vicariate of the Confessing Church. This letter was, by the way, one of the few times he explicitly mentions the topic of theodicy. He does not know, he writes, whether or not the question of theodicy will surface as vehemently during this war as it did during the previous one.

But the pervading, definitive theme of this letter is the question of death, and in it Bonhoeffer expresses very personal reflections about death. He introduces the subject by observing, "Death has once again entered our midst" (DBW 15, 271). He then distinguishes between death that results from external causes and death that dwells within us. By external causes he meant the brutal, bare fact of death that comes to us unexpectedly from an outside source. Indwelling death is specific to each one of us and has to do with the love of Christ and other human beings. "We die this death daily in Jesus Christ, or else we reject it," he writes; it is in prayer that we can express our feeling "that death comes to us from the outside only when we have become ready for it through this personal death . . . ; then our death is in reality only a transition to the fullness of God's love" (ibid.).

Three basic characteristics become crystallized in Bonhoeffer's reflections about death, and we encounter these time and again in his writings. They are by their very nature so intimately linked to one another that it is difficult to distinguish between them. Nevertheless, they can each be described individually.

The first characteristic is an unemotional "Yes" to the fact of death. The world as a whole and the lives of all human beings go their way under the sign of ephemerality. The "Law of Death," the "doom of death" (DBW 10, 501) is written in the Book of Life. In one of his sermons written in 1928 he said that "*Death is where the world no longer laughs*" (ibid.). It is the bitterest fact of life that we must die, and Bonhoeffer never tried to view this fact through rose-colored spectacles. He loved life far too much for that. At the same time, he respected the inescapability of death and rejected any kind of camouflage or detour around the omnipresent illusion that we can close our eyes to our own mortality: "The hour of death is determined for each of us, and it will find us no matter where we turn," he wrote on May 21, 1944 (DBW 8, 446).

The second characteristic is the inner, lifelong accommodation we each make to our own death, a process of becoming familiar with it and accepting it whenever it may come. This includes hope for a congruence between death that comes to us from without and death that exists within us. In an essay entitled "Danger and Death," written at the turn of the year 1942 for his friends in the Resistance, Bonhoeffer affirms: "The thought of death has become more and more our companion in the last few years. . . . We can no longer hate death so much; we have seen something good in its countenance, and have nearly made our peace with it" (DBW 8, 37). This, however, is no precipitate readiness to die, no bowdlerization or musical setting for the break death implies. The longing for meaning is not muzzled; "We naturally want to see a bit of meaning in the bits and pieces of our lives," he writes (ibid.). But in spite of all his love for life, he communicates an imperturbability, which may have been born out of his experiences as a conspirator: "We love life still; nevertheless, death cannot surprise us any longer" (ibid.). At the end of this passage he expresses the hope that he will not encounter his own death abruptly and without preparation, but in the fullness of life; he closes with the words, "We ourselves, not external circumstances, will turn our death into that which it can become: a death freely consented to" (ibid.). One of the opportunities available to man as a species is to reconcile himself to the fact that he must die, and with respect to his own personal journey unto death he writes, "Each individual's death is the most intimate aspect . . . , the unsurpassable and irreplaceable *intimus* of his personal life,"[4] and this is true above all for the children of God.

It is as if Bonhoeffer had concretely integrated into his own life the abstract perception that the shadow of death is a shadow vital to all living beings. And that one's own death is part of one's own life, that a conscious acceptance of death is part of the totality of one's life. Moreover, acknowledgment of death implies more intensity in life; indeed it is death that makes it possible to live: "One may ask whether Bonhoeffer is not hinting here that *consent to death* liberates us to *live fully and wholeheartedly*."[5]

The third characteristic of Bonhoeffer's attitude toward death is the unquenchable hope that God's reality will set its seal on the emptiness and ineffectuality of death, by triumphing over it. In the Easter sermon he preached in Barcelona in 1928, he declared that "The heart of the Easter proclamation is: God is the death of death; God lives, and thus Christ lives as well; death had no hold over Him against the overriding power of God" (DBW 10, 465). For Bonhoeffer, *the* certainty of faith is that of participating in this conquest of death once and for all. The result was his sense that death is a transition, a new beginning; and this sense developed even before he found himself in irrevocable nearness to death. This is what he was referring to, for example, when he wrote in Tegel Prison at the end of August 1944 about the certainty that "our joy lies hidden in suffering, our life in dying" (DBW 8, 573). In saying this, his intent was neither to glorify suffering nor make a mystery out of death, but to express the reverse side of the proclamation that the resurrection "shattered the law of death" (DBW 12, 270). For Bonhoeffer, the hope of resurrection is the central axis of Christian faith. It was the alpha and omega, the basis and implication, the cause and effect of his trust in God. God is present both in life *and* in death—or He is not present at all. Resurrection is the pledge of His reality; it vitiates the ultimate destruction that gives meaning to death. His confidence in being safe and secure even in death, because of and in God's present and presence, constituted the very root of Bonhoeffer's faith.

His theology of life was matched by his theology of death. Both were anchored in the hope of resurrection based on Christ's own resurrection, and both had resurrection as their goal. The same law applies to life and death. In the section of his *Ethics* manuscript entitled "The Last and Next-to-Last Things," Bonhoeffer summed up this inseparable core of the Christian proclamation and Christian existence as follows: "It is unrealistic to play off a theology of incarnation, a theology of the cross, or a theology of resurrection against one another without absolutizing any one of them; and it is also just as great a mistake to proceed in this way when reflecting about Christian life. . . . Christian life means that being a human being is validated by the Incarnation; it means that judgement and pardon have been validated by the cross; it means living a new life through the validity of the resurrection. The one cannot be valid without the other" (DBW 6, 149–50).

It is no wonder that traces of thought about the presence of death can be found with more than usual frequency throughout the texts Bonhoeffer wrote in Tegel Prison. In the incomplete drama he wrote we are struck by the obtrusion of an enigmatic figure, who represents "the most widespread and influential company on earth," upon one of the protagonists (DBW 7, 53). This figure is none other than death, and it dominates the long dialogue that follows.

Of course, in his letters and notes in *Resistance and Surrender* we find thoughts about death and dying that are inextricably linked to Bonhoeffer's concrete situation. It is impossible here to abstract from his interpretation of the path he took in life. He attempts to formulate this interpretation while being fully aware of the fact that this task can only be done in retrospect, that an overview of life is perhaps possible only after-the-fact but never before-the-fact. In a note he wrote on a piece of paper in May 1943, he spoke about "The wait—but e.g., fully at peace with *death*." He wrote his last will and testament in September 1943 "in thankful awareness of having lived a rich and fulfilled life" (ibid., 163).

It would, however, be a mistake here to speak in visual clichés of a hero of faith, an imaginary epitome of Christian martyrdom, who goes serenely to meet his death. Bonhoeffer's actual confrontation with death did not lead him to take his leave prematurely by inwardly turning his back on life. The letters he wrote from Tegel Prison, both in *Resistance and Surrender* and those he wrote to Maria von Wedemeyer, document this once and for all. They give us a close-up view of a "flesh and blood" man. Bonhoeffer longed for the end of his imprisonment and the war. He longed for his fiancée; he wanted to marry, to have children, to work. In a nutshell: he wanted to live, to have a future. But there is also a measure of ambivalence in the letters in *Resistance and Surrender* (DBW 8, 364). In spite of all his hope for a future life in *this* world, Bonhoeffer wrote to Bethge on April 11, 1944, after an often-discussed date for his release from prison had just retreated far into an unforeseeable future, that "If my present status should turn out to be the concluding point of my life, it would have a meaning I think I could understand; on the other hand, all of it could also be a thorough preparation for a new beginning in a life marked by marriage, peace, and a new field of work" (ibid., 391). But there was to be no new beginning in this life for Bonhoeffer, for whom life would truly end in his annihilation.

In prison, Bonhoeffer was able to endure the constant awareness that his lifeline was running side by side with a line leading to death. He knew that his life was being lived out "on *this* side of the precipice" (DBW 8, 500) but that it could be ended at any time, either unannounced or with the prelude of a death sentence—in any case, violently. Nevertheless he made no attempt to turn the hope of resurrection into a grandiose declaration of the certainty of salvation, thus sweeping both the fear of death and the longing for life under a rug. He did not view the hope of resurrection as a pat formula to be kept in readiness for the event of death, to be used to water down something that cannot be watered down. He concluded a long letter he wrote on April 30, 1944[6] with these words: "At the limit of our capabilities I find it better to remain silent and not try to solve the unsolvable. A belief in resurrection *is not* the 'solution' to the problem of death" (ibid., 408).

For Bonhoeffer, this belief nevertheless remained the quintessence of the Christian view of death, especially in contrast to other interpretations: "To come to terms with dying does not mean to have no problems with death. Mastery over the act of dying is within the bounds of human capabilities; mastery over death itself is resurrection," he wrote at Easter 1944 (DBW 8, 368). Similarly, this seems to be the sense of his warning against turning the cross and suffering into a life principle; this can engender an "unhealthy methodism which robs suffering of its contingency, its character as a divine gift" (ibid., 549).

For the believer, suffering can also be contingent—a random, inexplicable chance event lying somewhere between sense and senselessness. Moreover, Bonhoeffer does not view belief in God's greatness as a solution to every problem; indeed, he perceives suffering as absolutely not an invariably "wise" and necessary act of divine dispensation. On the contrary, it may remain incomprehensible, it can make us despair, it can go against all reason and meaning. It is, "God knows," not always plausible, much less the logical culmination, in a chain of divine decisions. Neither Job from the land of Uz nor Jesus from Galilee saw the divine logic of suffering; they despaired of God *and* held fast to Him—against all reason. In post-biblical times, Tertullian formulated his *credo quia absurdum est,* "I believe because it is absurd." In this sense, freedom and faith go together. For Bonhoeffer, man's freedom in the moment of suffering also consists in and becomes comprehensible precisely in that man lays it in God's hands. Thus he concludes: "In this sense, death is the crown of human freedom" (ibid.).

In August 1944, he again turned to these thoughts in his poem "Stations on the Way to Freedom," when he described trials, human actions, suffering, and death as the milestones on the highroad to human freedom (DBW 8, 570ff). His descriptions can perhaps be interpreted as a way of experience often viewed in the history of mysticism as a way "in steps, stages, or way stations."[7] The last verse, entitled "Death," begins with the line "Now come, thou Highest Feast 'fore everlasting freedom" and ends with "And dying see Thee in God's face" (ibid., 572).

It would appear from all we know that Bonhoeffer himself experienced this liberation from fear as it became clear to him that his death was a foregone conclusion. The convoy of prisoners that included Bonhoeffer was quartered in a school building in the town of Schönberg at the beginning of April 1945, after an odyssey from one concentration camp to another, that is, from Buchenwald to Flossenbürg.[8]

At the request of his fellow prisoners, Bonhoeffer improvised a divine service on the Sunday after Easter. Shortly thereafter the door swung open, and "two civilians called out 'prisoner Bonhoeffer, get your things and come with us!'"[9] Bonhoeffer then said his last known words, asking his English fellow prisoner Payne Best to bring the following message to his friend Bishop Bell: This was "the end but also the beginning" of life for him; he believed together with him in the universal brotherhood of all Christians, whose victory is a certainty; he would never forget his friend's words at their last meeting.

The first part of this message for the bishop of Chichester probably contains Bonhoeffer's most often quoted statements, and carefully researched studies have been made to determine their exact wording.[10] One especially fascinating and very loving, but also historically and critically accurate, study mentions in this context the motto of another prisoner, Maria Stuart: *En ma fin est mon commencement*,[11] "in my end is my beginning." However Bonhoeffer phrased his sentence—"This is the end, for me the beginning of life" or "For me this is the end but also the beginning"—it expresses in a nutshell his deep certainty of the reality of God. It was also on this day, Low Sunday in the church calendar, April 8, 1945, exactly one month before the final capitulation of the so-called Thousand Year Reich and the end of the war in Germany, that Bonhoeffer was brought to Flossenbürg and murdered a few hours later, at the break of dawn on April 9. We have no way of knowing his inner sensations as he met death. But there is every indication that the certainty spoken about immediately after the beginning of the war (DBW 15, 271), namely, that death "is indeed merely a transition to the fullness of God's love" had not abandoned him, and that for him too the human dread of death melted away before the promise of God's nearness—and not vice versa.

24

Future Memories

We are workers, not master builders,
ministers, not messiahs.
We are prophets of a future that is not our own.
Amen.

Oscar Arnulfo Romero

Bonhoeffer fascinated others involuntarily and spontaneously for a time, as a friend, brother, teacher, fellow man, conspirator, and fellow traveler through time. But a time came when this fascination changed, without diminishing in impact, and became—one might say—a "fascination with stepping into the gap."

In contrast to many Christians whose motto of faith in action had been more or less "surrender *without* resistance," Bonhoeffer was *the* countercultural model for the postwar generation—postwar in the wider sense; in other words, for those who experienced the war only as children and those born during and immediately after the war. The encounter with *Resistance and Surrender* was a seminal theological and political experience for the present author as well. Within Protestantism, it was Bonhoeffer above all who did what we and our elders had not done; who drew the conclusions we and our elders had not drawn; in short, he stepped into the gap and bore the burden in the past, while becoming a prototype of hope for the future. The seed was sown for what we might call "the Bonhoeffer effect" as one generation relays the baton to the next.

In the 1950s and early 1960s, Bonhoeffer was rediscovered—step by step and often amidst much controversy—in theology and the church, in schools and church communities, by those whose *confessio* and *professio* it is to make faith and theology communicable and comprehensible, including the "little flock" of women theologians (whose numbers are slowly growing).

This was followed by the so-called laity's discovery of Bonhoeffer—within Catholicism as well—and by the general public. This awareness, which was at one time sporadic, has long since become a continuum, an established state of affairs. Since the late 1960s, many teachers of theology have regarded Bonhoeffer's person and work, his life and theology, his ethics and personal commitment, almost as a matter-of-course wellspring of knowledge, convictions, and orientation, and this holds true for us today: Bonhoeffer as an epitome of Christian *and* political existence; Bonhoeffer, nonpareil in his own time, exemplary for a later time; Bonhoeffer, without whom today the views of the church, the proclamation of faith, and the teaching of theology would be impossible; Bonhoeffer, without a doubt the best-known Protestant theologian of the present, at least outside the confines of formal theology and beyond the confines of church, confession, and church communities.

This circumstance of course sets the stage for turning Bonhoeffer into an object of veneration. But we know at least one person—namely, Bonhoeffer himself—who regarded Bonhoeffer as anything but a saint or an icon to be placed on a pedestal.[1] The danger of idolizing or turning Bonhoeffer into an icon remains great, but it also remains contrary to his own view. As he once noted with respect to the Great Reformer, "Kierkegaard said it more than 100 years ago: Luther today would say just the opposite of what he said in his own day" (DBW 8, 179)! And how would Bonhoeffer himself revise this *bon mot* today?

The words "idol" and "icon," as we know, derive from Greek words that refer to a picture, image, or idol. But Bonhoeffer was a human being with weaknesses and strengths, hopes and fears, faith and doubts; there is no reason to heave him onto a silver pedestal of spotless admiration—unless we *want* to hold him at arm's length from ourselves and others (for every pedestal creates distance rather than affinity). Moreover, such idolizing would be not only un-Christian but also quite un-Protestant. A saint on a pedestal would inherently be far removed from us, an unattainable model having no real connection to our own lives. If we want to ensure that Bonhoeffer will not be forgotten, we must be clear about the fact that mummification and sacralization are also forms of forgetfulness.

Another form of forgetfulness would be to marginalize Bonhoeffer through a gradual process that makes him—once again—"a theological vagrant," who exists "somehow on the outer limits of our church" (DBW 11, 117–18), as he said of himself in 1932. Will Bonhoeffer once again become a borderline case in church and theology? Three developments have the potential to diminish Bonhoeffer's impact: here we will refer to them as the "renaissance of religion," the "forgotten God," and the "generation gap."

Since the 1980s, we have witnessed a renaissance of religion, not only outside the walls of church and theology but also *intra muros*, that is, within the church and theology. One may welcome this development or regret it. But in any case it hampers, hinders—even precludes—interpretation and/or discussion of what Bonhoeffer meant when he used the expressions religious *a priori*, religion-less age, and non-religious interpretation of the Bible. Theologians today respond to the question "Where do you stand on the subject of religion?" quite differently from their forebears, and the history of this crucial question within Evangelical theology, along with the answers, remains to be written. At a time when "feelings," the "experience" of God, a new "interiority," and religious fatalism have risen—so to speak—from the ashes and again come to the fore in many places, there is the danger that Bonhoeffer will be relegated to a back shelf in theology and the church. In itself, this renaissance of religion is beneficial, for there can be no doubt that emotion and spirituality have been largely banned from the language of Protestantism far too long. But when this is used as justification for separating the theological and political dimensions of human life one from the other, and for reinterpreting the relationship between faith and society as if they were two different worlds, leaving the church and theology at the mercy of an illusionary, other-worldly form of piety, then it is only (theo-)logical that a man like Dietrich Bonhoeffer will figure only as a footnote in theology and the history of the church.

The second development that has the potential to bring about Bonhoeffer's marginalization is the "forgotten God." The most radical form of atheism is one example of this attitude, as is the denial of God's existence in our concrete being and actions—the attitude of the man for whom God is no longer present even as a question. Other examples include the complete disappearance of the question of theodicy and a cool denial of—or even total indifference toward—the question of God's reality. Still another is the monotonous, indifferent response to these questions found in individual biographies of faith, assuming that faith even exists. Bonhoeffer—in a time of postmodern second thoughts—is a contradiction of terms.

The third development that has the potential either to marginalize Bonhoeffer's thought and impact, or to reinforce it, is the generation gap. The continuum mentioned above can no longer be taken for granted; the "ugly historical gap" cannot be skipped over. The Second World War—and even more, the First World War—have receded in the consciousness of today's children and young adults to the point that they have become more or less a matter of historical indifference. But it would be absurd to cultivate an attitude of reproach here.

Yet another development is the notion that the year 2000 is a sort of magical expiration date. Things that come to mind when we think of National Socialism or Fascism, world war and persecution of the Jews, collaborators and accessories, conspiracy and resistance, are consigned to a place "back in the previous century," thus making them once and for all "has-been."

Where do we ourselves stand with respect to the project of re-membrance? Do we want to accept the risk of forgetting? Attempts to rescue a collective social memory are nonsensical in and of themselves, but not when the goal is to establish an orientation for life in the future. Here we must of course be aware that all memory is a reconstruction of reality, an interpretation of past reality by those who are *still* living, those who have *survived*. What we do with memories determines whether they foster forgetfulness or put the past permanently to rest. Theodor W. Adorno once said in a lecture that we are compelled to philosophize, in order to have no shame before those who have been murdered. The same could be said *mutatis mutandis* with respect to theology, the proclamation of faith, and—in particular—Dietrich Bonhoeffer as part of that proclamation.

If we do not wish to fall victim to a tendency that makes either a statue or a borderline case of Bonhoeffer, we must ask ourselves the question: why not? Bonhoeffer can provide orientation and stability in any area of truth. He is an example of life and faith—no more and no less! Through Bonhoeffer, we see and experience the importance of living and believing each in our *own* way. Thus in each age transposing his political ethics into the present and the future is a worthwhile project. The bridge from the present to the past can indeed become a bridge to our own future inasmuch as we perceive and hold fast to the antinomies of faith: the suffering God *and* the God of promise; ethics as simple *and* devilishly difficult to practice in life; death as an enemy *and* a brother; the cry of abandonment on the cross *and* the certainty of God's reality at the end.

What Bonhoeffer presents as specific to the Christian faith is the perception of God and the world as one, and the perception of life that has its wellspring in this world in God, and in turn proceeds from this world back again to God. This is the *proprium* of his theology, his ethics, and his personal piety. The political Bonhoeffer is unthinkable without the theological Bonhoeffer, the worldly Bonhoeffer without the Bonhoeffer of deep faith, the later without the earlier Bonhoeffer. Any attempt to separate the one from the other does injustice to the ensemble of his faith and thought.

What is striking about Bonhoeffer is precisely continuity and integrity. His combination of mysticism and resistance, to borrow from Dorothee Sölle, his interlaced rationality and emotionality, his love of God and the world, and his own personal road of political protest within Protestantism are the elements of a model of Christian existence that has yet to become widely accepted.

Bonhoeffer was of great significance in particular for Christians who lived, and still live, in situations and systems of oppression.[2] Even persons in other religions felt strongly attracted to him; Pinchas Lapide, for example, mentioned the "fascination this man exerted" over him for years.[3] There is also a wealth of ecumenical potential in Bonhoeffer's work that has yet to be mined. In 1991, the Catholic theologian and Bonhoeffer scholar Ernst Feil wrote about Bonhoeffer that "It seems to me that an important contribution to ecumenism is present in Bonhoeffer's theology, one that both sides have not yet begun to identify and process."[4] As Bethge summed up in his biography, Bonhoeffer's "catholic" impact was apparent "wherever larger groups and cell groups experimented, where new structures for church communities were tried out and new forms of political solidarity were ventured; where . . . questions of atheism and cooperation with non-Christians were regarded as an acceptable part of humanized life together. It is there that Bonhoeffer proves to be the one who gives courage to sail out of the harbor before it becomes clogged with sand."[5]

Traces of the "Bonhoeffer effect" are found much too seldom in our church, in the world of ecumenism, and last but not least among non-Christians as well. While such traces may perhaps be better than nothing at all, we are called upon at least to follow them up and indeed to multiply their impact. They can immunize us against the re-emergence of an a-political Christian existence. They offer answers to the question of who Christ is for us today. They open up for us the possibility of a faith capable of embracing, without inner contradictions, both this concrete world and the reality of God immanent in and transcending it. Bonhoeffer is an inspiration toward Christian existence in a future world.

Bonhoeffer's self-confident, God-confident manner of believing went hand in hand with a natural openness and empathy for persons who thought quite differently from him. While actively working on behalf of tolerance, he did not mistake it for passivity or justification for an "anything goes" mentality. What we learn from him is a tolerance and an autonomy *sui generis,* along with empathy for men and women who despair before God and the world. Bonhoeffer's Christ-centered *and* autonomous ethics, his Christ-centered *and* (world-)open thought, his despairing *but* rock-solid hope in God, make him an example of faith in life and life in faith.

Just as it would be senseless and unrealistic to regard Bonhoeffer as obsolete, so it would likewise be an injustice to sacralize him. It would be much more appropriate in our real world to take him and his radicalness at his own word. It falls to us, the living, to interpret Bonhoeffer anew in the changed conditions of our time and to work out the further implications of this thought.

It is perhaps a utopian thought, but it may be that in the future Bonhoeffer's presence in our world will consist less in talking about him than in understanding his true meaning for our time. In other words, understanding him not only "through thoughts and words" *about* him but also through "works" as he envisioned them; that is, more authentically in correspondence with the real world.

Bonhoeffer himself was aware that he was neither one of the great thinkers nor one of the heroes of faith. And in any case there is little sense in trying to freeze him in a category. The purpose of this book has not been to point the way to *the one and only* path to understanding him, but to describe *a viable* path. Anyone who reads Bonhoeffer for himself will perhaps have the same experience as the present author during the writing of this introduction to the thought of a man whom I felt I already knew—namely, "astonishment time and again; astonishment at how different the man is, how multi-faceted, and not simply one way or the other, not a finished picture."[6]

But without a doubt, whoever reads him will also experience something else: Bonhoeffer's thought, especially that of his final years, is to be understood as conclusions drawn from his deepest personal faith, his theology, his personal and his political existence. *As such* and by their very nature they qualify as a model for future Christian existence.

Notes

Notes to Chapter 1

1. Christian Gremmels and Hans Pfeifer, *Theologie und Biographie: Zum Beispiel Dietrich Bonhoeffer* (Munich: Kaiser, 1983), 99, with reference to *Resistance and Surrender*.

2. On the development of Bonhoeffer's personal piety, see Herbert Rainer Pelikan, *Die Frömmigkeit Dietrich Bonhoeffers: Dokumentation, Grundlinien, Entwicklung* (Wien: Herder, 1982); and Werner Kallen, *In der Gewißheit seiner Gegenwart: Dietrich Bonhoeffer und die Spur des vermißten Gottes* (Mainz: Matthias-Grünewald, 1997).

3. See the Foreword to Otto Dudzus, ed., *Dietrich Bonhoeffer Lesebuch* (Munich: Kaiser, 1987), 8.

4. See Eberhard Bethge, *Dietrich Bonhoeffer: Eine Biographie* (8th ed.; Gütersloh: Kaiser, 1994); Eberhard Bethge, Renate Bethge, and Christian Gremmels, eds. *Dietrich Bonhoeffer: Sein Leben in Bildern und Texten* (Munich: Kaiser, 1986).

5. Eberhard Bethge, *Dietrich Bonhoeffer mit Selbstzeugnissen und Bilddokumenten* (17th ed.; Reinbek bei Hamburg: Rowohlt, 1999). See also Christian Feldmann, *"Wir hätten schreien müssen": Das Leben des Dietrich Bonhoeffer* (Freiburg im Breisgau: Herder, 1998); Edwin H. Robertson, *Dietrich Bonhoeffer: Leben und Verkündigung* (Göttingen: Vandenhoeck & Ruprecht, 1989); and Renate Wind, *Dem Rad in die Speichen fallen: Die Lebensgeschichte des Dietrich Bonhoeffer* (Weinheim, Basel: Beltz & Gelberg, 1990).

6. See Ernst Feil, *Die Theologie Dietrich Bonhoeffers: Hermeneutik, Christologie, Weltverständinis* (Munich: Kaiser, 1991).

7. See Ernst Feil, ed., *Internationale Bibliographie zu Dietrich Bonhoeffer* (Gütersloh: Chr. Kaiser and Gütersloher Verlagshaus, 1998).

8. Sabine Dramm, *Dietrich Bonhoeffer und Albert Camus: Analogien im Kontrast* (Gütersloh: Kaiser, 1998), 173.

9. Helmut Gollwitzer, *Krummes Holz—aufrechter Gang: Zur Frage nach dem Sinn des Lebens* (Munich: Kaiser, 1970), 13–14.

Notes to Chapter 2

1. See chapter 21.
2. See chapters 14 and 18.
3. On the inner and outer developments in Bonhoeffer's journey into the Resistance, see the corresponding chapters in Bethge, *Biographie*, 763ff. See also the sources referenced in chapter 18.
4. On the last phase of Bonhoeffer's life see Bethge, *Biographie*, 1001ff. See also chapter 23.

Notes to Chapter 3

1. See also the Afterword to DBW 8, 633–34 and 657–58.
2. Both texts are quoted from the Foreword of DBW 7, 15.
3. See my comments elsewhere under the chapter entitled "Facetten eines Lebens" in Dramm, *Bonhoeffer und Camus*, 71ff.
4. Thoroughly documented and discussed in Christian Gremmels and Wolfgang Huber, eds., *Theologie und Freundschaft, Wechselwirkungen: Eberhard Bethge und Dietrich Bonhoeffer* (Gütersloh: Gütersloher, 1994).
5. Bethge, *Biographie*, 491.
6. Reprinted in Eberhard Bethge, Renate Bethge, and Christian Gremmels, *Bietrich Bonhoeffer: Sein Leben in Bildern und Texten*, (Gütersloh: Gütersloher, 2005).
7. Reprinted in German translation in Bethge, Bethge, and Gremmels, *Leben in Bildern*, 137. See also DBW 13, 213–14 and 499–500. See also chapter 20.

Notes to Chapter 4

1. See also Feil, *Theologie Dietrich Bonhoeffers*. On this dimension of Bonhoeffer's theology, especially his theology during the Finkenwalde period, see Sabine Bobert-Stützel, *Dietrich Bonhoeffers Pastoraltheologie: Theologenausbildung im Widerstand zum "Dritten Reich"—dargestellt anhand der Finkenwalder Vorlesungen, 1935–1937* (Gütersloh: Kaiser, 1995).
2. On this subject see the works mentioned in Christian Gremmels, ed., *Bonhoeffer und Luther: Zur Sozialgestalt des Luthertums in der Moderne* (Internationales Bonhoeffer Forum 6; Munich: Kaiser, 1983).
3. Karl Barth, *Die Lehre von der Versöhnung, vol. IV/2* in *Die Kirchliche Dogmatik* (5 vols.; 2d ed.; Zürich: EVZ-Verlag, 1964), 725.
4. Bethge, *Selbstzeugnissen und Bilddokumenten*, 27.
5. Reprinted in DBW 11, 19 note 4.
6. Karl Barth, "An P. W. Herrenbrück 1952," in *Die mündige Welt: Dem Andenken Dietrich Bonhoeffers, Vorträge und Briefe* (5 vols.; Munich: Kaiser, 1955–1969). See DBW 11, 121.

7. Barth, *Lehre von der Versöhnung*, 725. See also chapter 9.

8. See the Afterword to DBW 2, 184.

9. Ibid., 185.

Notes to Chapter 5

1. It should be noted that the term "expressionism" is not used in this context without the awareness that it also has other connotations. Bonhoeffer, by the way, distanced himself as far as possible from this contemporary current of expressionism; see DBW 10, 325, editor's note 5. Regarding Bonhoeffer's use of the word "dialectic" in his earlier writings, see Feil, *Theologie Dietrich Bonhoeffers*, 119–20, who suggests that it would be better to call Karl Barth's dialectic theology "paradoxal theology," drawing attention in this context to Bonhoeffer's tendency to use paradoxical statements.

2. Bethge, *Biographie*, 214. See in this context chapter 4 as well as the beginning and end of the Afterword to DBW 3, 143–44 and 163.

3. On Bonhoeffer's partiality for the term "paradox" see also the editor's remark in DBW 4, 73 note 16.

4. Bethge, *Biographie*, 974.

5. See chapter 20.

Notes to Chapter 6

1. In full awareness that the term "reality" is extremely burdened from the very beginning—no less than the term "truth"—with philosophical, socio-cognitive, and theological connotations, it is used here in accordance with Bonhoeffer's own footnote in *Act and Being* (see DBW 2, 83 note 17). On Bonhoeffer's use and understanding of the term "reality," see the corresponding chapter in Feil, *Theologie Dietrich Bonhoeffers*.

2. On this subject in particular, see DBW 1, 133 and Feil, *Theologie Dietrich Bonhoeffers*, 141ff. See also chapter 9.

3. See DBW 2, 112. See also chapters 5 and 9.

4. Bethge, *Biographie*, 574 and 934; Dramm, *Bonhoeffer und Camus*, 71ff. See also chapter 3 of this book.

5. For an interpretation of this poem and others, see Johann Christoph Hampe, *Von guten Mächten: Gebete und Gedichte/Dietrich Bonhoeffer* (Gütersloh: Gütersloher Verlagshaus, 1976); and Jürgen Henkys, *Dietrich Bonhoeffers Gefängnisgedichte: Beiträge zu ihrer Interpretation* (Munich: Kaiser, 1986).

6. On this topic, see Feil, *Theologie Dietrich Bonhoeffers*, 65 and 101. See also chapter 16 of this book.

7. Christian Gremmels, "Dietrich Bonhoeffer," in *Religion in Geschichte und Gegenwart: Handwörterbuch für Theologie und Religionswissenschaft* (ed. Hans Dieter Betz et al.; 10 vols.; 4th ed.; Tübingen: Mohr Siebeck, 1998), especially 1:1684.

Notes to Chapter 7

1. Feil, *Theologie Dietrich Bonhoeffers*, 135.
2. Rainer Mayer, *Christuswirklichkeit, Grundlagen, Entwicklungen und Konsequenzen der Theologie Dietrich Bonhoeffers* (Stuttgart: Calwer, 1969).
3. See chapter 20.
4. See the summary and commentary by Craig L. Nessan and Renate Wind, *Wer bist Du, Christus? Ein ökumenisches Lesebuch zur Christologie Dietrich Bonhoeffer* (Gütersloh: Kaiser, 1998).
5. See chapter 10.
6. Bonhoeffer is basing his comments here on Mark 8:31–38.
7. On the *Ethics* as a whole, see chapter 11.
8. On the importance of Nietzsche in Bonhoeffer's thought as a whole, see Tiemo Rainer Peters, *Die Präsenz des Politischen in der Theologie Dietrich Bonhoeffers* (Munich: Kaiser; Mainz: Grünewald, 1976), 133ff. On Bonhoeffer's *Ethics*, see Peter Köster, "Nietzsche als verborgener Antipode in Bonhoeffers *ETHIK*," *Nietzsche-Studien*. 19 (1990).

Notes to Chapter 8

1. This is the basic "formula" that Bonhoeffer's dissertation revolves around. Both it and *Sanctorum Communio* as a whole are discussed in greater detail in chapter 9.
2. Wolfgang Huber, "Evangelischer Glaube und die Frage nach der Kirche," in *Das Wesen des Christentums in seiner evangelischen Gestalt: Eine Vortragsreihe im Berliner Dom* (Neukirchen-Vluyn: Neukirchener, 2000), 69.
3. See also chapters 4 and 24.
4. This vision will be discussed repeatedly.
5. See chapter 7.
6. On this text see also chapter 4.
7. Bonhoeffer's view of death is discussed in detail in chapter 23.
8. See Karl Barth, *Die Lehre von Gott*, Vol. II/2, in *Die Kirchliche Dogmatik* (5 vols.; 4th ed.; Zürich: EVZ, 1959).
9. See DBW 16, 277 note 2.

10. Gotthold Müller, "Ungeheuerliche Ontologie: Erwägungen zur christlichen Lehre über Hölle und Allversöhnung," *Evangelische Theologie* 34 (1974/3), 270.

11. This will be taken up again in chapter 10.

12. It is no coincidence that Feil's book, for one, closes with references to Bonhoeffer's thoughts on *Apokatastasis;* see Feil, *Theologie Dietrich Bonhoeffers,* 399.

13. See also chapter 22 on this subject.

14. Quoted according to Christian Gremmels and Heinrich W. Grosse, *Dietrich Bonhoeffer: Der Weg in den Widerstand, Mit Beiträgen von Eberhard and Renate Bethge et al.* (Gütersloh: Kaiser, 1996), 49–50.

15. See in particular Rom 11:30–33; 2 Cor 5:18–21; Eph 1:10 and 1:23; Col 1:15–23; 1 John 2:2, etc.

Notes to Chapter 9

1. Feil, *Theologie Dietrich Bonhoeffers,* 38 note 37.

2. See Bethge, *Biographie,* 166–67.

3. The latter has also been published in Gütersloh, "*Druck und Verlag von C. Bertelsmann*" (see the facsimile in DBW 2, 19), where it has now been reintegrated.

4. See chapter 4 note 7.

5. Quoted in the Foreword to DBW 1, 5.

6. Dietrich Goldschmidt, "Zur Religionssoziologie in der Bundesrepublik Deutschland," *Archives de Sociologie des Religions* 8 (1959; [Sonder-druck; Special printing]), 61.

7. See the Afterword to DBW 1, 314.

8. Concerning this "formula" and Bonhoeffer's transposition from Hegel in *Sanctorum Communio,* see Feil, *Theologie Dietrich Bonhoeffers,* 145ff.; Hans Pfeifer's comments in Gremmels and Pfeifer, *Theologie und Biographie,* 32–33; and Wolfgang Huber, "Wahrheit und Existenzform: Anregungen zu einer Theorie der Kirche bei Dietrich Bonhoeffer," in Ernst Feil and Ilse Tödt, eds., *Konsequenzen: Dietrich Bonhoeffers Kirchenverständnis heute* (Internationales Bonhoeffer Forum 3; Munich: Kaiser, 1980), 92ff.

9. See the Afterword to DBW 12, 476. On this topic in general, see Ilse Tödt, ed., *Dietrich Bonhoeffers Hegelseminar 1933: Nach den Aufzeichnungen von Ferenc Lehel* (Internationales Bonhoeffer Forum 8; Munich: Kaiser, 1988).

10. See von Soosten, in DBW 1, 320.

11. See Reuter in DBW 1, 163.

12. Ibid., 164.

13. See on this subject Feil, *Theologie Dietrich Bonhoeffers,* 38–39 notes 39–40. On *Sanctorum Communio* as a whole see ibid., 29ff. and 141ff.; on *Act and Being* as a whole see ibid., 38ff. and 149ff.

14. Quoted in the Foreword to DBW 2, 12.

15. See in particular two comprehensive scientific studies: Christiane Tietz-Steiding, *Bonhoeffers Kritik der verkrümmenten Vernunft: Eine erkenntnistheoretische Untersuchung* (Tübingen: Mohr Siebeck, 1999); and Jürgen Boomgaarden, "Das Verständnis der Wirklichkeit: Dietrich Bonhoeffers Systematische Theologie und ihr philosophischer Hintergrund," in *Akt und Sein* (Gütersloh: Kaiser, 1999).

16. See Reuter in DBW 2, 185.

17. See also chapter 6.

18. On thoughts of universal reconciliation and the eschatology of *Apokatastasis* (DBW 2, 160), see chapter 8.

19. Foreword to DBW 2, 8 and Bonhoeffer's letter to Helmut Rößler dated August 7, 1928 (DBW 10, 92).

Notes to Chapter 10

1. On the history of the writing of *Discipleship,* see Bethge, *Biographie,* 515ff; on *Discipleship,* see also ibid., 519; and Feil, *Theologie Dietrich Bonhoeffers,* 177ff. and 270ff.

2. See Bethge, *Biographie,* 167.

3. Barth, *Die Lehre von der Versöhnung,* 604.

4. See von Weizsäcker, in Barth, *Die Lehre von der Versöhnung,* 347 and 346. See also Carl Friedrich von Weizsäcker, "Gedanken eines Nichttheologen zur theologischen Entwicklung Dietrich Bonhoeffers (1976)" in *Der Garten des Menschlichen: Beiträge zur geschichtlichen Anthropologie* (Munich: C. Hanser, 1977), 346–47.

5. See DBW 4, e.g., 23, 37–38, etc.; on Kierkegaard's influence on Bonhoeffer as found in *Discipleship,* see Feil, *Theologie Dietrich Bonhoeffers,* 277 note 39 and the Afterword to DBW 4, 319.

6. Søren Kierkegaard, *Die Tagebücher* (trans. and ed. Hayo Gerdes; Düsseldorf: E. Diederich, 1980), 315.

7. See chapter 8.

8. On Bonhoeffer's worldview in *Discipleship* and the contradictions there, as well as his later worldview, see Feil, *Theologie Dietrich Bonhoeffers,* 270ff.

9. See chapter 15.

10. See my own reflections on this question in Sabine Dramm, "Jenseits der Diesseitigkeit? Mystik bei Dietrich Bonhoeffer," in *Christliche Mystik als Thema ökumenischer Theologie und Praxis: Konturen-*

Konkretionen-Konsequenzen (Arnoldshainer Texte 114; ed. Hermann Düringer; Frankfurt am Main: Haag & Herchen, 2001).

11. The special parallels between Theresa of Avila and Dietrich Bonhoeffer were pointed out in the 1980s by Schlingensiepen. For more on this subject and the interpretation of Bonhoeffer as a mystic see also Kallen, *In der Gewißheit.*

12. See Dorothee Sölle, *Mystik und Widerstand: "Du stilles Geschrei"* (Munich: R. Piper, 2000.), 108. See also chapter 23.

13. See von Weizsäcker, "Gedanken eines Nichttheologen," 347.

14. See von Weizsäcker, "Gedanken eines Nichttheologen," 347. See also chapter 12.

15. On this subject, see Bethge, *Biographie,* 535.

Notes to Chapter 11

1. See Bethge, *Biographie,* 793 and 804.

2. See the supplemental volume to the *Ethics* in DBW 6a, and the Foreword and Afterword in DBW 6, in particular 9ff. and 447ff.

3. See also chapter 8.

4. See the Afterword in DBW 6, 438.

5. See chapter 9. See also Bethge, *Biographie,* 89, 94, 102, etc. There was also personal contact between Bonhoeffer's parents and the brothers Alfred and Max Weber.

6. See chapter 18.

7. Max Weber, "Politik als Beruf (1919)," in *Gesammelte Politische Schriften* (ed. Johannes Winckelmann; 5th ed.; Tübingen, J. C. B. Mohr [Paul Siebeck], 1988), 551.

8. Ibid., 552.

9. Dramm, *Bonhoeffer und Camus,* 118.

10. See Dramm, *Bonhoeffer und Camus,* 82ff.

11. See chapter 13. As the most recent edition of the *Ethics* correctly notes, the manuscript *Das natürliche Leben* marks "the first time that a German Protestant theologian of the twentieth century developed a theological ethics of human rights and basic rights" (DBW 6, 217 note 151).

Notes to Chapter 12

1. Feil, *Theologie Dietrich Bonhoeffer,* 289.

2. See von Weizsäcker, "Gedanken eines Nichttheologen," 347. See also chapter 10.

3. Afterword to DBW 8, 654.

4. Thus formulated in the title of Köster's study of Nietzsche's influence on Bonhoeffer's *Ethics,* "Nietzsche als verborgener Antipode."

5. Bonhoeffer's sources of "inspiration" in Life Affirmation philosophy are studied by Peters, *Präsenz des Politischen,* 128ff. See also Feil, *Theologie Dietrich Bonhoeffers,* 132 note 20.

6. Bethge, *Biographie,* 801.

7. Bethge, *Biographie,* 973 note 175. For greater detail see Feil, *Theologie Dietrich Bonhoeffers,* 355ff. See also chapter 21 of this book.

Notes to Chapter 13

1. Quoted by Gremmels and Grosse, *Der Weg in den Widerstand,* 37.

2. See also chapter 3.

3. Pinchas E. Lapide, "Bonhoeffer und das Judentum," in *Verspieltes Erbe? Dietrich Bonhoeffer und der deutsche Nachkriegsprotestantismus* (ed. Ernst Feil; Internationales Bonhoeffer Forum 2; Munich: Kaiser, 1979), 124.

4. See also chapter 11.

5. Thus an editorial footnote in the new edition of the *Ethics* (DBW 6, 181 note 55).

6. See Bethge, *Biographie,* 174; Feil, *Theologie Dietrich Bonhoeffer,* 191; and DBW 3, 114 note 3.

Notes to Chapter 14

1. This will be studied in detail in chapter 18.

2. This situation too will be analyzed in greater detail in chapter 18.

3. This situation too will be analyzed in greater detail in chapter 18.

4. On this sentence see also chapters 7 and 10.

5. Yorick Spiegel, "Dietrich Bonhoeffer und die 'preußisch-protestantische Welt," in *Verspieltes Erbe? Dietrich Bonhoeffer und der deutsche Nachkriegsprotestantismus* (ed. Ernst Feil; Internationales Bonhoeffer Forum 2; Munich: Kaiser, 1979), 68.

6. Thus expressed in the German summary of de Lange's Dutch dissertation, *Grond onder de voeten,* 468. The English translation of the title is *Solid Ground under His Feet: The Middle-Class Way of Life of Dietrich Bonhoeffer.*

7. Ibid., 470.

8. Thus, for instance, Klaus Michael Kodalle, *Dietrich Bonhoeffer: Zur Kritik seiner Theologie* (Gütersloh: Gütersloher Verlagshaus, 1991) on the one hand, and Georg Huntemann, *Der andere Bonhoeffer: Die Herausforderung des Modernismus* (Wuppertal: R. Brockhaus, 1989) on the other.

9. See Bethge, *Biographie*, 57.

10. Ibid., 153.

11. See chapter 20.

12. Bethge, *Selbstzeugnissen und Bilddokumenten*, 117.

13. Tiemo Rainer Peters, "Jenseits von Radikalismus und Kompromiß: Die politische Verantwortung der Christen nach Dietrich Bonhoeffer," in *Verspieltes Erbe? Dietrich Bonhoeffer und der deutsche Nachkriegsprotestantismus* (ed. Ernst Feil; Internationales Bonhoeffer Forum 2; Munich: Kaiser, 1979), 105.

14. Kodalle, *Zur Kritik seiner Theologie*, 44.

15. See chapter 15.

16. See chapter 18 here concerning this essay as a whole.

17. See Bethge, *Biographie*, 272ff.

18. On this subject see also chapters 4 and 8.

Notes to Chapter 15

1. More on this in chapter 18.

2. On this subject see Hans Pfeifer, ed., *Frieden—das unumgängliche Wagnis: Die Gegenwartsbedeutung der Friedensethik Dietrich Bonhoeffers* (Internationales Bonhoeffer Forum 5; Munich: Kaiser, 1982).

3. Martin Heimbucher, *Christusfriede—Weltfrieden: Dietrich Bonhoeffers kirchlicher und politischer Kampf gegen den Krieg Hitlers und seine theologische Begründung* (Gütersloh: Kaiser, 1997), 16.

4. See also chapter 14.

5. Thus the sober comment of the editor in DBW 10, 387–88 note 18.

6. On Bonhoeffer's personal ecumenical commitment see also chapter 16.

7. Eberhard Bethge, "Dietrich Bonhoeffers Weg vom 'Pazifismus' zur Verschwörung," in *Frieden—das unumgängliche Wagnis: Die Gegenwartsbedeutung der Friedensethik Dietrich Bonhoeffers* (ed. Hans Pfeifer; Internationales Bonhoeffer Forum 5; Munich: Kaiser, 1982), 118–19.

8. Afterword to DBW 12, 499.

Notes to Chapter 16

1. Gremmels and Pfeifer, *Theologie und Biographie*, 37.

2. On the general significance of "church" for Bonhoeffer, see, for example, Ernst Lange, "Kirche für andere: Dietrich Bonhoeffers Beitrag zur Frage einer verantwortbaren Gestalt der Kirche in der Gegenwart, 1967," in *Kirche für die Welt: Aufsätze zur Theorie kirchlichen* (ed. Ernst Lange; Munich: Kaiser; Gelnhausen: Burckardthaus, 1981); Huber, "Wahrheit und Existenzform"; and chapters 8 and 9.

3. See chapter 6.

4. Lange, "Kirche für andere," 38.

5. Huber, "Wahrheit und Existenzform," 122–23.

6. On this subject see the Afterword to DBW 16, 681–82.

7. On the message for Bell, see also chapters 10 and 23.

8. Quoted in the Foreword to DBW 14, 10.

9. Huber, "Wahrheit und Existenzform," 113.

10. Feil, *Theologie Dietrich Bonhoeffers*, 61.

11. Karl Dietrich Bracher, *Stufen der Machtergreifung* (Frankfurt am Main: Ullstein, 1974), 443.

12. See chapter 17 for more details.

13. See, for example, Bethge, *Biographie*, 363ff.

14. On Bonhoeffer's Fanø call for peace see chapter 15.

15. See Karl Kupisch, *Das Zeitalter der Revolutionen und Weltkriege: 1815–1945* (vol. 5 in *Kirchengeschichte;* 5 vols.; Stuttgart: Kohlhammer, 1975), 63.

16. Bethge, *Biographie*, 325 and 374.

Notes to Chapter 17

1. Winfried Meyer, *Unternehmen Sieben: Eine Rettungsaktion für vom Holocaust Bedrohte aus dem Amt Ausland/Abwehr im Oberkommando der Wehrmacht* (Frankfurt am Main: Hain, 1993), 8.

2. Thus the short title of Eberhard Bethge, "Dietrich Bonhoeffer und die Juden," in *Konsequenzen: Dietrich Bonhoeffers Kirchenverständnis heute* (Internationales Bonhoeffer Forum 3; ed. Ernst Feil and Ilse Tödt; Munich: Kaiser, 1980).

3. See on this subject, for instance, Lapide, "Bonhoeffer und das Judentum" and Bertold Klappert, "Weg und Wende Dietrich Bonhoeffers in der Israelfrage," in *Ethik im Ernstfall: Dietrich Bonhoeffers Stellung zu den Juden und ihre Aktualität* (Internationales Bonhoeffer Forum 4; eds. Wolfgang Huber and Ilse Tödt; Munich: Kaiser, 1982).

4. See on this subject as a whole, for instance, the corresponding chapter in Keith W. Clements, *Freisein wozu? Dietrich Bonhoeffer als ständige Herausforderung* (Bonn: Pahl-rugenstein, 1991), 189ff.

5. Lapide, "Bonhoeffer und das Judentum," 118.

6. See Bethge, *Biographie*, 57–58. See also chapter 14.

7. Wolfgang Gerlach, *Als die Zeugen schwiegen: Bekennende Kirche und die Juden* (2d ed.; Studien zu Kirche und Israel 10; Berlin: Instut Kirche und Judentum, 1993), 61.

8. This has been studied in detail by Bonhoeffer researchers. See Wolfgang Huber and Ilse Tödt, eds., *Ethik im Ernstfall: Dietrich Bon-*

hoeffers Stellung zu den Juden und ihre Aktualität (Internationales Bonhoeffer Forum 4; Munich: Kaiser, 1982).

9. Heinz Eduard Tödt, "Judendiskriminierung 1933: der Ernstfall für Bonhoeffers Ethik," in *Ethik im Ernstfall: Dietrich Bonhoeffers Stellung zu den Juden und ihre Aktualität* (ed. Wolfgang Huber and Ilse Tödt; Internationales Bonhoeffer Forum 4; Munich: Kaiser, 1982), 175.

10. Quoted from Gerlach, *Als die Zeugen schwiegen,* 414.

11. The realm of ethical questions includes the question, "What kind of person is qualified to put his hand between the spokes of the wheel of history?" See Bertold Klappert, "Weg und Wende," 96–97; Tödt, "Judendiskriminierung 1933," 182; and Max Weber himself, "Politik als Beruf (1919)," 545.

12. Kierkegaard, *Die Tagebücher,* 53.

13. See on this subject also chapter 16.

14. On the date see Bethge, "Dietrich Bonhoeffer und die Juden," 195–96.

15. Lange, "Kirche für andere," 43.

16. Christine-Ruth Müller, *Dietrich Bonhoeffers Kampf gegen die nationalsozialistische Verfolgung und Vernichtung der Juden: Bonhoeffers Haltung zur Judenfrage im Vergleich mit Stellungnahmen aus der evangelischen Kirche und Kreisen des deutschen Widerstandes* (Munich: Kaiser, 1990), 326.

17. On this complex of topics as a whole see Meyer, *Unternehmen Sieben.*

18. See on this subject also chapters 8, 16, and 20.

19. Bethge, "Bonhoeffer und die Juden," 212.

Notes to Chapter 18

1. See the preceding chapter and Lapide, "Bonhoeffer und das Judentum," 118.

2. Eberhard Bethge, "Zwischen Bekenntnis und Widerstand: Erfahrungen in der Altpreußischen Union," in *Der Widerstand gegen den Nationalsozialismus: Die deutsche Gesellschaft und der Widerstand gegen Hitler* (ed. Jürgen Schmädeke and Peter Steinbach; Munich: R. Piper, 1985), 286.

3. Ekkehard Klausa, "Politischer Konservativismus und Widerstand," in *Widerstand gegen den Nationalsozialismus* (ed. Peter Steinbach and Johannes Tuchel; Berlin: Akademie Verlag, 1994), 231.

4. Ibid.

5. Winfried Meyer, "Staatsstreichplanung, Opposition und Nachrichtendienst: Widerstand aus dem Amt Ausland/Abwehr im Oberkommando der Wehrmacht," in *Widerstand gegen den Nationalsozialismus* (ed. Peter Steinbach and Johannes Tuchel; Berlin: Akademie Verlag, 1994), 321.

6. For example, Hans Mommsen, "Der Widerstand gegen Hitler und die deutsche Gesellschaft," in *Der Widerstand gegen den Nationalsozialismus: Die deutsche Gesellschaft und der Widerstand gegen Hitler* (ed. Jürgen Schmädeke and Peter Steinbach; Munich: R. Piper, 1985), 9.

7. Klaus-Jürgen Müller, "Nationalkonservative Eliten zwischen Kooperation und Widerstand," in *Der Widerstand gegen den Nationalsozialismus: Die deutsche Gesellschaft und der Widerstand gegen Hitler* (ed. Jürgen Schmädeke and Peter Steinbach; Munich: R. Piper, 1985), 24.

8. Heinz Eduard Tödt, "Der Bonhoeffer-Dohnanyi-Kreis in der Opposition und im Widerstand gegen das Gewaltregime Hitlers (Zwischenbilanz eines Forschungsprojekts)," in *Die Präsenz des verdrängten Gottes: Glaube, Religionslosigkeit und Weltverantwortung nach Dietrich Bonhoeffer* (ed. Christian Gremmels and Ilse Tödt; Internationales Bonhoeffer Forum 7; Munich: Chr. Kaiser, 1987), 262.

9. Christoph Strohm, *Theologische Ethik im Kampf gegen den Nationalsozialismus: Der Weg Dietrich Bonhoeffers mit den Juristen Hans von Dohnanyi und Gerhard Leibholz in den Widerstand* (Munich: Kaiser, 1989), 346.

10. Meyer, *Unternehmen Sieben*, 458.

11. See on this subject chapter 14.

12. Tödt, "Bonhoeffer-Dohnanyi-Kreis," 238.

13. Meyer, "Staatsstreichplanung," 331.

14. Bethge, *Biographie*, 835.

15. See on this subject the Afterword to DBW 16, 690ff. as well as, for example, the classic book on resistance, Peter Hoffmann, *Widerstand, Staatsstreich, Attentat: Der Kampf der Opposition gegen Hitler* (4th ed.; Munich: R. Piper, 1979), 268ff. See also the recent work of Ian Kershaw, *Hitler: 1936–1945* (Stuttgart: Deutsche Verlags-Anstalt, 2000), 872–73.

16. See, for example, Bethge, "Weg vom 'Pazifismus'"; and Bethge, "Zwischen Bekenntnis und Widerstand."

17. See, for example, Strohm, *Theologische Ethik im Kampf,* who focuses on a particular area in tracing the path up to 1938; and, with a different focus, Müller, *Dietrich Bonhoeffers Kampf.*

18. See Gremmels and Grosse, *Der Weg in den Widerstand.*

19. Mommsen, "Der Widerstand gegen Hitler," 18.

20. So, for example, in DBW 6, 224–25, 232–33, 274ff., and 279ff.

21. Meyer, "Staatsstreichplanung," 338.

Notes to Chapter 19

1. See Bethge, *Biographie.* See also Christian Gremmels, "Theologie am Ort der Gefangenschaft," in *Theologie und Biographie: Zum*

Beispiel Dietrich Bonhoeffer (Christian Gremmels and Hans Pfeifer, ed.; Munich: Kaiser, 1983), 95ff.; and the Foreword and Afterword to DBW 8.

2. Foreword to DBW 6, 11.

3. Wolf Krötke, "Teilnehmen am Leiden Gottes: Zu Dietrich Bonhoeffers Verständnis eines 'religionslosen Christentums,'" in *450 Jahre Evangelische Theologie in Berlin* (ed. Gerhard Besier and Christof Gestrich; Göttingen: Vandenhoeck & Ruprecht, 1989), 440.

4. Gremmels, "Theologie am Ort der Gefangenschaft," 114. See also Lange, "Kirche für andere," 52.

5. Tödt, "Der Bonhoeffer-Dohnanyi-Kreis," 259.

6. Eberhard Jüngel, *Gott als Geheimnis der Welt: Zur Begründung der Theologie des Gekreuzigten im Streit zwischen Theismus und Atheismus* (Tübingen: Mohr, 1977), 81.

Notes to Chapter 20

1. This question is a constant motif in Feil's major work on Bonhoeffer's theology and has also been raised independently and repeatedly in the interpretation of Bonhoeffer's thought. See Feil, *Theologie Dietrich Bonhoeffers*.

2. The collection published by Gremmels and I. Tödt in 1987 is especially important here. See Christian Gremmels and Ilse Tödt, *Die Präsenz des verdrängten Gottes: Glaube, Religionslosigkeit und Weltverantwortung nach Dietrich Bonhoeffer* (Internationales Bonhoeffer Forum 7; Munich: Kaiser, 1987) and the reader published by Peter H. A. Neumann, ed., *"Religionsloses Christentum" und "nicht-religiöse Interpretation" bei Dietrich Bonhoeffer* (Wege der Forschung 304; Darmstadt: Wissenschaftliche Buchgellschaft, 1990). See also Bethge, "Zwischen Bekenntnis und Widerstand," 395ff.

3. The entire third and last part of the above-mentioned work is entitled "Religionless Christianity in a World Come of Age" (Feil, *Theologie Dietrich Bonhoeffers*, 221). See also, for example, Ernst Feil's publications in 1978 and 1987: "Zur Wiederkehr der Religion: Ein kritischer Problembericht," *Herder-Korrespondenz* 32 (1978); and "Ende oder Wiederkehr der Religion? Zu Bonhoeffers umstrittener Prognose eines 'religionslosen Christentums,'" in *Die Präsenz des verdrängten Gottes: Glaube, Religionslosigkeit und Weltverantwortung nach Dietrich Bonhoeffer* (ed. Christian Gremmels and Ilse Tödt; Internationales Bonhoeffer Forum 7; Munich: Chr. Kaiser, 1987). See also his other essays, not mentioned individually here, in Neumann, ed., *"Religionsloses Christentum."*

4. See also chapter 12.
5. See Gandhi's letter to Bonhoeffer, reprinted in DBW 13, 213–14 and 499–500. See also chapter 3.
6. See on this subject also chapters 8, 16, and 17.
7. See on this subject chapter 4.

Notes to Chapter 21

1. This conclusion is based on Bethge's list of the works read by Bonhoeffer in prison. See Bethge, *Biographie*, 1054.
2. See on this subject chapter 12.
3. On this subject, see in particular the detailed research by Feil, *Theologie Dietrich Bonhoeffers*, 355ff.
4. This letter will be discussed in greater detail in chapter 22.
5. This was already mentioned in chapter 4.
6. This is discussed in greater detail in the commentary to DBW 8, 476 note 11.
7. See on this subject chapter 2.
8. See chapter 9.
9. Ott already wrote all that is necessary here in 1966. See Heinrich Ott, *Zum theologischen Erbe Dietrich Bonhoeffers*, in vol. 1 of *Wirklichkeit und Glaube* (2 vols.; Zürich: Vandenhoeck & Ruprecht, 1966), 90.

Notes to Chapter 22

1. The process for locating the source of this quotation is comprehensively described in the editor's remark in DBW 8, 530–31.
2. See on this subject also chapter 21.
3. On this poem see also chapter 8.
4. This is the title of a chapter in Bethge's excursus on the theology of *Resistance and Surrender*. See Bethge, *Biographie*, 958.
5. See Bethge, *Selbstzeugnissen und Bilddokumenten*, 111; and DBW 11, 148–49.
6. Dorothee Sölle, *Mystik und Widerstand*, 197.
7. Lapide, "Bonhoeffer und das Judentum," 122.
8. Ibid., 119.
9. Jürgen Moltmann, *Der gekreuzigte Gott: Das Kreuz Christi als Grund und Kritik christlicher Theologie* (Munich: Kaiser, 1972), 259.
10. Ibid., 49.
11. See Clements, *Freisein wozu?* 217ff.
12. Simone Weil, "Aufzeichnungen aus den Jahren 1940/42," in *Zeugnis für das Gute: Spiritualität einer Philosophin* (trans. and ed. Friedhelm Kemp; Zürich: Benziger, 1998), 215.

Notes to Chapter 23

1. The letter dictated by Walter Bonhoeffer, just before his death in a field hospital, is reprinted in Bethge, *Biographie*, 50–51.

2. See Sabine Leibholz-Bonhoeffer, *Vergangen, erlebt, überwunden: Schicksale der Familie Bonhoeffer* (8th ed.; Wuppertal: Kiefel, 1968; Gütersloh: Gütersloher Verlagshaus, 1995), 53.

3. Bethge, *Biographie*, 743.

4. Rainer Marten, *Der menschliche Tod: Eine philosophische Revision* (Paderborn: F. Schöningh, 1987), 10.

5. Volker Weymann, "Religiöses und religionsloses Christentum: Bemerkungen zu Kriterien christlicher Gotteserfahrung—im Anschluß an Dietrich Bonhoeffer (1974)," in *"Religionsloses Christentum" und "nicht-religiöse Interpretation" bei Dietrich Bonhoeffer* (ed. Peter H. A. Neumann; Wege der Forschung 304; Darmstadt: Wissenschaftliche Buchgellschaft, 1990), 390.

6. On this subject see in particular chapter 20.

7. Dorothee Sölle, *Mystik und Widerstand*, 108. See also chapter 10.

8. The last weeks and days of Bonhoeffer's life have been minutely reconstructed by his biographer. See Bethge, *Biographie*, 1026ff.

9. Ibid., 1037.

10. See Bethge, *Biographie*, 1037 note 54 and the editor's remark in DBW 16, 468.

11. See Jørgen Glenthøj, "Die letzten Worte Dietrich Bonhoeffers—das Motto von Maria Stuart?" in *Wie eine Flaschenpost: Ökumenische Briefe und Beiträge für Eberhard Bethge* (ed. Heinz Eduard Tödt., Munich: Kaiser, 1979), 103ff.

Notes to Chapter 24

1. See on this subject chapter 3.

2. See chapter 19. See also the Afterword to DBW 8, 658.

3. Lapide, "Bonhoeffer und das Judentum," 117–18.

4. Feil, *Theologie Dietrich Bonhoeffers*, 429, in the Afterword to the 4th edition of his 1971 work.

5. Bethge, *Biographie*, 999.

6. Max Frisch, *Stiller: Roman* (5th ed.; Frankfurt am Main: Suhrkamp, 1975), 150.

Bibliography

Text editions of Bonhoeffer's writings used in the preparation of this book. The superscription on the date refers to the edition.

DBW: *Dietrich Bonhoeffer Werke*. Edited by Eberhard Bethge et al. 17 vols. Munich and Gütersloh: Chr. Kaiser and Gütersloher Verlagshaus, 1986–1999. English: *Dietrich Bonhoeffer Works*. Vols. 1–5, 7. Edited by Geffrey B. Kelly. Translated by Daniel Bloeschard and James Burtness. Minneapolis: Fortress, 1996.

Vol. 1 (DBW 1): *Sanctorum Communio: Eine dogmatische Untersuchung zur Soziologie der Kirche*. Edited by Joachim von Soosten. 1986. English: *Sanctorum Communio: A Dogmatic Inquiry into the Sociology of the Church*. Edited by Clifford Green. Translated by Reinhard Krauss and Nancy Lukens. Minneapolis: Fortress, 1998.

Vol. 2 (DBW 2): *Akt und Sein: Transzendentalphilosophie und Ontologie in der systematischen Theologie*. Edited by Hans-Richard Reuter. 1986. English: *Act and Being*. Translated by Bernard Noble. New York: Octagon Books, 1983.

Vol. 3 (DBW 3): *Schöpfung und Fall*. Edited by Martin Rüter and Ilse Tödt. 1989, 2002^2. English: *Creation and Fall: A Theological Exposition of Genesis 1–3*. Edited by John de Gruchy. Translated by Douglas Bax. Minneapolis: Fortress, 1997.

Vol. 4 (DBW 4): *Nachfolge*. Edited by Martin Kuske and Ilse Tödt. 1994^2, 2002^3. English: *The Cost of Discipleship*. Edited by Geffrey B. Kelly and John Godsey. Translated by Barbara Green and Reinhard Krauss. Minneapolis: Fortress, 2001.

Vol. 5 (DBW 5): *Gemeinsames Leben: Das Gebetbuch der Bibel*. Edited by Gerhard Ludwig Müller and Albrecht Schönherr. 1987, 2002^2. English: *Life Together: Prayerbook of the Bible*. Edited by Geffrey B. Kelly. Translated by Daniel Bloesch and James Burtness. Minneapolis: Fortress, 1996.

Vol. 6 (DBW 6): *Ethik*. Edited by Ilse Tödt et al. 1992, 1998^2. English: *Ethics*. Edited by Clifford Green. Translated by Reinhard Krauss, Charles West, and Douglas Stott. Minneapolis: Fortress, 2005.

Vol. 6 (DBW 6a): *Annotated Supplement to Ethik.* Edited by Ilse Tödt. 1993.

Vol. 7 (DBW 7): *Fragmente aus Tegel.* Edited by Renate Bethge and Ilse Tödt. 1994. English: *Fiction from Tegel Prison.* Edited by Clifford Green. Translated by Nancy Lukens. Minneapolis: Fortress, 1971.

Vol. 8 (DBW 8): *Widerstand und Ergebung: Briefe und Aufzeichnungen aus der Haft.* Edited by Christian Gremmels et al. 1998. English: *Letters and Papers from Prison.* Edited by Eberhard Bethge. London: SCM Press, 1971.

Vol. 9 (DBW 9): *Jugend und Studium 1918–1927.* Edited by Hans Pfeifer with Clifford Green and Carl-Jürgen Kaltenborn. 1986. English: *The Young Bonhoeffer, 1918–1927.* Edited by Paul Matheny et al. Translated by Mary Nebelsick and Douglas Stott. Minneapolis: Fortress, 2003.

Vol. 10 (DBW 10): *Barcelona, Berlin, Amerika 1928–1931.* Edited by Hans Christoph von Hase et al. 1991.

Vol. 11 (DBW 11): *Ökumene, Universität, Pfarramt 1931–1932.* Edited by Eberhard Amelung and Christoph Strohm. 1994.

Vol. 12 (DBW 12): *Berlin 1932–1933.* Edited by Carsten Nicolaisen and Ernst-Albert Scharffenorth. 1997.

Vol. 13 (DBW 13): *London 1933–1935.* Edited by Hans Goedeking, Martin Heimbucher and Hans-Walter Schleicher. Gütersloh: Kaiser, 1994.

Vol. 14 (DBW 14): *Illegale Theologenausbildung: Finkenwalde, 1935–1937.* Edited by Otto Dudzus et al. 1996.

Vol. 15 (DBW 15): *Illegale Theologenausbildung: Sammelvikariate, 1937–1940.* Edited by Dirk Schulz. 1998.

Vol. 16 (DBW 16): *Konspiration und Haft, 1940–1945.* Edited by Jørgen Glenthøj, Ulrich Kabitz, and Wolf Krötke. 1996. English: *Conspiracy and Imprisonment, 1940–1945.* Edited by Mark S. Brocker. Translated by Lisa E. Dahill. Minneapolis: Fortress, 2006.

Vol. 17 (DBW 17): *Register und Ergänzungen.* Edited by Herbert Anzinger et al. 1999.

Other Literature

Barth, Karl, "An P. W. Herrenbrück 1952." In *Die mündige Welt: Dem Andenken Dietrich Bonhoeffers, Vorträge und Briefe.* 5 vols. Munich: Kaiser, 1955–1969.

———. *Die Lehre von Gott.* Vol. II/2 in *Die Kirchliche Dogmatik.* 5 vols. 4th ed. Zürich: EVZ, 1959.

—. *Die Lehre von der Versöhnung*. Vol. IV/2 in *Die Kirchliche Dogmatik*. 5 vols. 2d ed. Zürich: EVZ, 1964.

Bethge, Eberhard. *Dietrich Bonhoeffer: Eine Biographie*. 8th ed. Gütersloh: Kaiser, 1994. (Paperback: *Dietrich Bonhoeffer: Theologe, Christ, Zeitgenosse*. Munich: Kaiser, 1967). English: *Dietrich Bonhoeffer: A Biography*. Translated by Eric Mosbacher. Minneapolis: Fortress, 2000.

—. "Christlicher Glaube ohne Religion: Hat sich Dietrich Bonhoeffer geirrt? *Evangelische Kommentare* 8 (1975).

—. *Dietrich Bonhoeffer mit Selbstzeugnissen und Bilddokumenten*. 17th ed. Rowohlts Monographien 236. Reinbek bei Hamburg: Rowohlt, 1976, 1999.

—. "Dietrich Bonhoeffer und die Juden." In *Konsequenzen: Dietrich Bonhoeffers Kirchenverständnis heute*. Internationales Bonhoeffer Forum 3. Edited by Ernst Feil and Ilse Tödt. Munich: Kaiser, 1980.

—. "Dietrich Bonhoeffers Weg vom 'Pazifismus' zur Verschwörung." In *Frieden, das unumgängliche Wagnis: Die Gegenwartsbedeutung der Friedensethik Dietrich Bonhoeffers*. Internationales Bonhoeffer Forum 5. Edited by Hans Pfeifer. Munich: Kaiser, 1982.

—. "Zwischen Bekenntnis und Widerstand: Erfahrungen in der Altpreußischen Union." In *Der Widerstand gegen den Nationalsozialismus: Die deutsche Gesellschaft und der Widerstand gegen Hitler*. Edited by Jürgen Schmädeke and Peter Steinbach. Munich: R. Piper, 1985.

Bethge, Eberhard, Renate Bethge, and Christian Gremmels, eds. *Dietrich Bonhoeffer: Sein Leben in Bildern und Texten*. Munich: Kaiser, 1986. English: *Dietrich Bonhoeffer: A Life in Pictures*. Edited by Eberhard Bethge, Renate Bethge, and Christian Gremmels. Translated by John Bowden. London: SCM Press, 1986.

Bethge, Renate, and Christian Gremmels, eds. *Dietrich Bonhoeffer—Bilder aus seinem Leben*. Munich: Kaiser, 1986. English: *Dietrich Bonhoeffer: A Life in Pictures*. Edited by Renate Bethge and Christian Gremmels. Translated by Brian McNeil. Minneapolis: Fortress, 2006.

Bobert-Stützel, Sabine. *Dietrich Bonhoeffers Pastoraltheologie: Theologenausbildung im Widerstand zum "Dritten Reich"—dargestellt anhand der Finkenwalder Vorlesungen, 1935–1937*. Gütersloh: Kaiser, 1995.

Bonhoeffer, Dietrich, and Maria von Wedemeyer. *Brautbriefe Zelle 92: Dietrich Bonhoeffer Maria von Wedemeyer, 1943–1945*. Edited by Ruth-Alice von Bismarck and Ulrich Kabitz. 2d ed. Munich: C. H. Beck, 1995 (abgekürzt: Brautbriefe). English: *Love Letters from Cell 92: The Correspondence between Dietrich Bonhoeffer and Maria von*

Wedemeyer, 1943–1945. Translated by John Brown. Nashville: Abingdon Press, 1995.

Boomgaarden, Jürgen. "Das Verständnis der Wirklichkeit: Dietrich Bonhoeffers Systematische Theologie und ihr philosophischer Hintergrund." In *Akt und Sein.* Gütersloh: Kaiser, 1999.

Bracher, Karl Dietrich. *Stufen der Machtergreifung.* Frankfurt am Main: Ullstein, 1974.

Clements, Keith W. *What Freedom? The Persistent Challenge of Dietrich Bonhoeffer.* Bristol: Bristol Baptist College, 1990. German: *Freisein wozu? Dietrich Bonhoeffer als ständige Herausforderung.* Bonn: Pahl-Rugenstein, 1991.

Dramm, Sabine. *Dietrich Bonhoeffer und Albert Camus: Analogien im Kontrast.* Gütersloh: Kaiser, 1998.

———. "Jenseits der Diesseitigkeit? Mystik bei Dietrich Bonhoeffer." In *Christliche Mystik als Thema ökumenischer Theologie und Praxis: Konturen, Konkretionen, Konsequenzen.* Arnoldshainer Texte 114. Edited by Hermann Düringer. Frankfurt am Main: Haag & Herchen, 2001.

Dudzus, Otto, ed. *Dietrich Bonhoeffer Lesebuch.* Munich: Kaiser, 1987. English: *Bonhoeffer for a New Generation.* Edited by Otto Dudzus. London: SCM Press, 1986.

Feil, Ernst. *Die Theologie Dietrich Bonhoeffers: Hermeneutik, Christologie, Weltverständnis.* 4th ed. Munich: Kaiser, 1971, 1991.

———. "Ende oder Wiederkehr der Religion? Zu Bonhoeffers umstrittener Prognose eines 'religionslosen Christentums,' " In *Die Präsenz des verdrängten Gottes: Glaube, Religionslosigkeit und Weltverantwortung nach Dietrich Bonhoeffer.* Internationales Bonhoeffer Forum 7. Munich: Kaiser, 1987.

———. "Zur Wiederkehr der Religion: Ein kritischer Problembericht," *Herder-Korrespondenz* 32 (1978).

———, ed. *Internationale Bibliographie zu Dietrich Bonhoeffer.* Assisted by Barbara E. Fink. Gütersloh: Chr. Kaiser and Gütersloher Verlagshaus, 1998.

———, ed. *Verspieltes Erbe? Dietrich Bonhoeffer und der deutsche Nachkriegsprotestantismus.* Internationales Bonhoeffer Forum 2. Munich: Kaiser, 1979.

Feil, Ernst, and Ilse Tödt, eds. Konsequenzen: Dietrich Bonhoeffers Kirchenverständnis heute. Internationales Bonhoeffer Forum 3. Munich: Kaiser, 1980.

Feldmann, Christian. *"Wir hätten schreien müssen": Das Leben des Dietrich Bonhoeffer.* Freiburg im Breisgau: Herder, 1998.

Frisch, Max. *Stiller: Roman*. 5th ed. Frankfurt am Main: Suhrkamp, 1975.

Gerlach, Wolfgang. *Als die Zeugen schwiegen: Bekennende Kirche und die Juden*. 2d ed. Studien zu Kirche und Israel 10. Berlin: Instut Kirche und Judentum, 1993. English: *And the Witnesses Were Silent: The Confessing Church and the Persecution of the Jews*. Translated by Victoria Barnett. Lincoln: University of Nebraska Press, 2000.

Glenthøj, Jørgen. "Die letzten Worte Dietrich Bonhoeffers—das Motto von Maria Stuart?" In *Wie eine Flaschenpost: Ökumenische Briefe und Beiträge für Eberhard Bethge*. Edited by Heinz Eduard Tödt. Munich: Kaiser, 1979.

Goldschmidt, Dietrich. "Zur Religionssoziologie in der Bundesrepublik Deutschland." *Archives de Sociologie des Religions* 8 (1959): Special printing (Sonder-druck).

Gollwitzer, Helmut. *Krummes Holz—aufrechter Gang: Zur Frage nach dem Sinn des Lebens*. Munich: Kaiser, 1970.

Gremmels, Christian. "Dietrich Bonhoeffer." In *Religion in Geschichte und Gegenwart: Handwörterbuch für Theologie und Religionswissenschaft*, Vol. 1. Edited by Hans Dieter Betz et al. 10 vols. 4th ed. Tübingen: Mohr Siebeck, 1998.

———, "Theologie am Ort der Gefangenschaft." In *Theologie und Biographie: Zum Beispiel Dietrich Bonhoeffer*. Edited by Christian Gremmels and Hans Pfeifer. Munich: Kaiser, 1983).

———, ed. *Bonhoeffer und Luther: Zur Sozialgestalt des Luthertums in der Moderne*. Internationales Bonhoeffer Forum 6. Munich: Kaiser, 1983.

Gremmels, Christian, and Heinrich W. Grosse. *Dietrich Bonhoeffer: Der Weg in den Widerstand, Mit Beiträgen von Eberhard and Renate Bethge et al.* Gütersloh: Kaiser, 1996.

Gremmels, Christian, and Wolgang Huber, eds. *Theologie und Freundschaft, Wechselwirkungen: Eberhard Bethge und Dietrich Bonhoeffer*. Gütersloh: Gütersloher, 1994.

Gremmels, Christian, and Hans Pfeifer. *Theologie und Biographie: Zum Beispiel Dietrich Bonhoeffer*. Munich: Kaiser, 1983.

Gremmels, Christian, and Ilse Tödt, eds. *Die Präsenz des verdrängten Gottes: Glaube, Religionslosigkeit und Weltverantwortung nach Dietrich Bonhoeffer*. Internationales Bonhoeffer Forum 7. Munich: Kaiser, 1987.

Hampe, Johann Christoph. *Von guten Mächten: Gebete und Gedichte/ Dietrich Bonhoeffer*. Gütersloh: Gütersloher Verlagshaus, 1976. English: *Prayers from Prison: Prayers and Poems by Dietrich Bonhoeffer*.

Translated by John Bowden. London: Collins, 1977; Philadelphia: Fortress, 1978.

Heimbucher, Martin. *Christusfriede—Weltfrieden: Dietrich Bonhoeffers kirchlicher und politischer Kampf gegen den Krieg Hitlers und seine theologische Begründung.* Gütersloh: Kaiser, 1997.

Henkys, Jürgen. *Dietrich Bonhoeffers Gefängnisgedichte: Beiträge zu ihrer Interpretation.* Munich: Kaiser, 1986.

Hoffmann, Peter. *Widerstand, Staatsstreich, Attentat: Der Kampf der Opposition gegen Hitler.* 4th ed. Munich: R. Piper, 1979.

Huber, Wolfgang. "Evangelischer Glaube und die Frage nach der Kirche." In *Das Wesen des Christentums in seiner evangelischen Gestalt: Eine Vortragsreihe im Berliner Dom.* Neukirchen-Vluyn: Neukirchener, 2000.

———. "Wahrheit und Existenzform: Anregungen zu einer Theorie der Kirche bei Dietrich Bonhoeffer." In *Konsequenzen: Dietrich Bonhoeffers Kirchenverständnis heute.* Internationales Bonhoeffer Forum 3. Edited by Ernst Feil and Ilse Tödt. Munich: Kaiser, 1980.

Huber, Wolfgang and Ilse Tödt, eds. *Ethik im Ernstfall: Dietrich Bonhoeffers Stellung zu den Juden und ihre Aktualität.* Internationales Bonhoeffer Forum 4. Munich: Kaiser, 1982.

Huntemann, Georg. *Der andere Bonhoeffer: Die Herausforderung des Modernismus.* Wuppertal: R. Brockhaus, 1989.

Jüngel, Eberhard. *Gott als Geheimnis der Welt: Zur Begründung der Theologie des Gekreuzigten im Streit zwischen Theismus und Atheismus.* Tübingen: Mohr, 1977. English: *God as the Mystery of the World: On the Foundation of the Theology of the Crucified One.* Translated by Darrell Guder. Grand Rapids: Eerdmans, 1983.

Kallen, Werner. *In der Gewißheit seiner Gegenwart: Dietrich Bonhoeffer und die Spur des vermißten Gottes.* Mainz: Matthias-Grünewald, 1997.

Kershaw, Ian. *Hitler: 1936–1945.* Stuttgart: Deutsche Verlags-Anstalt, 2000.

Kierkegaard, Søren. *Die Tagebücher.* Translated and edited by Hayo Gerdes. Düsseldorf: E. Diederich, 1980.

Klappert, Bertold. "Weg und Wende Dietrich Bonhoeffers in der Israelfrage." In *Ethik im Ernstfall: Dietrich Bonhoeffers Stellung zu den Juden und ihre Aktualität.* Internationales Bonhoeffer Forum 4. Edited by Wolfgang Huber and Ilse Tödt. Munich: Kaiser, 1982.

Klausa, Ekkehard. "Politischer Konservativismus und Widerstand." In *Widerstand gegen den Nationalsozialismus.* Edited by Peter Steinbach and Johannes Tuchel. Berlin: Akademie Verlag, 1994.

Kodalle, Klaus Michael. *Dietrich Bonhoeffer: Zur Kritik seiner Theologie.* Gütersloh: Gütersloher Verlaghaus Gerd Mohn, 1991.

Köster, Peter. "Nietzsche als verborgene Antipode in Bonhoeffers *ETHIK.*" *Nietzsche-Studien* 19 (1990).

Krötke, Wolf. "Teilnehmen am Leiden Gottes. Zu Dietrich Bonhoeffers Verständnis eines 'religionslosen Christentums.'" In *450 Jahre Evangelische Theologie in Berlin.* Edited by Gerhard Besier and Christof Gestrich. Göttingen: Vandenhoeck & Ruprecht, 1989.

Kupisch, Karl. *Das Zeitalter der Revolutionen und Weltkriege: 1815–1945.* Vol. 5 in *Kirchengeschichte.* 5 vols. Stuttgart: Kohlhammer, 1975.

Lange, Ernst. "Kirche für andere: Dietrich Bonhoeffers Beitrag zur Frage einer verantwortbaren Gestalt der Kirche in der Gegenwart, 1967." In *Kirche für die Welt: Aufsätze zur Theorie kirchlichen Handelns.* Edited by Ernst Lange and Rüdiger Schloz. Munich: Kaiser; Gelnhausen: Burckardthaus, 1981.

Lange, Frederik, de. *Grond onder de voeten: Burgerlijkheid bij Dietrich Bonhoeffer, Een theologische studie.* Kampen: Van den Berg, 1985.

Lapide, Pinchas E. "Bonhoeffer und das Judentum." In *Verspieltes Erbe? Dietrich Bonhoeffer und der deutsche Nachkriegsprotestantismus.* Edited by Ernst Feil. Internationales Bonhoeffer Forum 2. Munich: Kaiser, 1979.

Leibholz-Bonhoeffer, Sabine. *Vergangen, erlebt, überwunden: Schicksale der Familie Bonhoeffer.* 8th ed. Wuppertal: Kiefel, 1968; Gütersloh: Gütersloher Verlagshaus, 1995. English: *The Bonhoeffers: Portrait of a Family.* Translated by Sabine Leibholz-Bonhoeffer. New York: St. Martin's Press, 1972.

Marten, Rainer. *Der menschliche Tod: Eine philosophische Revision.* Paderborn: F. Schöningh, 1987.

Mayer, Rainer. *Christuswirklichkeit, Grundlagen, Entwicklungen und Konsequenzen der Theologie Dietrich Bonhoeffers.* Stuttgart: Calwer, 1969.

Meyer, Winfried. "Staatsstreichplanung, Opposition und Nachrichtendienst: Widerstand aus dem Amt Ausland/Abwehr im Oberkommando der Wehrmacht." In *Widerstand gegen den Nationalsozialismus.* Edited by Peter Steinbach and Johannes Tuchel. Berlin: Akademie Verlag, 1994.

———. *Unternehmen Sieben: Eine Rettungsaktion für vom Holocaust Bedrohte aus dem Amt Ausland/Abwehr im Oberkommando der Wehrmacht.* Frankfurt am Main: Hain, 1993.

Moltmann, Jürgen. *Der gekreuzigte Gott: Das Kreuz Christi als Grund und Kritik christlicher Theologie.* Munich: Kaiser, 1972. English: *The Crucified God: The Cross of Christ as the Foundation and Criticism of*

Christian Theology. Translated by R. A. Wilson and John Bowden. New York: Harper & Row, 1974.

Mommsen, Hans. "Der Widerstand gegen Hitler und die deutsche Gesellschaft." In *Der Widerstand gegen den Nationalsozialismus: Die deutsche Gesellschaft und der Widerstand gegen Hitler.* Edited by Jürgen Schmädeke and Peter Steinbach. Munich: R. Piper, 1985.

Müller, Christine-Ruth. *Dietrich Bonhoeffers Kampf gegen die national-sozialistische Verfolgung und Vernichtung der Juden: Bonhoeffers Haltung zur Judenfrage im Vergleich mit Stellungnahmen aus der evangelischen Kirche und Kreisen des deutschen Widerstandes.* Munich: Kaiser, 1990.

Müller, Gotthold. "Ungeheuerliche Ontologie: Erwägungen zur christlichen Lehre über Hölle und Allversöhnung." *Evangelische Theologie* 34/3 (1974).

Müller, Klaus-Jürgen. "Nationalkonservative Eliten zwischen Kooperation und Widerstand." In *Der Widerstand gegen den Nationalsozialismus: Die deutsche Gesellschaft und der Widerstand gegen Hitler.* Edited by Jürgen Schmädeke and Peter Steinbach. Munich: R. Piper, 1985.

Nessan, Craig L., and Renate Wind. *Wer bist Du, Christus? Ein ökumenisches Lesebuch zur Christologie Dietrich Bonhoeffers.* Gütersloh: Kaiser, 1998. English: *Who Is Christ for Us?* Edited by Craig Nessan and Renate Wind. Translated by Craig Nessan. Minneapolis: Fortress, 2002.

Neumann, Peter H. A., ed. *"Religionsloses Christentum" und "nicht-religiöse Interpretation" bei Dietrich Bonhoeffer.* Wege der Forschung 304. Darmstadt: Wissenschaftliche Buchgellschaft, 1990.

Ott, Heinrich. *Zum theologischen Erbe Dietrich Bonhoeffers.* Vol. 1 in *Wirklichkeit und Glaube.* 2 vols. Zürich: Vandenhoeck & Ruprecht, 1966.

Pelikan, Herbert Rainer. *Die Frömmigkeit Dietrich Bonhoeffers: Dokumentation, Grundlinien, Entwicklung.* Wien: Herder, 1982.

Peters, Tiemo Rainer. "Jenseits von Radikalismus und Kompromiß: Die politische Verantwortung der Christen nach Dietrich Bonhoeffer." In *Verspieltes Erbe? Dietrich Bonhoeffer und der deutsche Nachkriegsprotestantismus.* Internationales Bonhoeffer Forum 2. Edited by Ernst Feil. Munich: Kaiser, 1979.

———. *Die Präsenz des Politischen in der Theologie Dietrich Bonhoeffers.* Munich: Kaiser; Mainz: Grünewald, 1976.

Pfeifer, Hans, ed. *Frieden—das unumgängliche Wagnis: Die Gegenwartsbedeutung der Friedensethik Dietrich Bonhoeffers.* Internationales Bonhoeffer Forum 5. Munich: Kaiser, 1982.

Robertson, Edwin H. *Dietrich Bonhoeffer: Leben und Verkündigung.* Göttingen: Vandenhoeck & Ruprecht, 1989.

Schlingensiepen, Ferdinand. *Im Augenblick der Wahrheit: Glaube und Tat im Leben Dietrich Bonhoeffers.* Munich: Kaiser, 1985.

Schmädeke, Jürgen, and Peter Steinbach, eds. *Der Widerstand gegen den Nationalsozialismus: Die deutsche Gesellschaft und der Widerstand gegen Hitler.* Munich: R. Piper, 1985.

Sölle, Dorothee. *Mystik und Widerstand: "Du stilles Geschrei."* 2d ed. Munich: R. Piper, 2000. English: *The Silent Cry: Mysticism and Resistance.* Translated by Barbara and Martin Rumscheidt. Minneapolis: Fortress, 2001.

———. *Stellvertretung: Ein Kapitel Theologie nach dem "Tode Gottes."* Stuttgart: Kreuz-Verlag, 1965. English: *Christ the Representative: An Essay in Theology after the Death of God.* Translated by David Lewis. Philadelphia: Fortress, 1967.

Spiegel, Yorick. Dietrich Bonhoeffer und die "preußisch-protestantische Welt." In *Verspieltes Erbe? Dietrich Bonhoeffer und der deutsche Nachkriegsprotestantismus.* Internationales Bonhoeffer Forum 2. Edited by Ernst Feil. Munich: Kaiser, 1979.

Steinbach, Peter, and Johannes Tuchel, eds. *Widerstand gegen den Nationalsozialismus.* Berlin: Akademie Verlag, 1994.

Strohm, Christoph. *Theologische Ethik im Kampf gegen den Nationalsozialismus: Der Weg Dietrich Bonhoeffers mit den Juristen Hans von Dohnanyi und Gerhard Leibholz in den Widerstand.* Munich: Kaiser, 1989.

Tietz-Steiding, Christiane. *Bonhoeffers Kritik der verkrümmten Vernunft: Eine erkenntnistheoretische Untersuchung.* Tübingen: Mohr Siebeck, 1999.

Tödt, Heinz Eduard. "Judendiskriminierung 1933: der Ernstfall für Bonhoeffers Ethik." In *Ethik im Ernstfall: Dietrich Bonhoeffers Stellung zu den Juden und ihre Aktualität.* Internationales Bonhoeffer Forum 4. Edited by Wolfgang Huber and Ilse Tödt. Munich: Kaiser, 1982.

———. "Der Bonhoeffer-Dohnanyi-Kreis in der Opposition und im Widerstand gegen das Gewaltregime Hitlers (Zwischenbilanz eines Forschungsprojekts)." In *Die Präsenz des verdrängten Gottes: Glaube, Religionslosigkeit und Weltverantwortung nach Dietrich Bonhoeffer.* Edited by Christian Gremmels and Ilse Tödt. Internationales Bonhoeffer Forum 7. Munich: Chr. Kaiser, 1987.

Tödt, Ilse, ed. *Dietrich Bonhoeffers Hegelseminar 1933: Nach den Aufzeichnungen von Ferenc Lehel.* Internationales Bonhoeffer Forum 8. Munich: Kaiser, 1988.

Weber, Max. "Politik als Beruf (1919)." In *Gesammelte Politische Schriften.* Edited by Johannes Winckelmann. 5th ed. Tübingen: Mohr Siebeck, 1988.

Weil, Simone. "Aufzeichnungen aus den Jahren 1940/42." In *Zeugnis für das Gute: Spiritualität einer Philosophin.* Translated and edited by Friedhelm Kemp. Zürich/Düsseldorf: Benziger, 1998.

von Weizsäcker, Carl Friedrich. "Gedanken eines Nichttheologen zur theologischen Entwicklung Dietrich Bonhoeffers (1976)." In *Der Garten des Menschlichen: Beiträge zur geschichtlichen Anthropologie.* Munich: C. Hanser, 1977.

Weymann, Volker. "Religiöses und religionsloses Christentum: Bemerkungen zu Kriterien christlicher Gotteserfahrung—im Anschluß an Dietrich Bonhoeffer (1974)." In *"Religionsloses Christentum" und "nicht-religiöse Interpretation" bei Dietrich Bonhoeffer.* Wege der Forschung 304. Edited by Peter H. A. Neumann. Darmstadt: Wissenschaftliche Buchgellschaft, 1990.

Wind, Renate. *Dem Rad in die Speichen fallen. Die Lebensgeschichte des Dietrich Bonhoeffer.* Weinheim and Basel: Beltz & Gelberg, 1990. English: *A Spoke in the Wheel: The Life of Dietrich Bonhoeffer.* Translated by John Bowden. Grand Rapids: Eerdmans, 1992.